GREENER LIVING

EDITORS
DR. MAMTA SHARMA   DR. HUKAM SINGH
DR. UPENDRA SINGH

PUSTAK BHARATI
TORONTO CANADA

Editors : Dr. Mamta Sharma
Dr. Hukam Singh
Dr. Upendra Singh

Book Title : Greener Living

Cover Picture : By Dr. Anil Kumar Chhangani, D.Sc.

Published by :
Pustak Bharati (Books India)
180 Torresdale Ave, Toronto Canada M2R 3E4
email : pustak.bharati.canada@gmail.com
Web : www.pustak-bharati-canada.com

Published for
Raj Rishi Government Autonomous College,
Alwar, Rajasthan, India

Financial Assistance
Rashtriya Uchchatar Shiksha Abhiyan
(RUSA-2.0)

Copyright ©2023

ISBN : 978-1-989416-12-9

© All rights reserved. No part of this book may be copied, reproduced or utilised in any manner or by any means, computerised, e-mail, scanning, photocopying or by recording in any information storage and retrieval system, without the permission in writing from the editors.

PREFACE

"Our planet is slowly dying, and if we don't do anything about it soon enough, it would eventually begin to deteriorate and everything would be used. The world would become a barren place without any resources. We need to cater to the needs of our planet, and we need to change our life styles so that it becomes beneficial to the planet. We need to become much more eco-friendly, so that no harm is dealt to the planet by our existence. Many people don't realize that they waste large amounts of energy and other resources in various unnecessary things that could otherwise be saved."

This series of books is an extension of the 3 days international conference on "**Multidisciplinary Approach Towards Sustainable Development and Climate Change for A Viable Future (Icmsdc-2022)**" held from 12th-14th August 2022 at Raj Rishi Government Autonomous College, Alwar, Rajasthan.

We are very happy and delighted to publish our series of books which are accumulation of research papers of knowledgeable experts in the field of sustainable development and climate change.

Climate change is the most significant challenge to achieving sustainable development, and it threatens to drag millions of people into grinding poverty. At the same time, we have never had better know-how and solutions available to avert the crisis and create opportunities for a better life for people all over the world. Climate change is not just a long-term issue. It is happening today, and it entails uncertainties for policy makers trying to shape the future.

There is a dual relationship between sustainable development and climate change. On the one hand, climate change influences key natural and human living conditions and thereby also the basis for social and economic development, while on the other hand, society's priorities on sustainable development influence both the greenhouse gas emissions that are causing climate change and the vulnerability.

Climate policies can be more effective when consistently embedded within broader strategies designed to make national and regional development paths more sustainable. This occurs because the impact of climate variability and change, climate policy responses, and associated socio-economic development will affect the ability of countries to achieve sustainable development goals. Conversely, the pursuit of those goals will in turn affect the opportunities for, and success of, climate policies.

With these books, we aim to reach to as many people as we can, and spread awareness about sustainable development and climate change and its in-depth analysis through our didactic research papers. We hope that the thought with which ICMSDC-2022 was executed is taken forward through this series of books and the inception of an idea of saving the environment is rooted in the minds of our readers.

The articles in these books have been contributed by eminent research scholars, scientists, academicians and industry experts whose contributions have enriched this book series. We thank our publisher, Pustak Bharati, Toronto, Canada for joining us in this initiative and helped in publishing this series of books.

Finally, we will always remain indebted to all our well-wishers for their blessings, without which ICMSDC-2022 and series of these book would have not come into existence.

Financial Assistance provided by Rashtriya Uchchatar Shiksha Abhiyan (RUSA-2.0) is gratefully acknowledged.

Dr. Mamta Sharma
Dr. Hukam Singh
Dr. Upendra Singh

Contents

Preface

1. Noise Pollution : An Outlook — 1
   Dr. Mamta Sharma
   Dr. Hukam Singh
   Dr. Upendra Singh

2. Role of Artificial Intelligence in Chemistry — 5
   Dr. Sudha Sukhwal Shringi

3. ग्लोबल वार्मिंग : प्रभाव एवं समस्या निदान — 11
   दयाचंद

4. Ayurveda and Healthcare : A Review — 19
   Archana Singh,
   Anjul Dadoria
   Suman Malik

5. Biocentrism : A Study in Environmental Ethics — 28
   Dr. Sadek Ali

6. Sustainable Development, Climate Change and Indian Economy — 41
   Pratibha Sharma
   Ashish Sharma

7. Degradation Kinetics and Antimicrobial Studies of Copper (II) Soap Complexes for Sustainable Development of Environment — 51
   Asha Meena

8. भारतीय अर्थव्यवस्था पर कोविड–19 का प्रभाव — 60
   डॉ. अरुणा कुमारी पलिया

9. Legal Aspects of Environmental Proction (A Study of Environmental Policy and Laws) — 69
   Dr Madhuri Gupta

10. Palladium Nanoparticles Synthesis and their Catalytic Application on Oxidation of Arginine in Aqueous Acidic Medium — 72
    Dhanraj
    Rashmi Gupta
    M. B. Yadav

11. Effects of Air Pollution on Human Health and Control — 84
    Measures of Air Pollution : A Bibliometric Analysis
    Rutuja Chothe
    Akanksha Botre
    Divya Patil
    Rohan Sawant

12. Studies of Electrical output in Photogalvanic Cell for — 103
    Energy Conversion and Storage
    Sushil Kumar Yadav

13. Political Governance and Covid -19 — 112
    Dr. Ranjana Garg

14. पर्यावरण संवर्धन एवं सतत् विकास (ऐतिहासिक परिप्रेक्ष्य) — 119
    मधु कुमावत

15. Synthesis of Aluminium (III) and Gallium (III) Complexes — 121
    with Biaoctive Schiff Bases and Their Spectral,
    Electrochemical and Biological Aspects
    Dr. Sunita yadav,
    Dr Neelam Gupta
    Prof. R.V. Singh

16. Health and Environment Impact of Air Pollution — 129
    Niharika Singh

17. Floristic diversity of Invasive weeds in Shirpur taluka of — 143
    Dhule district, Maharashtra state, India
    Rajni Kant Thakur and Kumar Ambrish

18. Optical Properties of Polyvinylpyrrolidone / — 155
    Polyvinylacetate Blend Films
    A. Rawat
    A. K. Agrawal
    Shivali Chauhan
    P. J. Singh

19. Sustainable Development Goals (SDGs) in India : — 174
    Achievements & Challenges
    Mrs. Sumitra Devi Sahu

20. Steam : Way forward the Future of Education — 192
    Mr. Neeraj Mohan Puri[1]
    Dr. Rashmi Tyagi[2]

1. Greener Living : At A Glance

Dr. Mamta Sharma*
Dr. Hukam Singh**
Dr. Upendra Singh ***

Introduction

Time to Start Green Living! Our planet is slowly dying, and if we don't do anything about it soon enough, it would eventually begin to deteriorate and everything would be used. The world would become a barren place without any resources. We need to cater to the needs of our planet, and we need to change our lifestyles so that it becomes beneficial to the planet. We need to become much more eco-friendly so that no harm is dealt to the planet by our existence. Now, we are certainly not doing anything like that and in order for us to be able to know what's right and what's wrong for the planet, we really need to open our eyes and look around. Global warming is rapidly becoming an increasing phenomenon, the glaciers are melting at a very fast rate. The instigators of global warming are just us. We have driven the planet to the extent that it has begun to harm itself. Every day, we use up large amounts of the resources of the planet to facilitate our lives, but do we realize who is going to replenish those resources? No, we don't. All we are intent on is making life easy for ourselves. However, the time has now come for us to make a move and change our lives so that we do not pose a threat, or become a source of harm to the planet. We need to analyse and see that whatever we are doing is according the needs of the planet or not. If it isn't, then we need to change and start green living so that the planet begins to replenish its resources and becomes the beautiful place it once was. Floods, earth quakes and all natural disasters are instigated because of us if you actually look at it in a wider sense, and all we think is that the planet is hurting us. It is not in any way trying to harm us, but these are just signs of things to come if we don't take care of our beloved planet. Many people have now begun to realize the message that is being conveyed and have begun green living so that they could be free of the guild of destroying the planet. You can start green living as well, and by following some simple guidelines, you could certainly be on your way in helping the planet. It is futile to think that one person can do nothing, but you should try and set an example for others to follow. Try being a source of inspiration to others so that they also being to adopt green living as well. Simple steps such as turning off the lights or electricity when not in use could go a long way in helping the planet, and it highly recommended that we now start to utilize our energy efficiently because it is high time that we begin to listen to the pleas of the planet and try to make life better for ourselves before things get out of hand and it all becomes too late. PAGE 4 The new decade is upon us, and many of us have the same goal in mind: to be more eco-friendly. Living a more sustainable lifestyle can be very rewarding – but also a bit daunting. Thankfully there are four easyto-follow stepping stones that we can apply to everyday life: reduce, reuse, recycle and repurpose.

Why Greener Living

Greener living is also called as sustainable living is a lifestyle that attempts to reduce an individuals or society's use of mother earth's natural resources and one's individual resources. Greener living in the 21st century can be described as "shifting to a renewable energy-based, reuse/recycle economy with a diversified transport system. Proponents of greener living often attempt to reduce their carbon footprint by altering methods of transportation, energy consumption and diet. They also aim to conduct their lives in ways that are consistent with sustainability, in natural balance and respectful of humanity's symbiotic association with ecology. The practice and general philosophy of ecological living is highly interrelated with the overall principles of sustainable development. According to Brundtland Commissions report the sustainable development is "development that meets the needs and aspirations of the present without compromising the ability of future generations to meet their own needs. As the human population grows so does the total consumption, material and energy. This, as it is the sum of the consumption of each person. Put another way, it is average consumption multiplied by population. As such, sustainable development also means that the population is kept at the same level or under the sustainable population limit. We need to adapt the practice of "ethical consumerism" which refers to buying things which are made ethically i.e. without harm to or exploitation of humans, animals or the natural environment. This generally entails favouring products and businesses that take account of the greater good in their operations. An extension of the idea, doing more with less, overlaps with the first part of Reduce, reuse and recycle. The slogan Reduce, Reuse and Recycle is an approach to the waste hierarchy that seeks to be as ecologically appropriate as possible and maximize the value and use out of a resource. It is sometimes shortened to "3R Principle" and sometimes, a fourth 'R' is added, such as 'Refuse', 'Remanufacture', 'Recover', 'Restore', 'Redesign', 'Repurposing', 'Rot' (compost), etc. Circular Economy for Productivity and Sustainability is way to adapt at larger scale for sustainable living. Productivity and Sustainability are interconnected in a way that inside activities of industry affect its outside environment. It is an economy where products are designed for durability, reuse and recyclability and thus almost everything gets reused, remanufactured, and, recycled into a raw material or used as a source of energy. It includes 3 R's (Reduce, Reuse and Recycle), Refurbishment, Recover, and Repairing of materials. Hence, Circular Economy focuses on increasing productivity in terms of more efficient utilization of resources. Currently, most of the countries follow a linear process in which raw materials are taken from the environment, turn in to new products which are then disposed of after use. Germany and Japan have used it as a binding principle for reorganizing its economy, whereas China even has a law on it. Greener living at individual scale is adopting Eco-friendly and sustainable attitude in day to day life i.e. instead of focusing on materialistic living one should focus on meaningful living which include Reduce The unnecessary and unwanted wasteful purchases, Avoiding waste is the preferable option for waste management, Avoid excessive use of paper, switch to online modes. Reuse the same item more than once in either the same way or modified way. It is the way to use the materials or items again. Recycle to make something new from a commodity that has been used earlier, Processing older items to produce something new in order to save energy and resources, There are several commodities for instance in your households, kitchens which could be recycled with a little polish perhaps. To conclude the theme we come to the conclusion that one should adapt sustainable living instead of materialistic living as our father of the nation Mr. M. K. Gandhi said " the earth has enough resources for our need but not for our greened.

References
Source of knowledge is the internet and it is highly acknowledged.

*Associate Professor (Zoology)
**Professor
*** Associate Professor (Chemistry)
Raj Rishi Government (Autonomous) College,
Alwar, Rajasthan 301001,India.
email : mamta810@gmail.com;
drhukamsingh63@gmail.com
dr.usingh09@gmail.com

2. Role of Artificial Intelligence in Chemistry

Dr. Sudha Sukhwal Shringi

Abstract

Artificial intelligence is a type of intelligence that synthesizes, perceives and interferes the information as demonstrated by machines. The use of artificial Intelligence is going to be rampant in every field of science and exploration in the coming times. With the rise of Machine learning and deep learning artificial intelligence is becoming more popular nowadays in every field. AI in chemistry studies can be very efficient and bring faster results and outputs with minimum waste.

Use of Artificial Intelligence in chemistry can be on drug discovery and development in the healthcare department. It can also help in the prediction of molecular properties, validation in retrosynthesis and reaction outcome predictions. While there are many advantages of using AI in chemistry there are potential disadvantages as well.

Keywords : Artificial Intelligence, Chemistry, Drug discovery, Robotic chemistry etc

Introduction :

Artificial Intelligence (AI) and chemistry are two fields that have seen rapid advancements in recent years. AI refers to the simulation of human intelligence in machines that are programmed to think and learn like humans. Chemistry, on the other hand, is the science that deals with the properties, composition, and structure of matter, as well as the changes it undergoes.

In recent years, there has been increasing interest in applying AI techniques to problems in chemistry, such as drug discovery, materials design, and chemical forecasting. The intersection of AI and chemistry allows for more efficient and accurate predictions, simulations, and automation of laboratory tasks. AI is the most important part of technology as it helps in collection and analyzing the data at low cost. Artificial intelligence (AI) is increasingly being used in the field of chemistry to improve and automate various aspects of research and development.

Advantage of AI in Chemistry

Some examples of how AI is being used in chemistry include:

Drug Discovery : AI algorithms can be used to screen large libraries of chemical compounds for potential drug candidates, reducing the time and cost of the drug discovery process.

Material Discovery : AI algorithms can be used to identify new materials with specific properties, such as high thermal conductivity or mechanical strength.

Predictive Modelling : AI algorithms can be used to predict the properties and behavior of chemical compounds, such as toxicity or reactivity, which can help to identify potential risks and guide the development of safer compounds.

Virtual Screening : AI algorithms can be used to virtually screen millions of compounds to identify the most promising candidates for further experimentation.

Data Analysis and Interpretation : AI algorithms can be used to analyze large sets of chemical data and extract meaningful insights, such as identifying patterns in data or detecting outliers, to accelerate the discovery of new compounds and phenomena.

Synthetic Planning : AI can help to plan and optimize synthetic routes for compounds, reducing the number of steps and reagents required, and increasing the efficiency of the synthetic process.

Robotic Chemistry : AI-controlled robotic systems can perform high-throughput experimentation and increase the speed and scalability of chemical syntheses.

Target Identification and Validation : AI algorithms can be used to analyze large sets of biological data, such as gene expression data, to identify potential targets for drug development. They can also help to validate these targets by analyzing data on the relationship between the target and the disease.

Lead Optimization : Once a potential drug candidate has been identified, AI algorithms can be used to optimize its properties, such as its chemical structure, to improve its efficacy and safety. This can include analyzing data on the compound's pharmacokinetics, toxicity, and pharmacodynamics, as well as its interactions with other molecules.

Chemistry Simulation : AI can be used in drug discovery by simulating chemical reactions, predicting the outcomes of chemical synthesis, and identifying new chemical reactions. This can be helpful for researchers to design chemical reactions, predict the outcomes of chemical reactions, and identify the best reagents to use in certain chemical reactions.

Predictive ADMET : AI can predict important pharmacokinetic and pharmacodynamic properties of drug candidates, such as absorption, distribution, metabolism, excretion, and toxicity (ADMET) which can help to identify potential risks and guide the development of safer compounds.

Overall, the use of AI in drug discovery has the potential to greatly accelerate the pace of scientific discovery and lead to the development of new and improved drugs. However, it's important to note that drug discovery is a complex and multi-faceted process, and AI is just one tool among many that researchers can use to advance it. More research is needed to fully realize the potential of AI in drug discovery and to develop AI algorithms that can effectively handle the complexity of biological systems.

AI technology is still in its infancy for certain areas of chemistry, and more research is needed to fully realize the potential of AI in this field. Nonetheless, it has the potential to revolutionize many aspects of chemistry, from discovering new drugs and materials to improving the efficiency and safety of chemical processes, and providing new insights into complex chemical systems.

Disadvantage of AI in Chemistry

While artificial intelligence (AI) has the potential to greatly improve many aspects of chemistry, including drug discovery and materials synthesis, there are also some potential disadvantages to its use in this field. Some of the main disadvantages include:

Lack of Transparency : AI algorithms, particularly those based on machine learning, can be difficult to interpret and explain, which can make it hard to understand how they arrived at their predictions and decisions. This lack of transparency can make it difficult to validate results and ensure that the AI system is making accurate predictions.

Lack of understanding of chemical processes: AI algorithms may not fully understand the underlying chemical processes that they are analyzing. This can lead to errors or inaccuracies in predictions and decisions.

Bias and errors in Data : AI algorithms learn from the data they are trained on, so any bias or errors in the data can be carried over into the predictions and decisions made by the AI system.

Over Reliance on AI : There is a risk of over reliance on AI in chemistry, where researchers might not fully understand the assumptions, limitations, and uncertainties of the AI model. This could lead to incorrect conclusions or decision-making based on the AI's predictions.

Ethical Concerns : AI has the potential to have a profound impact on society, especially in the field of chemistry. There is a need to carefully assess and mitigate its potential negative impacts and ethical implications.

High-Cost : Developing and implementing AI in chemistry can be an expensive process, especially for small-scale research or for companies that are just starting to explore AI applications.

Limited Generalizability : AI algorithms are often trained on specific sets of data and can struggle to make accurate predictions when applied to new data, especially when there is a lack of diversity in the training data. Therefore, AI models trained on one specific type of data may not be able to generalize to other types of data.

Difficulty of Validating Results : AI algorithms can be complex and it can be difficult to validate the results they produce. This can make it hard to understand the underlying assumptions and limitations of the model, which can make it hard to ensure that the results are accurate and reliable.

Job Displacement : As AI begins to take on more complex tasks and decision making, there is a risk that it will displace human jobs. This can be especially concerning in the field of chemistry, where AI-driven automation of laboratory tasks has the potential to reduce the number of jobs available to chemists.

Overhyping and Unrealistic Expectations : There is a risk that the hype around AI and its potential benefits may lead to unrealistic expectations, which can make it hard to justify the costs and resources required to implement AI in chemistry. This can make it hard for researchers to secure funding and support for their projects, and may lead to disappointment when the results don't match the initial expectations.

It's worth noting that these disadvantages of AI in chemistry should not be taken as a reason to avoid AI in this field, but rather a way to be aware of the limitations and uncertainties of AI model, this way they can be mitigated and proper decisions can be taken while utilizing AI.

Conclusion

Artificial Intelligence (AI) is a rapidly growing field that is having a significant impact on many industries, including chemistry. The ability of AI algorithms to analyze vast amounts of data, recognize patterns, and make predictions has the potential to revolutionize many aspects of chemistry, from drug discovery and materials synthesis to chemical process optimization.

By using AI algorithms to analyze data on materials properties, it is possible to identify potential new materials that have specific properties, such as high thermal conductivity or mechanical strength, much faster and more efficiently than traditional methods. This has the potential to greatly accelerate the development of new and improved materials.

Additionally, AI can be used in virtual screening of millions of compounds to identify the most promising candidates for further experimentation. This approach not only saves time and resources but also allows the discovery of new compounds and potential drug candidates that would be otherwise missed.

In summary, AI has the potential to revolutionize many aspects of chemistry, from discovering new drugs and materials to improving the efficiency and safety of chemical processes, and providing new insights into complex chemical systems.

References
1. "Artificial Intelligence and Machine Learning in Chemistry" by A.R. Raccuglia and K.R. Gustafson in Chemical Reviews (2020), vol. 120, issue 16, pp. 8197-8261. This review article provides an overview of the various applications of AI in chemistry, including drug discovery, materials design, and chemical forecasting.
2. "Artificial Intelligence in Chemistry: State of the Art and Future Directions" by L. Cronin and A.J. Mulholland in Chemical Society Reviews (2019), vol. 48, issue 7, pp. 1753-1772. This review article focuses on the current state of AI in chemistry and discusses future directions for the field.
3. "Chemical Informatics and Artificial Intelligence in Drug Discovery" by D.W. Hughes, D.R. Spring, and P. Willett in Nature Reviews Drug Discovery (2018), vol. 17, pp. 285-298. This review article provides an overview of the use of AI in drug discovery and its potential to accelerate the drug discovery process.
4. "Artificial Intelligence in Materials Science: Current Status and Future Directions" by M.R. O'Mara, J.C. Hautier, and G. Ceder in Nature Materials (2018), vol. 17, pp. 263-275. This review article discusses the current state of AI in materials science, its potential applications and future directions.
5. "AI in Chemistry: a review" by Y. Al-Rasheed in Journal of chemical information and modeling (2021) vol 61 issue 10, pp. 4821–4831. This review article discuss how AI and ML are used to accelerate chemical processes from drug discovery, process optimization, and prediction of chemical properties.

**Associate Professor,
Department of Chemistry,
Rajrishi College Alwar, Rajasthan, India
email : Sudhashringi@gmail.com**

Greener Living

3. ग्लोबल वार्मिंग : प्रभाव एवं समस्या निदान

दयाचंद

हाल ही के वर्षों तक ग्लोबल वार्मिंग को आमतौर पर संशय की दृष्टि से देखा जाता था, लेकिन अब यह एक कटु हकीकत के तौर पर हमारे द्वार पर दस्तक दे चुकी है और इसका प्रभाव हम साफ-साफ महसूस करने लगे हैं। दुनियाभर में तेजी से मिलते ग्लेशियर, समुद्र के जलस्तर में दर्ज की गई वृद्धि, विलुप्त होती वनस्पति और जीव-जंतुओं की प्रजातियां, मौसम के मिजाज में दिखने वाली उलट-पुलट यह विश्वास दिलाने के लिए काफी है कि इस दिशा में वक्त हमारे हाथ से खिसकता जा रहा है। दरअसल, हमारे सौर मण्डल में कई ग्रह या तो ज्यादा गर्म या ज्यादा ठण्डे होते है। लेकिन पृथ्वी का वातावरण मध्यम होता है। यही वजह है कि यहां पर जीवन संभव है। लेकिन पिछले काफी सालों में पृथ्वी का तापमान अस्थिर हो रहा है। कहने का मतलब है कि पृथ्वी का तापमान का औसत तापमान से ज्यादा बढ़ गया है और इसे ही ग्लोबल वार्मिंग कहा जाता है और यह सजीव जीवन के लिए एक बुरा संकेत है।

अर्थात् विभिन्न गतिविधियां के कारण जब पृथ्वी का तापमान लगातार बढ़ रहा हो, उसे ग्लोबल वार्मिंग कहते है। सूर्य की कई किरणें वायुमंडल से होती हुई पृथ्वी की सतह से टकराती है, और फिर परावर्तित होकर वापस लौट जाती है। लेकिन पृथ्वी का वायुमंडल कई वायु से मिलकर बना है। इसमें कुछ ग्रीनहाउस वायु भी शामिल है जैसे कार्बन डाइ आक्साइड, नाइट्रोजन आक्साइड, मिथेन आदि। यह वायु जब वायुमंडल में बढ़ जाए तो धरती के ऊपर एक आवरण बना लेती है। यही आवरण परावर्तित होकर लौटती किरणों के एक भाग को रोक देता है और इसी के कारण पृथ्वी का वातावरण लगातार गर्म हो रहा है। इसी को ग्लोबल वार्मिंग कहते है। दुनिया के कई बड़े वैज्ञानिकों के अनुसार 21वीं सदी की सबसे बड़ी समस्या ग्लोबल वार्मिंग है। वैज्ञानिकों ने इसकी मिसाल तृतीय विश्वयुद्ध दी है। उनके मुताबिक तृतीय विश्वयुद्ध से होने वाले नुकसान से 10 गुना ज्यादा ग्लोबल वार्मिंग का नुकसान होगा।

आसान शब्दों में समझें तो ग्लोबल वार्मिंग का अर्थ है 'पृथ्वी के तापमान में वृद्धि और इसके कारण मौसम में होने वाले परिवर्तन' पृथ्वी के तापमान में हो रही इस वृद्धि (जिसे 100 सालों के औसत तापमान पर 10 फारेनाईट आँका गया है) के परिणाम स्वरूप बारिश के तरीकों में बदलाव, हिमखण्डों और ग्लेशियरों के पिघलने, समुद्र के जलस्तर में वृद्धि और वनस्पति तथा जन्तु जगत पर प्रभावों के रूप के सामने आ सकते हैं। ग्लोबल वार्मिंग दुनिया की कितनी बड़ी समस्या है, यह बात एक आम आदमी समझ नहीं पाता है। उसे ये शब्द थोड़ा टेकनिकल लगता है। इसलिये वह इसकी तह तक नहीं जाता है, लिहाजा इसे एक वैज्ञानिक परिभाषा मानकर छोड़ दिया जाता है। ज्यादातर लोगों को लगता है कि फिलहाल संसार को इससे कोई खतरा नहीं है।

Greener Living

भारत में भी ग्लोबल वार्मिंग एक प्रचलित शब्द नहीं है और भाग-दौड़ में लगे रहने वाले भारतीयों के लिये भी इसका अधिक कोई मतलब नहीं है। लेकिन विज्ञान की दुनिया की बात करें तो ग्लोबल वार्मिंग को लेकर भविष्यवाणियाँ की जा रही हैं। इसको 21वीं शताब्दी का सबसे बड़ा खतरा बताया जा रहा है। यह खतरा तृतीय विश्वयुद्ध या किसी क्षुद्रग्रह (एस्टेराइड) के पृथ्वी से टकराने से भी बड़ा माना जा रहा है। विशेषज्ञ बार-बार चेतावनियां दे रहे हैं कि अगर अगले आठ-दस सालों में इस दिशा में कुछ सार्थक न किया गया तो भयावह भविष्य से हमारा सामना होगा। इस मसले पर बार-बार एक ही सवाल उठता है कौन इसके लिए ईमानदारी से पहल करे? जब अमेरिका जैसा विकसित देश जो पर्यावरण को बिगाड़ने में दुनिया में सबसे आगे है, वही इस मुद्दे को गंभीरता से नहीं लेता तथ गरीब और विकासशील देशों से कैसे उम्मीद की जा सकती है कि वे अपने विकास की बिना पर इस मामले में गंभीर रूख अख्तियार करें।

वायुमंडल में ग्रीन हाउस गैसों, खासकर कार्बन डाइ ऑक्साइड के उत्सर्जन में लगातार हो रही वृद्धि से उत्पन्न पृथ्वी की गरमाहट क्या गुल खिला सकती है, इसकी चेतावनी इस वर्ष के विश्व पर्यावरण दिवस की पूर्व संध्या पर संयुक्त राष्ट्र पर्यावरण कार्यक्रम (यूएनईपी) ने पेश की है। यूएनईपी की 'ग्लोबल आउटलुक फॉर आइस एंड स्नो' रिपोर्ट में कहा गया है कि ग्लेशियरों, हिम चादरों और हिम शिखरों के पिघलने से दुनिया की 40 प्रतिशत आबादी प्रभावित हो सकती हैं।

ग्लोबल वार्मिंग का यह प्रभाव समुद्री जल स्तर बढ़ने, सुखा पड़ने, पेयजल का संकट और सिंचाई के लिए पानी उपलब्ध न होने के तौर पर होगा। सबसे चिंता की बात यह है कि ग्लोबल वार्मिंग का प्रभाव एशियाई जनसंख्या पर अधिक पड़ेगा। करीब 1.5 अरब एशियाई इसकी चपेट में आयेंगे। न केवल समुद्रतटीय शहर डूब जाएंगे, बल्कि गंगा, ब्रह्मपुत्रा, नील व मीकांग जैसी बड़ी नदियों के किनारे बसे करोड़ों लोग इसकी चपेट में आयेंगे। मौजूदा दौर में पर्यावरणविदों और वैज्ञानिकों की सबसे बड़ी चिंता हिमनदों और ग्लेशियरों को पिघलने से रोकने की है। इसकी वजह यह है कि बर्फ और हिम पृथ्वी पर पड़ने वाली 70 प्रतिशत सूर्य ऊर्जा को प्रत्यावर्तित कर देती है, जबकि महासागर उस ऊर्जा को सोखकर गर्म लहरों की आवृत्ति को बढ़ा देते हैं। यदि ग्रीनलैंड और अंटार्कटिका का 20 प्रतिशत हिस्सा भी पिघला तो समुद्र का जल स्तर 5 मीटर बढ़ जाएगा। पिछले 200 सालों में ही ग्रीनलैंड की हिमचादरों के पिघलने की रफ्तार दो गुनी हुई है। दूसरी तरफ यह भी पाया गया कि उत्तरी गोलार्ध में इसी साल मार्च और अप्रैल में हिमाच्छादित क्षेत्रों में 7 से 8 प्रतिशत की कमी आई है।

ग्लोबल वार्मिंग के कारण होने वाले जलवायु परिवर्तन के लिये सबसे अधिक जिम्मेदार ग्रीन हाउस गैस हैं। ग्रीन हाउस गैसें, वे गैसें होती हैं जो बाहर से मिल रही गर्मी या ऊष्मा को अपने अंदर सोख लेती हैं। ग्रीन हाउस गैसों का इस्तेमाल सामान्यतः अत्यधिक सर्द इलाकों में उन पौधों को गर्म रखने के लिये किया जाता है जो अत्यधिक सर्द मौसम में खराब हो जाते हैं। ऐसे में इन पौधों को काँच के

Greener Living

एक बंद घर में रखा जाता है और काँच के घर में ग्रीन हाउस गैस भर दी जाती है। यह गैस सूरज से आने वाली किरणों की गर्मी सोख लेती है और पौधों को गर्म रखती है। ठीक यही प्रक्रिया पृथ्वी के साथ होती है। सूरज से आने वाली किरणों की गर्मी की कुछ मात्रा को पृथ्वी द्वारा सोख लिया जाता है। इस प्रक्रिया में हमारे पर्यावरण में फैली ग्रीन हाउस गैसों का महत्त्वपूर्ण योगदान है।

अगर इन गैसों का अस्तित्व हमारे में न होता तो पृथ्वी पर तापमान वर्तमान से काफी कम होता। ग्रीन हाउस गैसों में सबसे ज्यादा महत्त्वपूर्ण गैस कार्बन डाइ आक्साइड है, जिसे हम जीवित प्राणी अपने साँस के साथ उत्सर्जित करते हैं। पर्यावरण वैज्ञानिकों का कहना है कि पिछले कुछ वर्षों में पृथ्वी पर कार्बन डाइ आक्साइड गैस की मात्रा लगातार बढ़ी है। वैज्ञानिकों द्वारा कार्बन डाइ आक्साइड के उत्सर्जन और तापमान वृद्धि में गहरा सम्बन्ध बताया जाता है। सन 2006 में एक डाक्यूमेंट्री फिल्म आई– 'द इन्कन्वीनियेंट ट्रुथ' यह डाक्यूमेंट्री फिल्म तापमान वृद्धि और कार्बन उत्सर्जन पर केन्द्रित थी। इस फिल्म में मुख्य भूमिका में थे– अमेरिकी उपराष्ट्रपति 'अल गोरे' और इस फिल्म का निर्देशन 'डेविड गुन्हेम' ने किया था। इस फिल्म में ग्लोबल वार्मिंग को एक विभीषिका की तरह दर्शाया गया, जिसका प्रमुख कारण मानव गतिविधि जनित कार्बन डाइ आक्साइड गैस माना गया। इस फिल्म को सम्पूर्ण विश्व में बहुत सराहा गया और फिल्म को सर्वश्रेष्ठ डाक्यूमेंट्री का आस्कर एवार्ड भी मिला।

यद्यपि ग्लोबल वार्मिंग पर वैज्ञानिकों द्वारा शोध कार्य जारी है, मगर मान्यता यह है कि पृथ्वी पर हो रहे तापमान वृद्धि के लिये जिम्मेदार कार्बन उत्सर्जन है जोकि मानव गतिविधि जनित है। इसका प्रभाव विश्व के राजनीतिक घटनाक्रम पर भी पड़ रहा है। सन 1988 में 'जलवायु परिवर्तन पर अन्तरशासकीय दल' का गठन किया गया था। सन 2007 में इस अन्तरशासकीय दल और तत्कालीन अमेरिकी उपराष्ट्रपति 'अल गोरे' को शांति का नोबल पुरस्कार दिया गया। आई.पी.सी.सी. वस्तुतः एक ऐसा अन्तरशासकीय वैज्ञानिक संगठन है जो जलवायु परिवर्तन से जुड़ी सभी सामाजिक, आर्थिक जानकारियों को इकट्ठा कर उनका विश्लेषण करता है। आई.पी.सी.सी का गठन सन 1988 में संयुक्त राष्ट्र संघ की जनरल असेंबली के दौरान हुआ था। यह दल खुद शोध कार्य नहीं करता और न ही जलवायु के विभिन्न कारकों पर नजर रखता है। यह दल सिर्फ प्रतिष्ठित जर्नल में प्रकाशित शोध पत्रों के आधार पर जलवायु को प्रभावित करने वाले मानव जनित कारकों से सम्बन्धित राय को अपनी रिपोर्ट्स के जरिए सरकारों और आम जनता तक पहुँचाता है।

आई.पी.सी.सी. की रिपोर्ट के अनुसार मानवजनित ग्रीन हाउस गैसें वर्तमान में पर्यावरण में हो रहे तापमान वृद्धि के लिये पूरी तरह से जिम्मेदार हैं, जिनमें कार्बन डाइऑक्साइड की मात्रा सबसे ज्यादा है। इस रिपोर्ट में कहा गया है कि ग्लोबल वार्मिंग में 90 प्रतिशत योगदान मानवजनित कार्बन उत्सर्जन का है। जबकि प्रो. यू.

आर. राव अपने शोध के आधार पर कह रहे हैं कि ग्लोबल वार्मिंग में 40 प्रतिशत योगदान तो सिर्फ कास्मिक विकिरण का है। इसके अलावा कई अन्य कारक भी हैं जिनका ग्लोबल वार्मिंग में योगदान है और उन पर शोध कार्य जारी है।

भारतीय अंतरिक्ष एजेंसी द्वारा 'इसरो' के पूर्व चेयरमैन और भौतिकविद प्रो. यू. आर. राव अपने शोध-पत्र में लिखते हैं कि अंतरिक्ष से पृथ्वी पर आपतित हो रहे कास्मिक विकिरण का सीधा सम्बन्ध सौर-क्रियाशीलता से होता है। अगर सूरज की क्रियाशीलता बढ़ती है तो ब्रह्माण्ड से आने वाला कास्मिक विकिरण निचले स्तर के बादलों के निर्माण में प्रमुख भूमिका निभाता है। इस बात की पेशकश सबसे पहले स्वेन्समार्क और क्रिस्टेन्सन नामक वैज्ञानिकों ने की थी। निचले स्तर के बादल सूरज से आने वाले विकिरण को परावर्तित कर देते हैं, जिस कारण से पृथ्वी पर सूरज से आने वाले विकिरण के साथ आई गर्मी भी परावर्तित होकर ब्रह्माण्ड में वापस चली जाती है।

वैज्ञानिकों ने पाया कि सन 1925 से सूरज की क्रियाशीलता में लगातार वृद्धि हुई। जिसके कारण पृथ्वी पर आपतित होने वाले कास्मिक विकिरण में लगभग 9 प्रतिशत कमी आई है। इस विकिरण में आई कमी से पृथ्वी पर बनने वाले खास तरह के निचले स्तर के बादलों के निर्माण में भी कमी आई है, जिससे सूरज से आने वाला विकिरण सोख लिया जाता है और इस कारण से पृथ्वी के तापमान में वृद्धि का अनुमान लगाया जा सकता है। प्रो. राव के निष्कर्ष के अनुसार ग्लोबल वार्मिंग में इस प्रक्रिया का 40 प्रतिशत योगदान है जबकि कास्मिक विकिरण सम्बन्धी जलवायु ताप की प्रक्रिया मानव गतिविधि जनित नहीं है और न ही मानव इसे संचालित कर सकता है। इस तरह यह शोध आई.पी.सी.सी. के इस निष्कर्ष का खंडन करता है कि ग्लोबल वार्मिंग में 90 प्रतिशत योगदान मानव का है। अगर ग्लोबल वार्मिंग के अन्य कारकों का अध्ययन किया जाए तो ग्लोबल वार्मिंग में मानव-गतिविधियों का योगदान आई.पी.सी.सी. की रिपोर्ट की अपेक्षा बहुत कम होगा।

ग्लोबल वार्मिंग के प्रभाव :

गर्मी में वृद्धि : 1901 से लगातार दुनिया के अनेक स्थानों में असाधारण रूप से रिकार्ड गर्मी दर्ज की गयी है। तापमान बढ़ने और गर्म हवाओं के चलने से जहां बीमारियां बढ़ी है, वहीं इससे मौतों में बड़ी वृद्धि हुई है।

समुद्रों का बढ़ता जलस्तर : तापमान में बढ़ोत्तरी के चलते पर्वतीय ग्लेशियर तेजी से पिघल रहे हैं। इसके चलते समुद्र का पानी विस्तारित हो रहा है और दुनिया में समुद्रों का जलस्तर बढ़ रहा है। पिछले 100 सालों में समुद्र के जलस्तर में 4 से 10 इंच (10-20) सेंटीमीटर की वृद्धि हुई हैं। अनुमान है कि अगले 100 सालों में इसमें 1 से 3 फुट की वृद्धि होगी। इस स्तर में प्रत्येक एक फुट की वृद्धि से 50 से 100 फुट तटीय क्षेत्र खत्म हो जायेगा।

Greener Living

पिघलते ग्लेशियर : पिछले 150 सालों में दुनिया के ज्यादातर ग्लेशियर सिकुड़ रहे हैं। कम ऊँचाई पर स्थित ग्लेशियर लुप्त होते जा रहे हैं और वैज्ञानिकों के मुताबिक ग्लोबल वार्मिंग की मौजूदा प्रवृत्ति के चलते वर्ष 2100 तक ज्यादातर ग्लेशियरों का अस्तित्व ही खत्म हो जायेगा। ग्लेशियरों के सिकुड़ते रहने से गर्मियों में होने वाले जल प्रवाह में तेजी से कमी आयेगी और इससे बहुत क्षेत्रों में सिंचाई और ऊर्जा उत्पादन अस्त–व्यस्त हो जायेगा।

नंगे होते आर्कटिक और अंटार्कटिक : पिछले कुछ दशकों से कनाडा, अलास्का, साबेरिया और अंटार्कटिका के हिस्से औसत से ज्यादा गर्मी से गुजर रहे हैं। ग्रीनहाउस गैसों के स्तर में हो रही वृद्धि से ग्लोबल वार्मिंग का प्रभाव यहां स्पष्ट देखा जा रहा है। आर्कटिक और अंटार्कटिका की हिमचादरें लगातार पतली हो रही है।

ग्लोबल वार्मिंग के लक्षण :

फैलती बीमारियां : गर्म तापमान मच्छरों के लिए अनुकूल होता है, जिससे ये मलेरिया और डेंगू जैसी बीमारियों को तेजी से फैलाते हैं। तापमान बढ़ने से मच्छरों का फैलाव उन क्षेत्रों में भी होने लगता है, जहां पहले वे कभी नहीं होते थे।

बसंत का जल्दी आगमन : पिछले कुछ दशकों से दुनिया के अनेक हिस्सों में समय से पहले ही बसंत का आगमन देखा गया है। नदियों और झीलों का समय से पहले पिघलना, पेड़–पौधों में समय से पहले फूलों का खिलना, पक्षियों द्वारा सय से पहले अंडे देना आदि इसके उदाहरण है। बसंत का यह समय पूर्व आगमन जंतुओं की प्रवास प्रक्रिया को अस्त व्यस्त कर पारिस्थितिकीय प्रणाली में अनेक समस्याएं पैदा कर रहा है।

वनस्पति और जंतुओं का प्रभाव : देखा गया है कि जंतु और वनस्पतियां गर्म तापमान के कारण ऊँचाई की तरफ मुड़ते हैं। अध्ययनों में यह बात समाने आयी है कि गर्म मौसम की स्थितियों के चलते अनेक प्रजातियों ने अपना ठिकाना बदल दिया है। ऐसे में यदि ग्लोबल वार्मिंग की यही रफ्तार रही तो बहुत सी प्रजातियां नष्ट हो जायेंगी।

खतरे में मूंगा भित्तिया : ऑस्ट्रेलिया की ग्रेट बैरियर रीफ समेत 32 देशों में मूंगा भित्तियों पर ब्लीचिंग के कारण लगातार खत्तरा मंडरा रहा है। ब्लीचिंग तब होती है, जब सूक्ष्म काई खत्म होने लगती है। यही सूक्ष्म कार्ड जीवित मूंगों को पोषण और रंग प्रदान करती हैं। ब्लीचिंग तब होता है, समुद्र के पानी का तापमान 1.1 से 1.5 डिग्री सेल्सियस तक गर्म हो जाता है।

भारी बर्फवारी, बाढ़ और मूसलाधार वर्षा : गर्म जलवायु के कारण मौसम चक्र तेजी से प्रभावित हो रहा है। दुनिया के अनेक हिस्सों में असमय अति वृष्टि, बाढ़, जबर्दस्त बर्फबारी, मूसलाधार वर्षा होना अब सामान्य बात हो गयी है।

Greener Living

सूखा और आग : जलवायु के गर्म होने से बार बार सूखे की समस्या आने लगी हैं। निरंतर सूखे की स्थिति होने से जंगल आग से नष्ट हो जाते हैं।

ग्रीन हाउस गैस वो गैस होती है जो पृथ्वी के वातावरण में प्रवेश कर यहाँ का तापमान बढ़ाने में कारक बनती हैं। वैज्ञानिकों के अनुसार इन गैसों का उत्सर्जन अगर इसी प्रकार चलता रहा तो 21वीं शताब्दी में पृथ्वी का तापमान 3 डिग्री से 8 डिग्री सेल्सियस तक बढ़ सकता है। अगर ऐसा हुआ तो इसके परिणाम बहुत घातक होंगे। दुनिया के कई हिस्सों में बिछी बर्फ की चादरें पिघल जाएँगी, समुद्र का जल स्तर कई फीट ऊपर तक बढ़ जाएगा। समुद्र के इस बर्ताव से दुनिया के कई हिस्से जलमग्न हो जाएँगे, भारी तबाही मचेगी। यह तबाही किसी विश्वयुद्ध या किसी 'ऐस्टेरॉइड' के पृथ्वी से टकराने के बाद होने वाली तबाही से भी बढ़कर होगी। हमारे ग्रह पृथ्वी के लिये भी यह स्थिति बहुत हानिकारक होगी।

ग्रीन हाउस गैसों का उत्सर्जन : माना जा रहा है कि इसकी वजह से उष्णकटिबंधीय रेगिस्तानों में नमी बढ़ेगी। मैदानी इलाकों में भी इतनी गर्मी पड़ेगी जितनी कभी इतिहास में नहीं पड़ी। इस वजह से विभिन्न प्रकार की जानलेवा बीमारियाँ पैदा होंगी। हमें ध्यान में रखना होगा कि हम प्रकृति को इतना नाराज न कर दें कि वह हमारे अस्तित्व को खत्म करने पर ही आमादा हो जाए। हमें इन सब बातों का ख्याल रखना पड़ेगा।

आज हर व्यक्ति पर्यावरण की बात करता है। प्रदूषण से बचाव के उपाय सोचता है। व्यक्ति स्वच्छ और प्रदूषण मुक्त पर्यावरण में रहने के अधिकारों के प्रति सजग होने लगा है और अपने दायित्वों को समझने लगा है। वर्तमान में विश्व ग्लोबल वार्मिंग के सवालों से जूझ रहा है। इस सवाल का जवाब जानने के लिये विश्व के अनेक देशों में वैज्ञानिकों द्वारा प्रयोग और खोजें हुई हैं। उनके अनुसार अगर प्रदूषण फैलने की रफ्तार इसी तरह बढ़ती रही तो अगले दो दशकों में धरती का औसत तापमान 0.3 डिग्री सेल्सियस प्रति दशक के दर से बढ़ेगा, जो चिंताजनक है।

तापमान की इस वृद्धि से विश्व के सारे जीव–जंतु बेहाल हो जाएँगे और उनका जीवन खतरे में पड़ जाएगा। पेड़–पौधों में भी इसी तरह का बदलाव आएगा। सागर के आस–पास रहने वाली आबादी पर इसका सबसे ज्यादा असर पड़ेगा। जल स्तर ऊपर उठने के कारण सागर तट पर बसे ज्यादातर शहर इन्हीं सागरों में समा जाएँगे। हाल ही में कुछ वैज्ञानिक अध्ययन बताते हैं कि जलवायु में बिगाड़ का सिलसिला इसी तरह जारी रहा तो कुपोषण और विषाणु जनित रोगों से होने वाली मौतों की संख्या में भारी बढ़ोत्तरी हो सकती है।

जब किसी प्राकृतिक आपदा का पहाड़ टूटता है, तब उसकी चपेट में अमीर और गरीब दोनों ही आते हैं। प्रकृति भेदभाव नहीं करती, न खुशी में, न ही नाराजगी में। लेकिन जलवायु परिवर्तन पर पिछले कई सम्मेलनों में विकसित और विकासशील देशों ने एक दूसरे देशों पर आरोप लगाए हैं बजाय इस स्थिति को सुधारने की दिशा में। विकासशील देशों का कहना है कि पहले यह तय होना

चाहिए कि ग्रीन हाउस गैसों के उत्सर्जन के लिए विकसित देश कितने जिम्मेदार हैं। इनका तर्क है कि 1950 से पहले अमीर देश 95 प्रतिशत ग्रीन हाउस ग्लोबल वार्मिंग के लिए जिम्मेदार थे। 1950 से 2000 के बीच वे 77 प्रतिशत गैसो का उत्सर्जन कर रहे थे। इन देशों को यह तथ्य स्वीकार करना चाहिए।

लेकिन विकसित देश अपनी गलतियों को स्वीकार करने के लिए तैयार नहीं है। दरअसल विकसित देश विकासशील देशों की शर्त पर पर्यावरण का सुधार देखना चाहते है। अमेरिका आज ग्रीन हाउस गैसों के उत्सर्जन में पूरी दुनिया में नंबर एक है। रियो डि जेनेरियो के पृथ्वी सम्मेलन से आज तक जब भी ग्लोबल वार्मिंग और पर्यावरण प्रदूषण को लेकर उस पर जवाबदेही की बात उठी तो उसका गैर–जिम्मेदाराना व्यवहार ही सामने आया। फिलहाल विकसित देशों की रणनीति यह है कि तेजी से उभर रही चीन, भारत और ब्राजील जैसी अर्थव्यवस्थाओं को इस बहाने घेरा जाये। इसलिए यूरोपीय संघ कहता है कि जब हम इन तीन देशों से कोई वादा करने को कहते हैं तो इसका मतलब यह नहीं कि ये भी वही सब कुछ करें, जो विकसित देश कर रहे हैं।

प्रलय की ओर बढ़ रही दुनिया के सभी देशों को समान रूप से इसकी भयावहता के बारे में विचार करना होगा। लेकिन स्वाभाविक रूप से जो ग्लोबल वार्मिंग के सबसे बड़े गुनाहगार हैं, उनकी जिम्मेदारी है कि वे गुनाह के मुताबिक इसकी भरपाई करने के लिए भी तैयार रहें।

ग्लोबल वार्मिंग : संभव है नियंत्रण : ग्लोबल वार्मिंग और ऊर्जा की बर्बादी पर अंकुश लगाने के लिए चलाए जा रहे जागरूकता अभियान '15 मिनट्स ऑफ रेस्माइट फॉर द प्लेनेट' के तहत पिछले कुछ वर्षों से एफिल टॉवर की स्पॉट लाइट पांच मिनट के लिए बंद की जा रही है। इसका उद्देश्य है कि ऊर्जा के उपयोग की शैली में व्यापक बदलाव लाकर ग्लोबल वार्मिंग की समस्या पर नियंत्रण संभव है।

इंटरगवर्नमेंटल पैनल ऑफ क्लाइमेट चेंज के अनुसार मौसम मॉडल यह भविष्यवाणी कर रहे हैं कि 21वीं सदी के अंत तक वैश्विक तापमान 1.4 डिग्री सेंटीग्रेड तक चढ़कर 5.8 डिग्री सेंटीग्रेड पहुंच जाएगा। इस संबंध में विशेषज्ञों का कहना है कि संसाधनों के उपयोग की शैली में व्यापक बदलाव लाकर ग्लोबल वार्मिंग की समस्या पर नियंत्रण संभव है। इस क्रम में वाहनों एवं अन्य उपकरणों की क्षमता में इजाफा करना जरूरी है ताकि कार्बन डाइ ऑक्साइड के उत्सर्जन पर भी नियंत्रण रखा जा सके। आईईए के अनुसार वातावरण का तापमान बढ़ाने वाली ग्रीन हाउस गैसों के उपार्जन में कमी की रणनीति को प्रभावी रूप से लागू करने के लिए अधिक माइलेज वाली कारों और बेहतर इमारतों के निर्माण पर करीब 2.4 ट्रिलियन डॉलर राशि व्यय की जरूरत होगी जबकि इसके जरिए कालातर में तेल और बिजली के खर्च में 8.1 ट्रिलियन डॉलर की कमी लाई जा सकती है।

पृथ्वी ने हमें हवा, पानी, अन्न और रहने के लिए जगह दी। आज वही पृथ्वी हमारे कर्मों के कारण ही धीरे–धीरे अपनी अस्तित्व खोती नजर आ रही हैं और

Greener Living

हम मूक दर्शक बने तमाशा देख रहे हैं। ग्लोबल वार्मिंग घुन की तरह है जो धीरे-धीरे पृथ्वी को नष्ट करती जा रही है। बहरहाल, जिस तरह से जलवायु में आये दिन दिखने वाले बदलाव को लोग महसूस कर रहे हैं और उन्हें लगने लगा है कि यह ग्लोबल वार्मिंग का ही प्रभाव है, और इस भयावह संकट के कारण पर्यावरण के प्रति जागरूकता जगाने की जरूरत है। सिर्फ सरकारें ही इस मामले में बदलाव नहीं ला सकती। सबको प्रकृति और पर्यावरण से आत्मीय संबंध बनाने होंगे। वैसे सही मायने में ग्लोबल वार्मिंग को रोकने का कोई इलाज नहीं है। इसके बारे में सिर्फ जागरूकता फैलाकर ही इससे लड़ा जा सकता है। स्कूली स्तर पर बच्चों को पर्यावरण का पाठ पढ़ाना होगा। तभी हम और हमारी पृथ्वी सुरक्षित रह पायेगी। हमें अपनी पृथ्वी को सही मायनों में 'ग्रीन' बनाना होगा। अपने 'कार्बन फुटप्रिंट्स' (प्रति व्यक्ति कार्बन उत्सर्जन को मापने का पैमाना) को कम करना होगा।

संदर्भ सूची :

1. सिंह, सवीन्द्र, पर्यावरण भूगोल का स्वरूप, प्रवालिका पब्लिकेशन्स, इलाहाबाद, 2016
2. शर्मा, एच.एस., शर्मा, एम. एल. एवं मिश्रा, आर. एन. भौतिक भूगोल, पंचशील प्रकाशन, जयपुर 2019
3. रिपोर्ट, दक्षिण एशिया के हॉटस्पॉट : तापमान और वर्षण में परिवर्तन का जीवन-स्तर पर प्रभाव, विश्व बैंक समूह, 2018,
4. नारायण, सुनीता (पर्यावरणविद्), जलवायु परिवर्तन के अवश्यंभावी प्रभाव, बिजनेस स्टैण्डर्ड, दिनांक 14.8.18
5. सक्सेना, के. जी., जलवायु परिवर्तन और सम्पोषणीय विकास, योजना, प्रकाशन विभाग, दिल्ली, दिसम्बर 2015
6. आर्थिक समीक्षा 2020-21, भारत सरकार
7. दैनिक भास्कर, राजस्थान
8. इण्डियन एक्सप्रेस
9. योजना
10. कुरुक्षेत्र
11. प्रतियोगिता दर्पण
12. इण्डिया टुडे
13. आउटलुक
14. प्रतियोगिता दर्पण

सहायक आचार्य, राजनीति विज्ञान,
बाबू शोभाराम राजकीय कला महाविद्यालय, अलवर
email : dayachanddagur@gmail.com

4. Ayurveda and Healthcare : A Review

Archana Singh,
Anjul Dadoria
Suman Malik

Abstract

Ayurveda is a science of life with a holistic approach to health and personalized medicine. Health is defined as a state of equilibrium with one's self (svasthya) but which is inextricably linked to the environment. Ayurveda is a traditional Indian medicinal system being practiced for thousands of years. Considerable research on pharmacognosy, chemistry, pharmacology and clinical therapeutics has been carried out on ayurvedic medicinal plants. Many of the major pharmaceutical corporations have renewed their strategies in favor of natural products in medicine discovery, though it is equally important to follow systems of clinical trials to monitor biological applications before preparing the formulations. The present review highlights various fields of research including literary, fundamental, drug, pharmaceutical, and clinical exploration in Ayurveda.

Keywords : Ayurveda, Health, Therapeutics, Pharmacognosy, Pharmacology

1. Introduction about Ayurveda

The name "Ayurveda" is derived from two words in Sanskrit, "ayuh" meaning "life" or "longevity" and "veda" meaning "science" or "sacred knowledge." Ayurveda's definition therefore roughly translates as "the science of longevity" or "the sacred knowledge of life." Ayurveda is not simply about taking an herbal formula and waiting for the results. Instead, it encourages you to be an active participant in your own journey toward healing.

The practice of Ayurveda as a medicine is believed to date back to over five thousand years, during the Vedic period of ancient India. Ayurveda recognizes five elements as the fundamental building blocks of nature: Earth, Water, Fire, Air, Ether (Space). Every substance contains all five of these elements. That said, in a given substance, one or two elements are typically predominant over the others.

1.1 The Doshas and Your Ayurvedic Body Type

Then there are the three doshas (bodily humors): vata, pitta, and kapha. The doshas, or some combination of them, can be identified in various seasons, climates, landscapes, activities, plants, and animals.

All three doshas are present in everyone, but the ratio between them varies a great deal from one person to the next. There is a combination of doshas we are born with, called ourconstitution, Ayurvedic body type, or prakriti in Sanskrit. We also have a state of balance (vikriti) which represents the doshas that are elevated within our body at a given time.

Constitutional Types :

Ayurveda recognizes seven basic constitutional types :

Vata-Typev : A greater amount of vata, lesser amounts of pitta and kapha.

Pitta-Typevb: A greater amount of pitta, lesser amounts of vata and kapha.

Kapha-Typev : A greater amount of kapha, lesser amounts of vata and pitta.

Vata-Pitta-Type (or Pitta-Vata) : Greater amounts of both vata and pitta, a lesser amount of kapha.

Pitta-Kapha (or Kapha-Pitta) : Greater amounts of both pitta and kapha, a lesser amount of vata.

Kapha-Vata (or Vata-Kapha) : Greater amounts of both vata and kapha, a lesser amount of pitta.

Tridoshic (or Vata-Pitta-Kapha-Type) : Equal amounts of all three doshas within the body.

Your constitution influences your physiology, your likes and dislikes, your tendencies and habits, your mental and emotional character, and your vulnerabilities toward imbalance and disease.

1.2 Imbalances

Discovering your current state of balance will show you the present level of the doshas in your system. A vata imbalance occurs when vata is in excess. This can cause fear, anxiety, physical and emotional constriction, ungroundedness, poor circulation, constipation, dry skin, cracking joints, emaciation, insomnia, twitches, tremors, and other abnormal movements.

A pitta imbalance occurs when pitta is in excess. This can cause anger, jealousy, inflammation, excessive heat, heartburn, loose stools, migraines, rashes, bruising, bleeding disorders, sharp hunger, an overactive metabolism, and difficulty sleeping.

A kapha imbalance occurs when kapha is in excess. This can cause attachment, greed, resistance to change, lack of motivation, heaviness in the mind and body, excessive sleep, depression, a sluggish metabolism, congestion, water retention, hardening of the arteries, and the formation of masses and tumors.

A delicate balance between biophysiological forces (dosha) and constitution (prakriti) is said to determine health and disease. Ayurveda's principle therapeutic aim is to harmoniously restore that balance. Ayurveda has an extensive pharmacopoeia, predominantly herbs and minerals. Ayurvedic formulations, often complex with several herbal-mineral ingredients, are governed by well-described pharmacological principles of preparation, compatibility and administration. In some complex, well-controlled physicochemical processes convert raw metals and minerals into potent medicines known as bhasmas.

2. Ayurveda in Healthcare

Ayurveda emphasizes prevention and health promotion and provides treatment for disease. It considers the development of consciousness to be essential for optimal health and meditation as the main technique for achieving this. Treatment of disease is highly individualized and depends on the psychophysiological constitution of the patient. There are different dietary and lifestyle recommendations for each season of the year. Common spices are utilized in treatment, as well as herbs and herbal mixtures, and special preparations known as Rasayanas are used for rejuvenation, promotion of longevity, and slowing of the aging process. A group of purification procedures known as 'Panchakarma' removes toxins from the physiology. Whereas Western allopathic medicine is excellent in handling acute medical crises, Ayurveda demonstrates an ability to manage chronic disorders that Western medicine has been unable to.

It may be projected from Ayurveda's comprehensive approach, emphasis on prevention, and ability to manage chronic disorders that its widespread use would improve the health status of the world's population.

Use of plants as a source of medicine has been an ancient practice and is an important component of the health care system in India. In India, about 70 percent of rural population depends on the traditional Ayurvedic system of medicine. Most healers/practitioners of the traditional systems of medicine prepare formulations by their own recipes and dispense to the patients. Alternative medicines are being used by those people who do not use or cannot be helped by conventional medicinal system.

2.1 Ayurvedic Approaches in Osteoarthritis

While science has no definite answers about what causes osteoarthritis, researchers have identified several factors involved in the development and course of osteoarthritis. Some of these factors include inflammation, biomechanical imbalances that put stress on the joints, and cellular disorders that lead to the abnormal breakdown of cartilage. It is important that the approach we use in treating osteoarthritis address as many of these factors as possible.

Given the only moderate effectiveness and potential side effects of conventional treatment, both patients and health care professionals are seeking out alternative therapies, including those offered by the ancient healing system known as Ayurveda. This paperfocuses at the three main modalities Ayurveda uses to treat osteoarthritis and other disorders: herbal treatments, meditation, and yoga.

Ayurvedic Herbal Treatments

Ayurveda offers many herbal treatments for the treatment of OA. These plants have documented anti-inflammatory properties without the side effects of commonly prescribed medications. For example, at a recent meeting of the American College of Rheumatology, a study was presented that showed an herbal Ayurvedic therapy to be as effective in treating knee osteoarthritis as a commonly prescribed medication (Celebrex) and glucosamine – and with fewer side effects. The ACR stated thatAyurveda offers "safe and effective treatment alternatives" for OA.

The herbs boswellia, turmeric, ashwagandha, ginger, triphala, guggulu, and shatavari have all been shown to decrease inflammation by interfering with the production of inflammatory chemicals in the body.

Interestingly, some data suggests that it may protect the stomach against non-steroidal anti-inflammatories (NSAIDs). Although current studies for its use in treating osteoarthritis are few, curcumin/turmeric is a promising option in the treatment of OA.

Ashwagandha : Ayurvedic herb, ashwagandha (*Withaniasomnifera*), has known anti-inflammatory effects. In a study published in 2007, the extract of this herb was found to suppress the production of pro-inflammatory molecules (TNF-alpha and two interleukin subtypes). In one study, the anti-inflammatory effect of ashwagandha was comparable to taking the steroid hydrocortisone.

Ginger : The anti-inflammatory effects of ginger (*Zinziber officinale*) have also been documented. Ginger works as an anti-inflammatory by interfering with an enzyme (cyclooxygenase) that produces inflammatory chemicals in the body. There is some data showing that ginger has a moderate beneficial effect on OA of the knee. Further research is needed to determine the extent of ginger's effectiveness in treating OA.

Triphala : The Ayurvedic herb triphala has been used in India for thousands of years for treatment of osteoarthritis. Triphala is a formulary that consists of three herbs (amalaki, haritaki, and bibhitaki). Preliminary studies show that the herbs in triphala have anti-inflammatory effects.

Guggulu : In addition, the herb guggulu (*Commiphora guggul*) has been shown to be a potent inhibitor of the enzyme NF-kB, which regulates the body's inflammatory response. There are several studies that show decreased inflammation and joint swelling after administration of extracts of guggulu resin.

2.2 Ayurveda for Bronchial Asthma

Difficulty in breathing or shortness of breath may be simply termed as Swasa (Asthma). It may be primary - originating from respiratory system, secondary - originating from other systems of the body but the impact is on respiratory system.

Bronchial Asthma is a chronic inflammatory disease of airway. It leads to recurrent episodes of wheezing, breathlessness, tightness of chest and cough particularly at night or early morning. As per Ayurveda, Swasa is mainly caused by the Vata and Kapha doshas. Swasa is broadly classified into five types in Mahaswasa (Dyspnoea major), UrdhvaSwasa(ExpiratoryDyspnoea), Chinnaswasa (Chyne-stroke respiration), Kshudraswasa (Dyspnoea minor), Tamakaswasa (Bronchial Asthma).

Causes
As per Ayurveda the causes of TamakaSwasa are as follows:
- Intake of dry, cold, heavy, incompatible food and irregular intake of food
- Excessive Intake of black gram, beans, sesame, meat of aquatic animals.
- Intake of cold water and exposure to cold climate
- Exposure to dust, smoke and wind
- Excessive exercise
- Trauma to throat, chest and vital organs.

Treatment modalities in Ayurveda
As per the Ayurveda Bronchial Asthma is Vatakaphaja disease, it begins in the stomach, progresses to the lungs and bronchi. Hence the aim of treatment is to move the excess Kapha back to stomach and then eliminate it. For this purpose, following methods are adopted.
- Swedana (Sudation)
- Vamana (Therapeutic emesis)
- Virechana (Therapeutic purgation)

These procedures will be followed as per the need of individual patient. Practice of Pranayama, laxatives, light diet in the night and use of warm water will helps in the treatment of Asthma.

Specific Do's and Don'ts
Do's (Pathya)
(i) Godhuma (wheat), Old rice, Mudga (green gram), Kulattha (Horse gram), Yava (barley), Patola (snake gourd)
(ii) Use of Garlic, Turmeric, Ginger, Black pepper
(iii) Luke warm water, Goat milk, Honey
(iv) Respiratory exercise, Pranayama, Yoga

Don'ts (Apathya)
(i) Heavy, cold diet, Masha (black gram), Deep fried items, Mustard leaves, Fish
(ii) Exposure to Cold & Humid atmosphere
(iii) Sweets, Chilled water, Stored food items, Curd
(iv) Suppression of natural urges
(v) Excessive physical exertion
(vi) Exposure to Smoke, Dust and fumes, Pollutants and Pollens

2.3 Ayurveda for Skin Diseases

Skin disease is a common ailment, and it affects all ages from the neonate to the elderly and causes harm in a number of ways. Beside this, people suffering from skin disease suffer from social stigma. Ayurveda has given prime importance to *ahara* (diet) and *vihara* (lifestyle) in the maintenance of health and prevention of diseases. In the recent past, the relation between diet and skin ailments is well established in contemporary medicine. Ayurvedic literature has described skin diseases mainly under the spectrum of *Kushta*, the literary meaning of which is that which causes disfiguration. The Ayurvedic system of medicine describes a wide range of etiological factors for dermatological disorders.

All *Acharyas* have emphasized on *Shodhana* therapy for the management of *Kushta*. The therapy which expels out the morbid *doshas* from the body is known as *Shodhana*. By nature, *Kushta* is difficult to cure, but by the application of *Shodhana* therapy, cure of the diseases becomes easier due to removal of the root cause, hence *Shodhana* has great importance in *Bahudoshaavastha* (multifactorial condition).

According to Ayurveda, correcting skin diseases requires a multi-prong approach. Ayurveda recommends dietary changes to pacify the Dosha affected. Good food can help strengthen the digestive fire. This in turn helps block the formation of Ama or toxins that could harm the skin. The proper skincare, drinking sufficient water, and Yoga, and exercise are needed to help in effective skincare. Ayurvedic medicine for skin diseases can help manage skin problems.

Ayurvedic supplements for skin disorders use herbal ingredients that have a proven effect in helping manage skin problems. Some of the common ingredients used include :

1. Nyagrodha (*Ficus benghalensis*) : Extracts from the fig tree are anti-inflammatory in nature. It helps to manage skin diseases. It is helpful in managing Kapha and Pitta Doshas.

2. Ashwatha (*Ficus religiosa*) : This is the peepal tree. It is one of the traditional supplements helpful in managing skin diseases.

3. Raktachandana (*Pterocarpus santalinus*) : Popularly known as sandalwood, this Ayurvedic herb is helpful in managing acne and other skin conditions.

4. Haridra (*Curcuma longa*) : Known as turmeric, this is a powerful way to help improve skin health. It helps to reduce toxins on the skin and can help treat skin infections.

5. Keram (Coconut oil) : Coconut oil is used as a base to make oils to help manage skin diseases. Coconut oil is helpful in managing skin inflammation and itching. It is a natural moisturizer that helps to protect the skin and help prevent it from drying.

6. Vidpala (*Wrightia tinctoria*) : Also known as Kutaja, this is one of the powerful Ayurvedic ingredients that are helpful to manage psoriasis and dermatitis.

7. Sariba(*Hemidesmus indicus*) : This Ayurvedic herb helps manage burning in the skin. It is helpful in balancing the vitiation of all the three Doshas. It helps purify the blood and helps reduce toxins that cause skin diseases.

8. Kumkuma (*Crocus sativus*) : Saffron is helpful to improve skin complexion and tone. It helps maintain all three Doshas. It is anti-inflammatory and antioxidant in nature. It helps reduce pimples.

9. Manjistha (*Rubiacordifolia*) : Manjistha is a well-known herb that is helpful in the management of eczema, psoriasis, pimples, and dark spots. It helps improve skin health.

Conclusion

Every human has all three doshas with one of them in a prevailing position. Temporary disbalance in one of them can lead to certain short-term diseases, while long-term untreated disbalance can be a reason for chronic illnesses. All because continuous imbalances exhaust people, leaving them not enough energy to restore without respective medical treatment. Such exhaustion is called Ama. As

Ayurveda is a well-established medical system, one should expect the doctor to be able to determine main dosha and develop a treatment program based on medical records and current complaints. Mindful application of Ayurvedic practices can effectively reduce symptoms and suppress disease triggers to prevent or slow down further progression.

Acknowledgement :
The authors are thankful to DST, New Delhi for granting FIST program to the college.

References:
1. https://main.mohfw.gov.in/
2. https://www.ncbi.nlm.nih.gov/
3. Sharma, H., Chandola, H. M., Singh, G., &Basisht, G. (2007). Utilization of Ayurveda in health care: An approach for prevention, health promotion, and treatment of disease. Part 1- Ayurveda, the science of life. *Journal of Alternative and Complementary Medicine*, 13(9)(9), 1011–1019. doi:10.1089/acm.2007.7017-A, PubMed: 18047449
4. Pandey, M. M., & Rastogi Subha, R. A. K. S., & Rawat, A. K. (2013). Indian traditional ayurvedic system of medicine and nutritional supplementation. *Evidence-Based Complementary and Alternative Medicine: eCAM*, 2013, article ID 376327, 12 pages. doi:10.1155/2013/376327
5. https://www.integrativepractitioner.com/practice-management/news/an-ayurvedic-approach-to-osteoarthritis
6. https://ijatm.org/index.php/ijatm/article/view/110
7. https://www.keralaayurveda.biz/blog/all-you-need-to-know-about-skin-diseases-and-remedies

Department of Chemistry,
Sadhu Vaswani (Autonomous) College,
Sant Hirdaram Nagar (Bairagarh),
Bhopal, M.P. (India)
email : **drsingharchana@rediffmail.com**

5. Biocentrism : A Study in Environmental Ethics

Dr. Sadek Ali

Abstract

Apart from many ethical issues biocentrism is another important issue. Biocentrism gives important on all living life in respect of value oriented philosophy. Environmental ethics means ethical discussion on environmental events and in this regard many theories had been originated. Biocentrism transcends anthropocentrism. While anthropocentrism argues in favor of a world-view centering solely on humans and recognizes value only in human beings, biocentrism regards every living being in the nature as having intrinsic value that is value in itself and thus goes beyond speciesist anthropocentricity.

Keywords : Anthropocentric, transcendental, intrinsic value, biocentric.

Introduction

Environmental ethics mainly associated with the ethical discourses on environmental entities. We know environment not only confined within the human being rather environment is constituted by the biotic and abiotic or inert elements. In this regard, in contemporary environmental philosophy there are originated three leading theories namely-Anthropocentrism, Biocentrism and Ecocentrism. Anthropocentrism is mainly men-centric view, biocentrism is broad concept, it is not confined within human being rather all living entities, including non-human animals, planets etc. Ecocentrism is the holistic environmental theory and according to this theory not only the living beings are subject matter of this theory rather the whole ecosystem, including the abiotic part of the nature, is worthy of moral consideration.

Apart from three theories of the contemporary environmental philosophy biocentrism is the main discussion part in this writing and try to show how ethics can play the role in environment to save the living and inert entities. Paul Taylor was the pioneer of the biocentric thought and claimed that all living things have intrinsic or inherent value and so they are holding in the central position in the environmental ethics.

Speciesist anthropocentrism has been identified by the majority of environmental philosophers and other environmentalists as the root-cause of the present day eco- crisis. And it is often said that contemporary environmental philosophy has set out its journey by questioning this moral anthropocentrism. It is regarded as a systematic bias in traditional Western attitude to the non-human world or the nature in general. There have, however, recently developed some important views rejecting this attitude, and this development has strongly influenced the ways in which humans interpret their relationship with other species and with the nature and ecosystems. One such world-view we find in contemporary environmental philosophy is Biocentrism that considers all living beings to have moral value and humans to be one among innumerable species of organisms that live on the earth. 'Biocentrism' is a term that has more than one meaning. In environmental philosophy, however, it refers to the life-centric nature-view. It means that all living beings on the earth, including humans, have moral value. It recommends well-being of all life in the biosphere.

But it may be noted here that biocentrism also refers to the scientific position that life and consciousness forms the basis of observable reality, and thereby is the basis of the universe itself. For example, American scientist Robert Lanza proposed a theory in 2007, where he upholds this view that life and biology are central to being, reality, and the cosmos— life creates the universe rather than the other way around. This biocentrism of Robert Lanza asserts that current theories of the physical world do not work, and can never be made to work, until they fully account for life and consciousness. While physics is considered fundamental to the study of the universe, and chemistry is the fundamental to the study of life, biocentrism places biology before the other sciences to produce a 'theory of everything'.

Of course, the reception of Lanza's theory has been mixed. Critics have questioned whether the theory is falsifiable. Lanza has argued that future experiments, such as scaled-up quantum superposition, will either support or contradict the theory. Anyhow, this is a theory of cosmology, while we are interested in environmental philosophy and ethics. In environmental philosophy biocentrism is well-defined as the belief that all forms of life are equally valuable and only human is not the center of existence on the earth.

Anyhow, biocentrism transcends anthropocentrism. While anthropocentrism argues in favor of a world-view centering solely on humans and recognizes value only in human beings, biocentrism regards every living being in the nature as having intrinsic value that is value in itself and thus goes beyond speciesist anthropocentricity. This view asserts that we have an obligation to the whole biotic community. The central claim of biocentrism is that our moral obligation extends beyond humans to include all living beings. This obligation is direct, not merely indirect obligation to the living beings *via* humans. We are morally obliged, e.g., to preserve endangered species, not only because present and future humans would find life of diminished value unless we do that, but also because they are living beings with intrinsic/inherent value, the fact that demands our moral respect.

Australian philosopher Richard Routley (Sylvan) gives a good example in favour of biocentrism in his paper 'Is there a Need for a New, an Environmental Ethic? (1973) It goes by the name 'last man argument', where Routley asks us to imagine a hypothetical situation in which the 'last man', surviving a world catastrophe, acts to ensure the elimination of all other living beings and the destruction of all the landscapes after his demise. From the anthropocentric point of view, the 'last man' would do nothing morally wrong, since his destructive actin question would not cause any damage to the interest and well-being of humans, who would by then have disappeared. Nevertheless, Routley points out, there is a moral intuition that the imagined last act would be morally wrong. An explanation for this judgment, he gives, is that those non-human objects in the environment whose destruction is ensured by the 'last man' have intrinsic value, a kind of value independent of their usefulness for humans. From his critique, Routley concluded that the main approach in traditional western moral thinking was unable to allow the recognition that natural things have intrinsic value and that the tradition required overhaul of a significant kind. Anyhow, our common intuition is that it *does* matter to destroy the last form of life, and this is taken as evidence that non- human life has value independent of the existence of conscious valuers-and that this value is relevant to the assessment of the moral standing of living things.

Classical Biocentrism

Paul Taylor is the champion of this biocentric view of Nature, to whom we owe for its classical version. But the first life-centered concern in Western ethics is found, perhaps, in Albert Schweitzer's *Civilization and Ethics* published in 1923. Schweitzer's biocentric point of view is illustrated in terms of 'Reverence for Life'. He sees this as stemming from a fundamental 'will-to-live', inherent in all living beings. In self-conscious beings, like us, this will-to-live establishes a drive towards both self-realization and empathy with other living beings. He formulates his world-view in this way: 'I am life which wills to live, and I exist in the midst of life which wills to live.' Just in my own will-to-live there is a yearning for more life, the same obtains in each the will-to-live around me equally, whether it expresses itself or remains unvoiced. According to Schweitzer, all life is sacred and we should live accordingly, keeping in mind that each and every living being is inherently valuable 'will-to-live'. In nature one form of life falls prey upon another. But, human consciousness holds an awareness of, and sympathy for, the will of other beings to live. As a moral human being, he strives to rise above from this predator- prey relation so far as it is possible. Actually, as living beings with moral consciousness, we are not only concerned with our own life but also for the lives of other living beings and the environment in which we live in. According to him, 'It is good to maintain and cherish life; it is evil to destroy and check life.' (A. Schweitzer. "Reverence of Life" *Environmental Ethics: Readings in Theory and Practice,* P. 132) we have to choose to live up to this moral conscience; and our world-view must derive from this life-view, not *vice versa*. Respect for life, overcoming coarser impulses and hollow doctrines, leads the individual to live in the service of other people and of every living creature. In contemplation of the will-to-life, respect for the life of others becomes the highest principle and the defining purpose of humanity.

The fundamental principles of morality which we seek as a necessity for thought is not, according to Schweitzer, a matter of galvanizing the traditional moral views and norms, but also of expanding and extending the moral horizon. Morality, accordingly, is, in its unqualified form, extended responsibility with regard to anything living. He writes: "A man is really ethical only when he obeys the constraint laid on him to help all life which he is able to succour, and when he goes out of his way to avoid injuring anything living. He does not ask for how far this or that life deserves sympathy as valuable in itself, nor does he ask how far it is capable of feeling. To him life as such is sacred" (Ibid).

It may be mentioned here that Schweitzer received the 1952 Nobel Peace Prize for his philosophy of 'Reverence for Life'. Schweitzer's 'reverence for life' philosophy upholds that all living beings have intrinsic or inherent value. The intrinsic value of nature can and should be appealed to as the basis for human ethics. And the attitude of reverence for life would establish the connections between ethics and nature. According to Schweitzer, ethics begins when we recognize these connections, we feel awe and respect in the fact of living beings that commands our reverence and that compels us to strive to promote and preserve life in all its forms.

Anyhow, Schweitzer's assertion 'I am will-to-live' reminds us of Schopenhauer as his forerunner in the philosophy of 'willing' and 'will' in general. Of course, Schweitzer somehow individualizes this 'will to live', and this is something like this: I am life which wants to live amidst of lives which want to live! According to Schweitzer, I first of all experience the will to live and living in my own feeling and organism and I come to rationally respect this will also in other living beings, if I respect this will to live in myself. I am therefore forced or driven to acknowledge some such will to living also in other living beings around me and have to appreciate and respect this in the same way as in my own case. The transfer from the respect for my own will to living to the reverence for life of the other beings is grounded by certain methodological or meta-ethical principle of equality or equalitarianism, being a certain kind of inference by analogy, which Schweitzer however emphasizes as being '*denknotwendig*' (necessary in thinking). This kind of necessity and equalitarianism would and should lead me to respect and revere any other life and living being independently from any constraints or perspectives of speciesism, egotism or other partisan view-points.

Anyhow, as already stated, Paul Taylor is the best proponent of contemporary biocentric view of nature. Taylor's is, perhaps, the most comprehensive attempt to articulate and defend a biocentric position in environmental discourse. His biocentric world-view first comes to the fore with the publication of the article, 'The Ethics of Respect for Nature' in *Environmental Ethics* in 1981. It was then followed by a full-fledged book titled **Respect for Nature : A Theory of Environmental Ethics**, which he published in the year 1986. The core of Taylor's position is the claim that all living things and beings have inherent value and so merit moral respect. According to him, to say that an entity has a good of its own is simply to say that, without reference to any other entity, it can be benefited or harmed. This good is 'objective', in the sense that it is independent of what any conscious being happens to think about it. Anyhow, to say that each living being has a good of their own or something has inherent worth is, according to Taylor, to invoke two principles: the principle of *moral consideration* and the principle of *intrinsic value*.

The principle of *moral consideration* means that every living being that has a good of its own merits moral consideration. And the principle of *intrinsic value* states that the realization of the good of an individual is intrinsically valuable. This means that its good is *prima facie* worthy of being preserved or promoted as an endin itself and for the sake of the entity whose good it is. The combination of these two principles constitutes the fundamental moral attitude which Taylor calls 'respect for Nature'.

The first principle of moral consideration states that all living things deserve the concern and attention of all moral agents simply by virtue of their being members of the earth's community of life. From the moral point of view, their good must be taken into account whenever it is affected for better or worse by the behavior of some agents. This provision stands for all, no matter what species the creature belongs to. The good of each entity is accorded some value and so acknowledged as having some weight in the deliberations of all rational agents. However, it may be necessary for such an agent to act in ways contrary to the good of this or that particular organism in order to further other's good, including human good. But the principle of moral consideration prescribes that, with respect to each being an entity having its own good, every individual deserves moral consideration.

On the other hand, the principle of intrinsic value asserts that, irrespective of what kind of entity it is in other respects, if it is a member of the earth's biotic community, the realization of its good is something intrinsically valuable. This signifies that the good of the entity concerned is worthy of being preserved or attended to, and this intrinsic/inherent value is an end in itself and for the sake of the entity concerned. While we consider an entity as having intrinsic or inherent value, we deny that it can be treated as a mere object, or as an entity whose value completely depends on being instrumental in promoting another's good.

Though these two principles seem nearer to each other, they are not identical. While the principle of moral consideration affirms that all living beings deserve the concern and consideration of all moral agents simply by virtue of their being members of the earth's community of life, the principle of intrinsic value states that if some entity is a member of the earth's biotic community, the realization of its good is something *intrinsically* valuable, its good is worthy of being respected, and this intrinsic value is an end in itself, and as such, it is for the sake of the entity concerned. According to Taylor, when rational, autonomous agents regard such entities as possessing inherent worth, they place intrinsic value on the realization of their good and so hold themselves responsible for performing actions that will have this effect and for refraining from actions having the contrary effect. Not only that, then they subscribe to the principles of moral consideration and of intrinsic value and so conceive of wild living beings as having that kind of worth. On Taylor's judgment, "such agents are *adopting a certain ultimate moral attitude toward the natural world*. This is the attitude I call "respect for Nature".

Respect for nature thus signifies a life-centered world-view of environmental philosophy. This ethics of respect for nature has three basic elements: a belief system, an ultimate moral outlook, and a set of rules of duty and standards of character. These elements are connected with each other in the following manner. The belief system underlying this attitude of respect for nature is called 'the biocentric outlook on Nature'. As Taylor explains, the belief system provides a certain outlook on nature which supports and makes intelligible an autonomous agent's adopting, as an ultimate moral attitude, the attitude of respect for nature. Living things and beings are viewed as the appropriate objects of the attitude of respect, and are, accordingly, regarded as entities possessing inherent/intrinsic worth. One then places intrinsic value on the promotion and protection of their good. As a consequence of this, one makes a moral commitment to abide by a set of rules of duty and to fulfill certain standards of good character.

This ethics of respect for nature is symmetrical with a system of human ethics grounded on 'respect for person'. This has three aspects: The first is a conception of oneself and others as persons, as centers of autonomous choice. Second, there is an attitude of respect for person as person. It is adopted as an ultimate moral attitude in which every person is regarded as having inherent worth or human dignity. Third, there is an ethical system of duties which are acknowledged to be owed by everyone to everyone. These duties are forms of conduct in which public recognition is given to each individual's inherent worth as a person. Accordingly, the biocentric outlook on nature implies all these four things:

(1) Humans are members of the earth's community of life on the same terms as all the non-human members are.
(2) The earth's natural ecosystems are seen as complex web of interconnected and interdependent elements.
(3) Each individual organism is conceived of as a teleological centre of life, pursuing its own good in its own way.
(4) Humans are not superior to any other living thing.

While thus formulating the biocentric outlook, Taylor takes cognizance of the fact of our being an animal species to be a fundamental feature of our existence. He and his supporters do not deny the significant differences between ourselves and other species, but they wish to keep in the forefront of our consciousness the fact that, in relation to our planet's natural ecosystems, we are but one species population among many others. Our origin lies in the same process of evolution that gives rise to all other species and that we are confronted with similar environmental conditions that confront the members of other species. The so-called laws of natural selection, of adaptation and of genetics apply simultaneously with all of us as members of the biological community.

If we have a deep watch on the happenings in the nature, we would see that each animal and plant is like us in having a good, a *telos* of its own. Although our human good (e.g., of value and significance of human life, including the exercise of individual autonomy in choosing our own particular value-system) is not exactly similar to the good of a non-human animal or plant, it cannot be maintained that their good can go without the biological necessities for survival and physicalhealth.

Again, the possibility of the extinction of the human species makes us aware of another aspect in which we should not consider ourselves in better position than other species. Our well-being and survival is dependent upon the ecological health and wellbeing of various animals and plants communities, while their survival and health does not depend on human wellbeing. Rather, many wild animals and plants would be greatly benefited if all human beings disappear from the earth. The depletion of their habitats by human beings in the name of 'development' would then cease. The anthropogenic pollution of the land, air and water would come to an end. Ecosystems could gradually return to their balance, suffering only some natural disruptions. All these imply that our presence is not so much needed from the community standpoint.

Let us come to the *second* component of biocentric worldview, which sees the natural world as an organic system. To accept the biocentric outlook and regard ourselves and our place in the world from its perspective is to see the whole natural order of the earth's biosphere as a complex but unified web of interconnected organisms, objects, and events. The ecological relationship between any community of living things and their environment forms an organic whole of functionally interdependent parts. Such dynamic, but at the same time, relatively stable structures such as food-chains, predator-prey relations, plant succession in a forest, are self-regulating energy-recycling mechanisms that preserve the equilibrium of the whole.

And for this, while we think of the well-being of the biotic communities—of humans, animals and plants, we should be careful for the ecological equilibrium. When one views the realm of nature from this biocentric perspective, one should never forget that in the long run the integrity of the entire biosphere of our planet isessential to the realization of the good of its constituent communities of life, both human and non-human. This holistic view of the earth's ecological systems, according to Taylor, does not by itself constitute a moral norm. These are facts of biological reality, rather a set of causal connections put forth in empirical terms. Its ethical implications for our treatment of the natural environmental lie entirely in the fact that our knowledge of these casual connections is an essential means to fulfilling the ends we set for ourselves in adopting the attitude of respect for Nature.

In order to explain the *third* component of the biocentric outlook Taylor reiterates that each individual organism is to be conceived of as a teleological center of life. The organism comes to mean something to be one as a unique, irreplaceable individual. The final culmination of this process is the achievement of a genuine understanding of the biocentric point of view and with that understanding; ability would crop up to take that point of view. Conceiving of a living being as a center of life, one is able to look at the world from its perspective.

Understanding living beings as teleological centers of life does not necessitateassociating them with human characteristics. We need not consider all of them as having consciousness like us. Some of them may be aware of the world around them and others may not. Nor need we deny that different kinds and levels of awareness are exemplified when high level consciousness in some form or other is present. But be they conscious or not, all are equal teleological centers of life in the sense that each is a unified system of goal-oriented activities directed toward their preservation and well-being.

The denial of human superiority as the *fourth* component of the biocentric outlook on nature is perhaps the most important idea in establishing the justifiability of the attitude of respect for nature. The concept of human superiority is strictly human point of view, that is, from a point of view in which the good of humans is taken as the standard of judgment. Because of that, all we need to do is to look as the capacities of non-human animals from the standpoint of their good to find a contrary judgment of superiority. In each case, the claim to human superiority would be rejected from a non-human standpoint.

Another key exponent of biocentrism is Robin Attfield. He takes trees as an example of non-sentient life and seeks to establish whether and why they might also be morally considerable. He likewise maintains trees have a good of their own, but, for him, it is not sufficient to show that trees merit moral consideration. There are further differences between his position and that of Taylor. Taylor appeals to the rational and scientific merits of biocentricism in support of the moral status of trees, while Attfield appeals to analogy with morally significant human interests, such as the interests that derive from their capacities for nutrition, growth, and respiration.

Again, as to how the good of a non-human can be the ground of an obligation for moral agents, the answer turns on its good having intrinsic/inherent value. It is worth distinguishing between approaches which are qualified and unqualified in their commitment to the intrinsic/inherent value of the good of non-rational beings. A representative of the qualified view is Robin Attfield. For Attfield, whatever has a good of its own has moral standing, i.e., merits moral consideration. His position is that if we grant consideration to humans then we cannot consistently deny it to other living beings, and the onus is on a would-be opponent of this view to name some morally relevant differences between humans and other living beings which would justify considering humans as moral patients and non-humans not. He believes that this will prove hard to do. Anyhow, Attfield's qualified view does not deny that there might well be a preponderant need most of the time to treat plants, and, perhaps, some other creatures, as resources, valuable though their lives are in themselves. For Attfield, the moral standing of a being is established separately and prior to any judgements as to its moral significance. All beings which have moral standing have intrinsic/inherent value, but some of them will have very little of it—indeed, too little to be a determinant of any obligation of a moral agent. It, therefore, appears that a qualified approach may not necessarily lay the ground for claiming anything more than a frankly anthropocentric one.

Robin Attfield does not think that we owe moral respect to all living beings, as not all lives are worthwhile. He also is not egalitarian even with regard to those lives that are owed moral respect. The most compelling reason for preserving trees refers first to the interests of humans, and then to those of other sentient animals. He concludes that while some degree of respect is due to almost all life, the interest of other non-sentient life will always have a relatively low priority. Even then, Attfield and Taylor agree on the point that things and beings without good of their own cannot merit moral consideration in their own right, and that only living beings have goods of their own.

Concluding Remarks

On the basis of the above consideration it is clear to say that in environmental ethics not only discuss the human value for their superiority and as occupied in the central position on the earth but it equally gives much more emphasized on other living being on the earth that's why biocentrism comes into discussion. In environmental ethics there are so many 'ism' was raised to discuss the whole world perfectly. Apart from anthropocentrism, biocentrism is another important theory that gives much important on the all living being for the sake of human being. So to live the human species, other lives have valued equally as human being. In this regard Paul Taylor gives two important principles namely-*moral consideration and intrinsic value*. Both principles emphasized on to respect for nature and give emphasized intrinsic value on all the living being. On the other hand, Robin Attifield also gives important on intrinsic value and said that every living being has intrinsic value for its own nature. So biocentrism is significant theory apart from anthropocentrism.

References
1. Albert Schweitzer. "Reverence for Life." (2008). *Environmental Ethics: Readings in Theory and Application.* Louis P. Pojman & Paul Pojman, eds. Belmont: Thomson Wadsworth.
2. Attifield, R., and Belsey, A. eds. (1994). *Philosophy and the Natural Environment,* Cambridge: Cambridge University Press.
3. Bentham, Jeremy. (1962). *The Priciples of Morals and Legislation.* London.
4. Elliot, Robert, ed. (1998). *Environmental Ethics.* Oxford: Oxford University Press.
5. Jardins, Joseph R., Das. (1997). *Environmental Ethics: An Introduction to Environmental Philosophy.* Belmont: Wadsworth Publishing Company.
6. Naese, Arne. (2003). *Ecology, Community and Lifestyle: Outline of an Ecology.* Trans. David Rothenberg. Cambridge: Cambridge University Press, 2003.
7. Peter Singer. *Practical Ethics.* 2nd ed. (1933). Cambridge: Cambridge University Press.
8. Singer, Peter. (1983). *Animal Liberation: Towards an End to Men's Inhumanity to Animals.* Wellingborough: Thorson Publishers.

**Assistant professor,
Department of Philosophy,
University of Gour Banga, Malda,
West Bengal
email : ugb.sadek@gmail.com**

6. Sustainable Development, Climate Change and Indian Economy

Pratibha Sharma[1]
Ashish Sharma[2]

Abstract

A popular phrase today is "sustainable development." It is a set of guidelines for achieving human development goals while simultaneously maintaining the capacity of natural systems to deliver the natural resources and ecosystem services that are essential to the economy and society. The United Nations adopted the 17 interconnected sustainable development goals in 2015 in an effort to reorient the global economy away from social exclusion, environmental threats, and inequality and toward addressing the environmental, political, and economic issues that our planet is currently facing. The 13th of these 17 Sustainable Development Goals, "take urgent action to combat climate change and its impact," is stated as the main objective of the goal. The world's most pressing problem is climate change because of how it negatively affects everything. Climate change and the Earth's temperature are being affected more and more by human actions like the combustion of fossil fuels and the clearing of rainforests. This increases the greenhouse effect and causes global warming by adding enormous amounts of greenhouse gases to those already existing in the atmosphere. Human health, lifestyle, livelihood, and economy have all gotten worse as a result of climate change. In order to understand the evolution and historical development of sustainable development goals, their impact on the Indian economy, and the steps that the economy sector has taken to prevent or mitigate the negative effects of climate change, this research paper will examine both of these aspects.

Keywords : Sustainable Development Goals, Climate Change, Environment, Social, Economic, Global warming.

Introduction :
Economic viability, environmental preservation, and social equality are the three pillars of sustainability. Harmonizing three key

factors—economic growth, social inclusion, and environmental protection—is essential for sustainable development. These factors are all interrelated and essential for the health of people and communities. Living sustainably enhances our standard of living, safeguards our ecology, and protects natural resources for future generations. Table-1 depicts the three pillars in terms of 3 Ps called Planet, people and profit.

Table-1. 3 Pillars of Sustainability

In the business sector, sustainability is linked to an organization's all-encompassing strategy that considers everything from customer service to production and logistics. All countries are now concerned about sustainability. The Sustainable Development Goals (SDGs) or Global Goals were approved by the United Nations in 2015 to reorient the global economy away from social exclusion, environmental risks, and inequality to address the environmental, political, and economic difficulties our planet is now experiencing. In order to eradicate poverty, safeguard the environment, and secure prosperity by 2030, the 193 members of the United Nations, or 193 nations, agreed the Transforming the World: The 2030 Agenda for Sustainable Development, which consists of 17 interconnected Goals and 169 objectives.

The Brundtland Report, issued by the UN World Commission on Environment and Development in 1987, introduced the phrase "sustainable development," which was later defined as "development that meets the needs of the present without compromising the ability of future generations to meet their own needs." In order to be sustainable, a balance must be struck between economic development, environmental protection, and social well-being.

Greener Living

Current demands must be met without sacrificing those of future generations.

Long-term modifications to weather and temperature patterns are referred to as climate change. These changes could occur naturally, for instance through fluctuations in the solar cycle. But since the 1800s, burning fossil fuels like coal, oil, and gas has been the primary cause of climate change, which is mostly attributable to human activity. Increased and more severe droughts, storms, heat waves, rising sea levels, melting glaciers, and warmer oceans may directly injure animals, ruin their habitats, and have a disastrous impact on people's lives and societies. Sea ice loss, a faster increase in sea level, and longer, more severe heat waves are just a few of the effects of global climate change that scientists have long anticipated will occur. The use of fossil fuels like coal, gas, and oil is the primary contributor to climate change, according to overwhelming evidence. When fossil fuels are used, carbon dioxide is released into the atmosphere, warming the earth. The destruction of rainforests and the burning of fossil fuels are only two examples of human actions that have a growing impact on the climate and temperature of the Earth. This increases the amount of greenhouse gases already in the atmosphere, amplifying the greenhouse effect and contributing to global warming.

Research Objectives :

The Research objectives are :

1. To analyse the evolution of the sustainable development goals and how it impact the world.
2. To study the reasons of climate change and its impact on Indian Economy.
3. To study the prevent, corrective, mitigation and adaptive measures to overcome adverse effects of climate change on Indian Economy.

Research Methodology :

This research is of descriptive nature. Qualitative and fundamental research is conducted to explain sustainable development goals and climate change as well as their impact on Indian economy. This research paper is based on secondary data which is collected from websites, newspapers, and books.

Sustainable Development Goals and Climate Change :
Sustainable development refers to the idea of achieving human development goals while also preserving the capacity of natural systems to deliver the resources and ecosystem services that are essential to the economy and society. Although the idea of sustainable development has been important since the beginning of time, it can be argued that its importance grows with each passing day since humankind's population keeps growing but its access to natural resources does not. Global concerns for the careful use of the existing resources have long been highlighted in light of this situation.

The Sustainable Development Goals (SDGs) and the Millennium Development Goals (MDGs) are the most recent manifestations of these issues (SDGs). Following the SDGs were the MDGs. The MDGs signalled a crucial global mobilisation to advance a number of crucial socioeconomic issues everywhere. Despite the MDGs' relative efficacy, not all of the eight objectives' targets were met when the programme was in place for 15 years (2000–2015). As a result, the SDGs were introduced to carry on the development agenda. The 2030 Agenda (SDGs), which are a call to action to protect the environment, reduce poverty, and ensure human well-being, was endorsed by the UN as part of this new development blueprint.The following succinct objectives are what the 17 SDGs essentially aim to accomplish.

Universal access to basic services like water, sanitation, and renewable energy; the creation of inclusive education systems and decent employment opportunities; the eradication of poverty and hunger; the promotion of innovation and resilient infrastructure that will enable communities and cities to produce and consume goods in a sustainable manner.

Reduce global inequalities, particularly those related to gender; conserve the environment by battling climate change and safeguarding ocean and land ecosystems; and encourage cooperation between various social actors to foster a peaceful atmosphere and assure ethical production and consumption.People, planet, prosperity, peace, and partnerships are the five main themes of

Greener Living

Agenda 2030, which spans the 17 SDGs. They are designed to address the underlying causes of poverty and address issues like hunger, health, education, gender equality, water and sanitation, energy, economic growth, industry, innovation & infrastructure, inequalities, sustainable cities & communities, consumption & production, climate change, natural resources, peace & justice, and so on. From the SDGs, it may be inferred that sustainable development seeks to achieve social advancement, environmental balance, and economic growth. Goal 13, out of 17 sustainable development goals, "take urgent action to combat climate change and its impact," is stated as the main objective of the goal.Climate change is affecting every country on every continent. It is disrupting national economies and affecting lives. Weather patterns are changing, sea levels are rising, and weather events are becoming more extreme.Climate plays an important role in determining the livingconditions, food, agricultural economy, etc. of a particular nation. More than 50% people in India depend on agriculture for their livelihood. At present, the whole world, including India, is facing the problem of climate change. Many changes are taking place in the environment such as increase in temperature, decrease in rainfall, change in the direction of winds, etc.

Source : The United Nations (Website)

Climate Change : Present Scenario :

Climate, which includes factors like temperature, humidity, and air pressure, is the long-term mean of a certain location's climatic conditions.Although the climate is largely stable, climate change refers to the current process of regional and global climate change brought on by both natural and human sources.Long-term climate change has led to these changes, which not only have local and regional effects but also have a wider influence on the entire planet.The Northern Hemisphere's average temperature increased dramatically throughout the course of the second half of the 20th century compared to the previous 500 years, according to the Intergovernmental Panel on Climate Change (IPCC).Over the past ten years, the rate of Antarctica's ice melting has quadrupled. The sea level has risen globally during the past century by around 9 inches.The fact that the oceans are becoming more acidic supports this. In actuality, an additional 2 billion tons of $CO2$ are being absorbed by the ocean's top layer every year.From one century to the present, the temperature in India has risen by around 3°C.

Climate change is a result of both natural and human factors, with human causes making a larger contribution.One of the main causes of the rise in the earth's average temperature is the growth in emissions of greenhouse gases such carbon dioxide, methane, nitrous oxide, sulphur dioxide, etc.This is also caused by changes in land use, such as rising surface albino.Other factors contributing to climate change include deforestation, animal husbandry, increased agriculture, the use of nitrogen fertilisers in agriculture, and others.Changes in solar radiation, tectonic circulation, volcanic eruptions, etc. are examples of natural causes.

Climate Change and Agriculture :

Climate change has had a significant detrimental influence on agriculture. It is important to note that the majority of India's agriculture relies on rain, therefore the monsoon's unpredictability continues to affect it. The monsoon has become increasingly unpredictable as a result of climate change. The odd rainfall distribution is also causing certain areas to experience both droughts and floods at the same time.In addition to this, floods in northeast India, cyclones in eastern coastal regions, a drought in the northwest, and a rise in the frequency and power of heat waves in central and northern regions all occur. A decrease in soil moisture and an increase in the severity of pest and disease infestation. The majority of food crops, including wheat, rice, and soybeans, have revealed a lack of protein and other crucial nutrients as a result of the atmosphere's increased CO_2 concentration. Hot waves have become more intense as a result of climate change, which has also reduced milk production and decreased fertility in animals while also making them more susceptible to illness. Up to 2015, India's food grain output was lost by around 125 million tonnes, according to the Food and Agriculture Organization (FAO). The Indian summer monsoon's strength may only rise by 10% by the year 2100, according to estimates. The Indian Agricultural Research Institute (IARI) claims that every 1°C increase in temperature results in a 4-5 million tonne decline in wheat yield. The Indo-Gangetic plains' wheat output can be lowered by up to 51% as a result of excessive heat. Climate change is having a detrimental impact on agricultural productivity since fewer pollinating pests like butterflies and bees are present.

Climate Change and Indian Economy :

one unit of rise in temperature might slow middle-income emerging economies' economic development by 0.9% annually. The economics of middle- and low-income countries will be most affected by climate change. Climate change may require spending 5-20% of the yearly global GDP to reduce its evidence, according to an estimate. In 15 years, climate change may render 45 million Indians extremely impoverished, impeding economic growth, according to a World Bank assessment. Coral reefs may be at danger as a result of rising sea temperatures. An estimated $375 billion worth of products and services are produced annually by Coral Reef. Income inequality will rise as a result of climate change, and both domestic and international migration.

Climate Change and Preventive actions :

The Paris Climate Agreement was established in 2015, and its main clauses are related to keep the temperature at or below 2°C (pre-industrial levels), preferably 1.5°C. Provision of help also initiated as Developed nations will have to give $100 billion to poorer nations. At Cop-23 of the United Nations Framework on Climate Change, the action plan was initially accepted

(UNFCCC). The creation of the International Solar Alliance are also approved. The COP-25 pledged to carry out the terms of the Paris Agreement.

The Indian Prime Minister declared that the country's aim of 175 GW of renewable energy capacity by the end of 2022 will be increased to 450 GW. Execution of National Action Plan on Climate Change's eight missionsis initiated. India's declaration of its intended Nationally Determined Contribution (INDC) take place. By the year 2030, it is a plan to generate 40% or more of the installed electric power capacity from non-fossil fuel sources and by 2030, plan to establish a carbon sink that can absorb 2.5–3 billion tonnes of CO_2.

Additionally, initiatives are being made through the implementation of programs like the Environment Impact Assessment, National Afforestation Program, Green Skill Development Program, and Promotion of Organic Farming, among others.

Conclusion

The globe has been warming quickly, which is mostly due to the rising concentration of CHGs. more specifically, carbon dioxide. The combustion of fossil fuels and deforestation are generally acknowledged as the two main causes of the rise in CO_2 concentration. The international community has acknowledged the need to reduce global warming, which will need a shift away from using fossil fuels and reaching carbon emission zero. This necessitates a fundamental shift in how mankind lives going future. Indian for significant investments in water storage improvements to water gathering methods and irrigation systems. The optimal use of ground water resources will also need to be encouraged. Improvements in hydro-meteorological systems for weather forecasting and the construction of flood warning systems, improved urban planning to prepare for climate-related calamities. Sustainable development approaches and practices should take precedence. In the pertinent field, it is necessary to encourage research and development. India also has to create homegrown green technologies at the same time. The preservation of the environment and its resources must be put into action and integrated into daily life. Nature gives us life. In exchange, we must prioritize protecting and preserving nature.

References :
Adve, N. (2019) 'Impacts of global warming in India: narratives from below' in N.K. Dubash (ed.) India in a warming world: integrating climate change and development. Oxford: Oxford University Press.
Ali, A. (1999) 'Climate change impacts and adaptation assessment in Bangladesh' Climate Research 12(2): 109–116 (www.academia.edu/2266271/Climate_change_impacts_and_adaptation_assessment_in_Bangladesh).
Ali, S.A., Aadhar, S., Shah, H.L. and Mishra, V. (2018) 'Projected increase in hydropower production in India under climate change' Scientific Reports 8 (https://doi.org/10.1038/ s41598-018-30489-4).
Arcanjo, M. (2019) The future of water in India. Climate Institute (http://climate.org/thefuture-of-water-in-india/).
Birthal, P.S., Khan, M.T., Negi, D.S. and Agarwal, S. (2014) 'Impact of climate change on yields of major food crops in India: implications for food security' Agricultural Economics Research Review 27(2): 145–155 (https://doi.org/10.5958/0974-0279. 2014. 00019.6).
BClimate Transparency (2020) India, country profile 2020. Climate Transparency Report 2020 (www.climate-transparency.org/wp-content/uploads/2020/11/India-CT-2020-WEB.pdf).
Dubash, N.K. (2013) 'The politics of climate change in India: narratives of equity and cobenefits' WIREs Climate Change 4: 191–201 (https://doi.org/10.1002/wcc.210).
Mazdiyasni, O., Agha Kouchak, A., Davis, S.J. et al. (2017) 'Increasing probability of mortality during Indian heat waves' Science 3(6): e1700066 (https://doi.org/10.1126/sciadv.1700066).
Mirza, M.M.Q. (2011) 'Climate change, flooding in South Asia and implications' Regional Environmental Change 11: 95–107 (https://doi.org/10.1007/s10113-010-0184-7).
Mishra, V., Smoliak, B.V., Lettenmaier, D.P. and Wallace, J.M. (2012) 'A prominent pattern of year-to-year variability in Indian summer monsoon rainfall' Proceedings of the National Academy of Sciences USA 109: 7,213–7,217 (https://doi.org/10.1073/ pnas. 1119150109).
Murali, M., Riyas, M.J., Reshma, K.N. and Santhosh, K. (2020) 'Climate change impact and vulnerability assessment of Mumbai

city, India' Natural Hazards 102: 575–589 (https://doi.org/ 10.1007/ s11069-019-03766-2).

Sarthi, P.P., Agrawal, A. and Rana, A. (2014) 'Possible future changes in cyclonic storms in the Bay of Bengal, India under warmer climate' International Journal of Climatology 35(7): 1,267–1277 (https://doi.org/10.1002/joc.4053).

The drishti Vision, IAS.

The United Nation.

[1]Assistant Professor (A.B.S.T.)
[2]M. Sc. (Chemistry)
**Seth RL Saharia Govt. PG College,
Kaladera, Jaipur (Raj.),**
email : **parikhandal@gmail.com
ashishsharma@gmail.com**

7. Degradation Kinetics and Antimicrobial Studies of Copper (II) Soap Complexes for Sustainable Development of Environment

Asha Meena

Abstract

Copper (II) soap complexes of nitrogen and sulphur containing ligands have great importance in industrial, biological and pharmacological field with various applications. In relevance of aforesaid applications, the primary purpose of this study to determine the different thermal degradation steps of newly synthesized copper (II) sesame thiourea complex by using Coats-Redfern and Piloyan-Novikova equations for evaluating kinetic parameters such as activation energy and pre-exponential factor. Copper (II) soap complex was synthesized with N and S containing ligand and characterized by elemental analysis, IR, NMR and ESR spectral techniques. Solid state kinetics has attracted the attention of scientific community not only due to its numerous applications in environment, energy, waste water treatment, pollution control and green chemistry but also due to their wide range of biological activities. Antimicrobial activities against *Staphylococus aureus* of these compounds also have been analysed which may provide an important account of information about their industrial utilization. These results reveals that nature of different nitrogen, oxygen and sulphur containing ligands coordinated with copper ion play a significant role in the inhibition activity.

Keywords : Sesame oil, Thiourea, Antimicrobial activities, Inhibition activity, *Staphylococus aureus*.

1. Introduction

The possible contamination of the environment by surfactants arising from the extensive use of detergent formulations has been reviewed. Oils consist of wide group compounds that are soluble in various organic solvents and insoluble in water. They have low density than water at normal room temperature range in consistency from solid to liquid, depending on their structure and composition[1-

2]. Surfactants degradation is a necessity, as because its toxicity is of concern now days in water contamination. Adsorption and thermal degradation can be used as an alternative but it does not totally eliminate or degrade the surfactant components. In recent times the coordination chemistry of nitrogen and sulfur containing ligands has reputed greater importance in view of the fact that several of these compounds have been found to be biologically active and have found use in medicine as well as in industry. Vegetable oil based lubricants are slowly replacing the mineral oil due to their extraordinary biodegradability and many other specific properties[3-9]. Copper soaps derived from edible and non-edible oils play a very important role in various fields due to their surface active properties[10-12]. Copper soaps have a tendency of complexation with 'nitrogen' and 'sulphur' containing ligands. Using thiourea as a ligand, complexation of synthesized Copper soaps has been done to obtain its thiourea complex[13-14]. These Copper sesame thiourea complex was thermally analyzed by using TGA technique to study kinetic parameters like activation energy, rate costant, order of decomposition reaction[15-16]. The present study deals with the evaluation of kinetic as well as thermodynamic parameters for the degradation of several steps[17-18]. Compounds containing nitrogen and sulfur atoms in the heterocyclic ring shows different types of activities. Metal complexes of the ligands containing sulfur and nitrogen as donor atoms are known to obtain bactericidal, antiviral and carcinostatic activities.

2. Experimental

Copper sesame soap was prepared by direct metathesis of corresponding potassium soap with slight excess of required amount of Copper sulphate at 50-55 °C. After washing with hot distilled water and the alcohol, the sample was dried at 80-100 °C and recrystallized with hot benzene at 50 °C twice.

$$\text{RCOOH} \xrightarrow[\text{EtOH}]{\text{KOH}} \text{RCOOK} \xrightarrow{\text{Cu}^{+2}} (\text{RCOO})_2\text{Cu}$$

The copper (II) soap complexes were prepared by reacting ethanolic solution of ligand with copper (II) soap in 1:1 molar ratio. The mixture was refluxed for about two hours with constant stirring. The solid precipitate was filtered, washed with hot distilled water and ethyl alcohol and dried in vaccum. The dried complexes were then purified and recrystallized with hot benzene twice. These complexes are solids and dark green or greenish brown in colour, which are soluble in various solvents such as benzene, ether and methanol-benzene mixture but are insoluble in water.

3 Results and Discussion
3.1 Thermal Analysis

Thermo-gravimetric method for kinetic analysis is reported here. Thermogravimetric analysis was carried out in range of 50 °C - 750 °C on Perkin Elmer Thermal Analysis apparatus from SAIF, IIT-Powai, Mumbai in nitrogen atmosphere at two different heating rate 10 °C min^{-1}. This technique measures the weight change in a complex as a function of temperature and time, in a controlled environment[19]. This technique is very useful to investigate the thermal stability of a Copper (II) sesame thiourea complex. The technique can be used in the examination of absorptive surfaces together with the nature and processes involved in the thermal decomposition[20] and oxidation process. The results of thermogravimetric analysis usually reported in form of curves relating the mass lost from the sample against temperature as depicted in Figure 1.

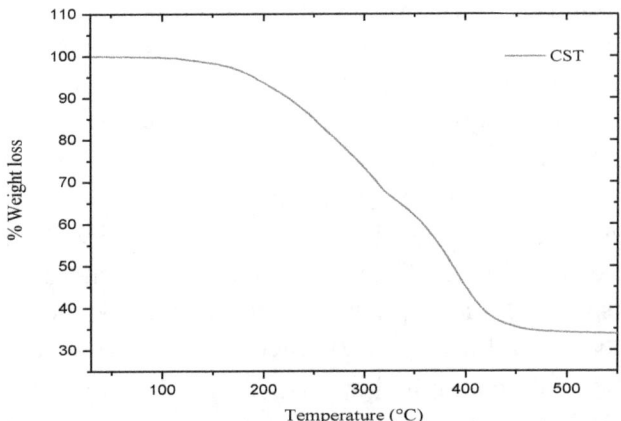

Figure-1: TGA of Copper (II) sesame thiourea complex at 10 degree.

On observation of thermal decomposition steps it was concluded that thermal degradation of Copper (II) sesame thiourea complex at 10 °C min^{-1}, first step is in the range of 150-250 °C. In the first step it may be suggest that decomposition of the unsaturated fatty acids begins. The long chain fatty acids produce volatile compounds, which are constantly removed by vapour generated during heating. Further, the second step of the thermal decomposition of complex in the range of 250-350 °C. The second step corresponds to decomposition of monounsaturated fatty acids such as oleic acid. The double bonds are broken, causing the long chain fatty acid molecules in the edible vegetable oil to become saturated. The third step in the thermal decomposition occurs in the temperature range of 350-450 °C, which may corresponds to the thermal decomposition of the saturated fatty acids such as palmitic acid.

3.2 Kinetic Parameters

The results of themogravimetric analysis have been applied in various equations like Coats-Redfern equation[21] and Piloyan-Novikova method[22] and then evaluate the energy of activation (E) for thermal degradation.

Coats-Redfern equation is an integral form of the rate equation. The method follows the rate low mentioned as follows :

$$log[-log(1-\alpha)/T2] = [logAR/\beta E(1-2RT)/E] - E/2.303RT \quad (1)$$

Where α stands for fraction of soap decomposed, K for the rate constant, E for the energy of activation of the reaction, β the heating rate, R the gas constant (R = 8.317 Jmol^{-1} K^{-1}) and A for the exponential or frequency factor and is usually assigned to independent of absolute temperature T.

The values of energy of activation using Coats- Redfern equation for the step have been evaluated from plots of $log\{[-log(1-\alpha)]/T^2\}$ V/S 1/T as depicted in Fig 2. The values of activation energies evaluated from the slope of these plots are recorded in Table 1 and are observed to be in following order:-Step III > Step II > Step I.

In Piloyan-Novikova method, the reaction order is not needed to be determined first. The rate of dissociation is given by the kinetic equation as follow :

$$\log [\alpha/T] = \log[ZR/E\beta] - E/2.303RT \quad (2)$$

The activation energy has been calculated from the straight line plot of log $[\alpha/T^2]$ versus 1/T as depicted in Fig 3, for Copper sesame thiourea complex.

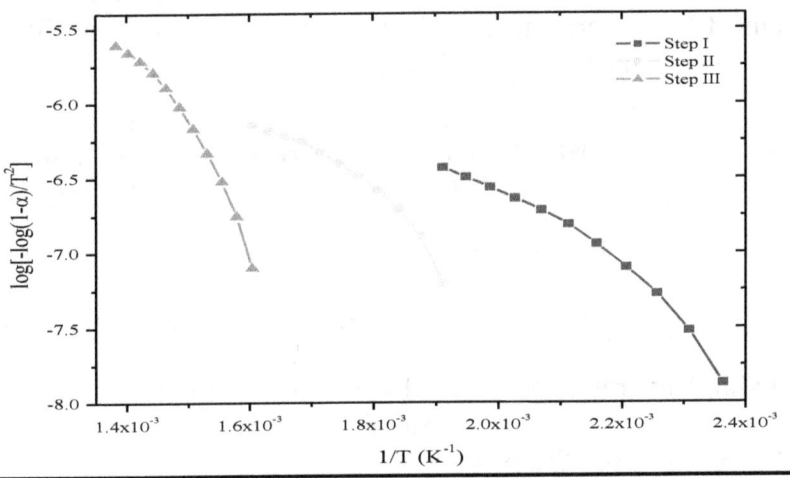

Figure-2: Coats-Redfern plot of Copper (II) sesame thiourea complex for different steps at 10 °C

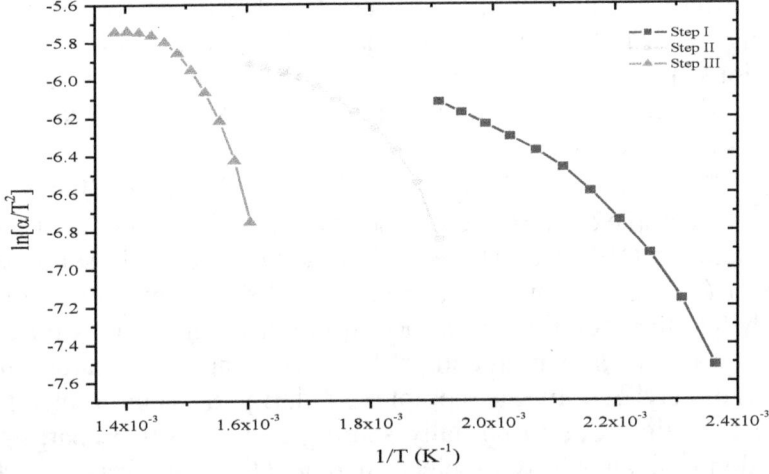

Figure-3: Piloyan-Novikova plot of Copper (II) sesame thiourea complex for different steps at 10 °C

A perusal of Table 1 reveals that the value of activation energy is highest for the third step and smallest for the first step. There was a good correlation between the activation energies evaluated by various equations and approximation methods however the values obtained by the approximation methods were higher than the values obtained by integral methods which can be ascribed the different mathematical treatment of the methods.

STEPS & EQUATIONS	COATS - REDFERN			HOROWITZ- METZGER			BROIDO			PILOYAN- NOVIKOVA		
	I	II	III	I	II	III	I	II	III	I	II	III
$10\ °C\ min^{-1}$	57.25	59.67	123.55	67.60	69.14	134.67	65.05	69.14	134.67	48.28	51.88	79.72

Table 1 Energy of activation Ea ($kJmol^{-1}$) of Copper(II) sesame thiourea complex at 10 °C.

3.3 Antimicrobial Study

Copper (II) sesame thiourea complex was screened for their antibacterial activity against *Staphylococcus aureus*. Mueller-Hinton agar medium was used for antimicrobial activity of complexes on two different concentrations by disk/ well diffusion susceptibility testing. After proper marking of plates, 50μl extracts from different dilutions prepared was loaded into the respective wells. The swabbed *Staphylococcus aureus* plates were kept for incubation at 37 °C for 24-48 hours.

Table 2 shows the biological activities of copper (II) sesame thiourea complex determined by screening against bacteria at 5×10^4 ppm and 2.5×10^4 ppm. The enhanced activity of newly synthesized copper (II) sesame thiourea complex can be explained on the basis of chelate formation, the presence of donor atoms such as nitrogen, sulphur and the structural compatibility with molecular nature of the toxic moiety[23]. In the complex, polarity of central metal ion reduces mainly due to partially sharing of its positive charge with the donor ligands and π- electron delocalization over the whole chelate ring. Such chelation could enhance the lipophilic character of the central metal atom, which consequently helps the penetration of the bacterial cell membranes and restricts further growth of the micro-organisms[24].

Compound	PC	C_1 (5×10^{4}ppm)		C_2 (2.5×10^{4}ppm)		NC
		24hrs	48hrs	24hrs	48hrs	
CST	34mm	6mm	6mm	6mm	6mm	NZI

Table 5 Zone of inhibition of two different concentrations of copper (II) sesame soap complexes (50µL/plate) against *Staphylococcus aureus*.

Conclusion

The present study clearly demonstrates that the values of energy of activation 'E' reveal that for all the equations applied the stepwise energy of activation follow the order: Step III > Step II > Step I. It may be suggested that the increase of activation energy for different steps in thermal decomposition of the system studied, occurred due to the possible break in the molecular bonds of unsaturated fatty acids, which are less stable than the molecular bonds of stable saturated fatty acids requiring higher activation energy of degradation. Biological studies demonstrated that copper (II) sesame thiourea complex are more powerful antimicrobial agents. The newly synthesized complexes should be more effective and possibly act through a distinct mechanism from those of well-known classes of antimicrobial agents to which many clinically relevant pathogens are now resistant.

References :
[1] F.D. Gunstone, Composition and Properties of Edible Oils, 2013
[2] J.N. Coupland, D.J. McClements, Physical properties of liquid edible oils, *J Amer Oil Chem Soc*, 1997, 74(12), 1559-1564.
[3] M. Stjerndahl and K.Holmberg, Synthesis and Chemical Hydrolysis of Surface-Active Esters, *J Surfact Deterg*, 2003, 6(4), 311-318.
[4] A.G. Souza, J.C.O. Santos, M.M. Conceicao, S.M.C. Dantas and S. Prasad, A thermoanalytic and kinetic study of sunflower oil. *Brazilian J. Chem. Engg*, 2004, 21(2), 265.

[5] A.G. Souza, M.M. Conceicao and R.O. Macedo, Thermoanalytical, kinetic and rheological parameters of commercial edible vegetable oils. *An. Assoc. Bras. Quim.,* 1998, 47, 361.

[6] J.C.O. Santos, A.V. Santos, A.G. Souza, S. Prasad and I.M.G.Santos, Thermal Stability and Kinetic Study on Thermal Decomposition of Commercial Edible Oils by Thermogravimetry. *J. Food Science,* 2002, 67(4), 1393.

[7] *S.S. Rathore, S.N. Saxena, R.K. Kakani, L.K. Sharma, D. Agrawal and B. Singh,* Genetic variation in fatty acid composition of fenugreek (*Trigonella foenum-graecum* L.) seed oil. *A.R.C.C.,* 2017, 40(4), 609-617.

[8] A.K. Sharma, R. Sharma, M. Saxena, Biomedical and antifungal application of Cu (II) soaps and its urea complexes derived from various oils. *J Trans Med Res.,* 2018, 2(2), 39-42.

[9] M.C. Dwivedi, S. Sapre, Total vegetable-oil based greases prepared from castor oil. *Wiley Online Library,* 2002, 19(3), 229-241.

[10] R.D. O'Brien, Fats and oils, *CRC Press, Washington,* 2nd *ed.,* 2000.

[11] A.K. Sharma, R. Sharma and A.Gangwal, Biomedical and Fungicidal Application of Copper Surfactants Derived From Pure Fatty Acid. *Organic & Medicinal Chem IJ.* 2018 6(1), 555-680.

[12] V.P. Mehta, P.R. Talesara, R. Sharma, A. Gangwal and R. Bhutra, Surface Tension Studies of Ternary System: Copper Soap Plus Benzene Plus Methanol at 313 K. *Ind. J. Chem.,* 2002, 41A, 1173-1176.

[13] R. Sharma, L.C. Heda and S. Sharma, Photocatalytic Degradation of Copper(II) Palmitates in Non Aqueous Media Using ZnO as Photocatalyst, *Tenside Surf. Det.,* 2015, 52(3), 512-516.

[14] R. Sharma, and S. Khan, Synthesis, Characterization and Antifungal Activities of Copper(II) Soaps and their Complexes Derived from Azadirecta Indica (Neem) and Pongamia Pinnata (Karanj) Oil. *Tenside Surf. Det.,* 2009, 46(3), 145-151.

[15] M. Stjerndahl, C.G. Van Ginkel, and K. Holmberg., Hydrolysis and biodegradation studies of surface-active esters, *J. Surfact Deterg,* 2003, 6(4), 319-324.

[16] Yu,Dawei and Utigard, A. Torstein, TG/DTA study on the oxidation of nickel concentrate. *Thermochemicia Acta,* 2012, 533, 56-65.

[17] A. Dhaundiyal, S. B. Singh, M. M. Hanon and R. Rawat, Determination of Kinetic Parameters for the Thermal Decomposition of *Parthenium hysterophorus*, 2018, 22, 5-21.
[18] C.D. Silva, C. Conceição, F.S. Trindade, A.G. Souza, C.D. Pinheir, J.C. Machado and P.F.A. Filho, Kinetic and Thermodynamic Parameters of The Thermal Decomposition of Zinc(II) Dialkyldithiocarbamate Complexes, J. Therm. Anal. Cal., 2004, 75, 583-590,
[19] S. Ramukutty, E. Ramachandran, Reaction Rate Models for the Thermal Decomposition of Ibuprofen Crystals, *J. Cryst. Pro. Tech.,* 2014, 4, 71-78.
[20] P. Tank, A.K. Sharma, R. Sharma, Thermal Behaviour and Kinetics of Copper (II) Soaps and Complexes Derived from Mustard and Soyabean Oil. *J Anal Pharm Res,* 2017 4(2), 00102.
[21] A.W. Coats and J.P. Redfern, Kinetic Parameters from Thermogravimetric Data II, *J. Poly. Sci.*, 1965, 3(11), 917-920.
[22] G.O. Piloyan, I.D. Pyabchikov and I.S. Novikova, Determination of Activation Energies of Chemical Reactions by Differential Thermal Analysis, *Nature (London),* 1966, 212, 1229.
[23] A.K. Sharma, R. Sharma and A.K. Gangwal, Antifungal activities and characterization of some new environmentally safe Cu (II) surfactants substituted 2-amino-6-methyl benzothiazole, Open Phar. Sci. J., 1-11 3-12, (2018).
[24] R. Bhutra, R. Sharma and A.K. Sharma, Antimicrobial Studies and Characterization of Copper Surfactants Derived from Various Oils Treated at High Temperatures by P.D.A. Technique, Open Pharm. Sci. J., 5, 2018, 36-44.

**Assistant Professor,
Department of Chemistry,
S. D. Govt. College, Beawar, Ajmer, Rajasthan,
email : a.beejal@gmail.com**

8. भारतीय अर्थव्यवस्था पर कोविड-19 का प्रभाव

डॉ. अरुणा कुमारी पलिया

COVID-19 महामारी के कारण विश्व भर की अर्थव्यवस्थायों में तीव्र गिरावट देखी गई, इस महामारी ने औद्योगिक क्षेत्र के विभिन्न घटकों (आपूर्ति शृंखला, मानव संसाधन आदि) को गंभीर रूप से प्रभावित किया और इसके साथ ही दैनिक खपत में भी भारी गिरावट देखने को मिली। इन चुनौतियों के कारण अर्थव्यवस्था में सुधार और इसे पुनः गति प्रदान करने को लेकर चिंताएँ बनी हुई थी। हालाँकी देश में COVID-19 महामारी के नियंत्रण हेतु लागू लाॅकडाउन के हटने के बाद देश की अर्थव्यवस्था में तीव्र सुधार के संकेत और स्पष्ट होते जा रहे हैं। आर्थिक क्षेत्र में यह सुधार विनिर्माण, कोल, स्टील आदि प्रमुख क्षेत्रों में भी देखने को मिला है। हालाँकी सेवा क्षेत्र के साथ कुछ अन्य क्षेत्रों में यह सुधार उतना प्रभावी नहीं रहा है, ऐसे में अर्थव्यवस्था को पुनः गति प्रदान करने के लिये कुछ बडे सुधारों की आवश्यकता होगी।

कोरोना वायरस का प्रकोप सबसे पहले 31 दिसंबर, 2019 को वुहान, चीन में हुआ था, कोरोना वायरस (CoV) वायरस का एक बडा परिवार है जो बिमारी का कारण बनता है, इससे आम सर्दी से लेकर Middle East Respiratory Syndrome (MERS-CoV) और Severe Acute Respiratory Syndrome (SARS-CoV) जैसी गंभीर बीमारियाँ हो सकती हैं। नॉवेल कोरोना वायरस, वायरस का एक नया प्रकार है जो कि अभी तक मानव में नहीं पाया गया था, हम इस तथ्य को नजरअंदाज नहीं कर सकते हैं कि चीन और दुनिया के अन्य देशों में COVID-19 के प्रकोप से वैश्विक स्तर पर आर्थिक मंदी, व्यापार, सप्लाई चैन का व्यवधान, वस्तुओं और लोलिस्टिक्स सहित अर्थव्यवस्था पर महत्वपूर्ण प्रभाव दिखाई दिया, पर हम एक वैश्विक कोविड-19 महामारी के बीच में हैं, जो देशों को दो तरह के झटके दे रही है :

स्वास्था झटका और आर्थिक झटका। बीमारी की प्रकृति को देखते हुए जो अत्यधिक संक्रामक हैं, उसके तरीके, प्रसार को शामिल करें जिसमें नीतिगत कार्रवाइयां शामिल हैं जैसे कि सामाजिक दूरी का लागू करना, घर पर आत्म-अलगाव संस्थानों, और सार्वजनिक सुविधाओं को बंद करना, गतिशीलता पर प्रतिबंध और यहां तक कि पूरे देश में लॉक डाउन करना। इन कार्यों से संभावित रूप से दुनिया भर की अर्थव्यवस्थाओं के लिए गंभीर परिणाम दिखाई दिये। दूसरे शब्दों में, रोग की प्रभावी रोकथाम के लिए किसी देश की अर्थव्यवस्था को अपने सामान्य कामकाज को रोकने की आवश्यकता होती है। इस एक गहरी और लंबी वैश्विक मंदी की आशंक पैदा कर दी है। 9 अप्रैल को, अंतर्राष्ट्रीय मुद्रा के प्रमुख फंड, क्रिस्टालिना जॉर्जीवा ने कहा कि वर्ष 2020 के बाद से सबसे खराब वैश्विक आर्थिक गिरावट देखी गई।

भारतीय अर्थव्यवस्था पर कोराना वायरस का प्रभाव

कोविड-19 महामारी का प्रकोप भारतीय अर्थव्यवस्था के लिए एक अभूतपूर्व आघात हैं। अर्थव्यवस्था कोविड-19 की चपेट में आने से पहले से ही एक खराब स्थिति में थी। दुनिया की प्रमुख अर्थव्यवस्थाओं के साथ-साथ भारतीय अर्थव्यवस्था भी गंभीर रूप से प्रभावित हुई है। लोगों और व्यवसायों पर महामारी का गहरा असर हुआ है। कुछ कारोबारों के लिए तो विनाशकारी परिणाम हुए हैं। उम्मीद हैं कि देश में आने वाले महीनों में सब कुछ पूरी तरह से ठीक हो जाएगा। हालांकि, यह समझना आवश्यक है कि पिछले कुछ महीनों में क्या हुआ, ताकि हम चुनौतियों का सही समाधान खोज संके।

फ्री मूवमेंट पार पाबंदी से सर्विस सेक्टर प्रभावित

वायरस (Corona Virus) फैलने के बाद से राज्य सरकारों ने लॉकडाउन लगाए और इससे फ्री-मूवमेंट पर पाबंदी लग गई। इसका सबसे बडा असर सेवा क्षेत्र पर पडा हैं। इसने बेरोजगारी बढाई है क्योंकि लोग सार्वजनिक परिवहन के माध्यम से अपने कार्य क्षेत्र तक यात्रा नहीं कर पा रहे थे। इसके अलावा, भारत में रोजगार का एक बडा हिस्सा असंगठित क्षेत्र में काम करता है, लॉकडाउन की वजह से काम की कमी ने प्रवासी मजदूरों को अपने गांव-शहर यानी गृह नगर लौटने को मजबूर किया। पर्यटन, रिटेल और आतिथ्य क्षेत्रों पर प्रतिकूल प्रभाव पडा है। अच्छी बात यह रही कि अनलॉक ने स्थिति में सुधार किया और मांग को काफी हद तक वापस लाया। कॉन्फेडरेशन ऑफ ऑल इंडिया ट्रेडर्स (सीएआईटी) के अनुसार, दिवाली के सीजन में मांग में 10.8% की बढोतरी देखी गई और बाजार में तेजी का रुख बना हुआ हैं।

वर्क फ्रॉम होम कल्चर विकसित

इस प्रकोप के कारण 'घर से काम' (Work form Home) और 'कहीं से भी काम करने' (Work form any where) के तरीके विकसित हुए जिसमें सोशल डिस्टेंसिंग (social distance) के मानदंड में बदलाव हुआ। यह कोविड-19 से पहले अकल्पनीय था, क्योंकि लोगों को काम करने के लिए शारीरिक रूप से रिपोर्ट करना पडता था। यह संगठनों और कर्मचारियों, दोनों के लिए पॉजिटिव रहा क्योंकि इसने कंपनियों को अपने फिक्स ओवरहेड्स को कम करने की अनुमति दी है, जबकि इससे कर्मचारियों को समय बचाने में मदद मिली। कर्मचारी भी लागत बचाने में सक्षम हुए क्योंकि वे अब अपने गृहनगर में रह रहे हैं। दूसरी ओर, कंपनियां रियल एस्टेट और अन्य ओवरहेड्स पर खर्च कम कर रही हैं। वे अब सक्रिय रूप से टियर-3 और टियर-4 शहरों से काम पर रख रहे हैं, क्योंकि कर्मचारियों को रीलोकेट करने की आवश्यकता नही हैं।

हेल्थ और फार्मा क्षेत्र में भी इनोवेशन

हेल्थ और फार्मा क्षेत्रो में स्टॉक की कीमतों में वृद्धि देखी गई क्योंकि कंपनियां बडी मात्रा में बिक्री हासिल करने में सक्षम थी। फार्मा और हेल्थ टेक

कंपनियां डिजिटल स्पेस (Digital Space) का अधिकाधिक इस्तेमाल कर रही हैं क्योंकि ग्राहक मौजूदा स्वास्थ्य संकट के दौरान अपनी दवाओं और स्वास्थ्य योजनाओं के लिए डॉक्टरों से परामर्श करने के लिए मोबाइल ऐप का उपयोग कर रहे हैं। वायरस के फैलने से पहले ही उद्योग विकास की गति पर था। कोविड-19 ने विकास का और तेज किया।

एफआईआई का प्रवाह बढा

कोविड-19 (Covid-19) संकट को सरकारों और केंद्रीय बैंको ने मौद्रिक और राजकोषीय उपायों (Fiscal stimulus) के साथ जवाब दिया हैं। जो वैश्विक वित्तीय संकट के चरम के दौरान घोषित की गई थी। इसके कारण विकसित अर्थव्यवस्थाओं में ब्याज दरें शून्य के करीब है। इससे वैश्विक तरलता में वृद्धि हुई, जिसके परिणामस्वरूप भारत सहित बडे उभरते बाजारों में एफआईआई का प्रवाह आया, क्योंकि हमें वित वर्ष 2021 में अब तक 2 लाख करोड रुपय से अधिक का प्रवाह प्राप्त हुआ है। इसने शेयर बाजारों में अपने ऑलटाइम हाई पर बेंचमार्क इंडेक्स ट्रेडिंग के साथ मजबूत बुलिश ट्रेड का भी नेतृत्व किया है। बाजार में रिकवरी की प्रमुख विशेषताओं में से एक खुदरा बिक्री में उल्लेखनीय वृद्धि हुई है क्योंकि निवेशकों ने बाजारों में प्रवेश करने के लिए सस्ते मूल्यांकन का लाभ उठाया।

वित्तीय समझदारी का गुण

महामारी ने हमें वित्तीय समझदारी (Financial smartness) के गुण सिखाए हैं। यदि आप नियमित निवेश (Investment) और लिक्विड फंड्स के साथ वित्तीय योजना बनाते हैं, तो वे अंततः ऐसे संकट काल में आपकी मदद करते है। न केवल वे आपको उनके साथ बेहतर तरीके से सामना करने के लिए सशक्त बनाते हैं, बल्कि बाजार में कोई अवसर सामने दिखने पर उसका लाभ उठाने में भी मदद करते हैं। इन सबसे ऊपर, यह आय का एक अतिरिक्त स्रोत बनकर उभरा है और आपको मुद्रास्फीति को हराने में मदद करता हैं।

कृषि क्षेत्र पर नकारात्मक प्रभाव

इस बार कोरोना की दूसरी लहर से ग्रामीण क्षेत्र भी अछूते नहीं रहे हैं। ग्रामीण इलाकों में बडी संख्या में लोग इस बार संक्रमण की चपेट में आए हैं। इससे इन क्षेत्रों की आर्थिक तस्वीर बदलने का खतरा बढ गया हैं। हालांकि ग्रामीण क्षेत्रों की अर्थव्यवस्था हालांकि कृषि आधारित मानी जाती है, लेकिन उससे अधिक दारोमदार गैर कृषि संसाधनों पर निर्भर है। लॉकडाउन की वजह से ग्रामीण क्षेत्रों में पैदा होने वाली उपज को सही बाजार नहीं मिल रहे हैं। शहरों में होटल, रेस्तरां, खानपान और मिठाई की दुकानें लंबे समय से बंद हैं शहरी क्षेत्रों के साथ ग्रामीण क्षेत्रों में भी शादी-विवाह और अन्य आयोजनों पर रोक लगी हुई हैं। इनमें उपयोग होने वाली सब्जियों, स्थानीय फलों, दूध और अन्य उपज की मांग में जबरदस्त कमी आई है। ग्रामीण इलाकों में छोटे और भूमिहीन किसानों की रोजी-रोटी का आधार डेयरी व सब्जियों की खेती होती है। दूध की 60

फीसदी बिक्री होटर, मिठाई व चाय की दुकानों पर होती हैं। संगठित क्षेत्र की निजी, सहकारी व सहकारी कंपनियों में मात्र 40 फीसदी ही खपत होती है। कई कंपनियों ने अपने दूध का कलेक्शन भी घटा दिया है जबकि दूध उत्पादन में कोई कमी नहीं आई है।

अप्रैल से जून तक गांवो में खेती का कार्य कम होने के कारण रूरल इंफ्रास्ट्रक्चर की परियोजनाएं किसानों की आजीविका के लिए मुफीद रहती हैं। लेकिन इस बार कोरोना की दूसरी लहर के चलते ग्रामीण सडक, आवसीय, सिचाई की परियोजनाएं, ग्रामीण विद्युतीकरण और जल संसाधन की परियोजनाएं लगभग ठप हो चुकी है। गांवों में सिर्फ मनरेगा का कच्चा काम ही हो रहा है। बाकी परियोजनाओं के लिए जरूरी कच्चे माल की आपूर्ति नहीं हो पा रही हैं लेकिन इन सभी हालातो के बावजूद कोविड–19 में मजबूती से उभरी भारतीय कृषि ने नयी आशा की किरण जगाई है।

भारत में शिक्षा पर COVID -19 (CORONA VIRUS) के प्रभाव

कोविड–19 ने शिक्षा ने शिक्षा के क्षेत्र पर कई प्रकार से प्रभाव दिखाया हैं। स्कूल और कॉलेज बंद कर दिए गए । स्कूल और कॉलेजों द्वारा ऑनलाइन प्लेटफार्म जैसे यूट्यब विडियों, मोबाइलो ऐप, वेबिनार, इत्यादि का उपयोग करके शिक्षा देने का प्रयास किया गया । विद्यार्थियों को अगली कक्षा में बिना किसी परीक्षा के प्रोन्नत (promote) करना पडा और विद्यार्थियों को पिछली कक्षाओं में मिले नंबर के आधार पर नंबर दिए गए। इससे विद्यार्थियों की शिक्षा गुणवक्ता पर नकारात्मक प्रभाव पडा और साथ ही साथ इसका बच्चों के भविष्य पर बुरा असर पडेगा।

कोरोना ने समाज के कमजोर वर्ग के छात्रों, ग्रामीण क्षेत्र के छात्रों और विकलांगों की शिक्षा पर बहुत बुरा असर डाला हैं। समाज के कमजोर वर्ग के और ग्रामीण क्षेत्र के विद्यार्थियों के पास ऑनलाइन शिक्षा प्राप्त करने के साधन जैसे लैपटॉप, स्मार्टफोन, हाई स्पीड इंटरनेट कनेक्शन इत्यादि उपलब्ध नहीं हैं।

औद्योगिक गतिविधियों में गिरावट

कोविड–19 महामारी के नियंत्रण हेतु लागू लॉकडाउन के कारण देश में औद्योगिक गतिविधियों पर गंभीर प्रभाव देखने को मिला। कृषि को छोड़कर लगभग सभी क्षेत्रों में नकारात्मक वृद्धि दर्ज की गई। औद्योगिक गतिविधियों गिरावट के साथ ही विद्युत की खपत में भारी कमी देखने को मिली, गौरतलब है कि मार्च(-8.7%), अप्रैल (-23.02%) मई (-14.9%) और जून (-10.9%) में विद्युत खपत में आई कमी देश में औद्योगिक गतिविधियों में गिरावट का स्पष्ट आँकड़ा प्रस्तुत करती हैं।

बेरोज़गारी में वृद्धि

लॉकडाउन के कारण औद्योगिक गतिविधियों के प्रभावित होने से शहरी रोज़गार में भारी गिरावट देखने को मिली, जिसके परिणामस्वरूप बेरोजगारी की दर अप्रैल माह में 23.52% और मई माह में 21.73% दर्ज की गई।

Greener Living

राजस्व में गिरावट

मार्च माह में लॉकडाउन की घोषणा के बाद सरकार के राजस्व में भारी गिरावट देखी गई। ध्यातव्य है कि मार्च माह में सरकार को जीएसटी के रूप में प्राप्त कुल राजस्व 97.597 करोड़ रुपय रहा, जबकी यह अप्रैल और मई माह में घटकर क्रमशः 32,000 करोड़ रुपय तथा 62,000 करोड़ रुपय (लगभग) तक पहुँच गया। राजस्व में हुई गिरावट के कारण सरकार के लिए औद्योगिक उत्पादन और खपत में हो रही गिरावट को कम करने के लिए बाहरी समर्थन प्रदान करना एक बड़ी चुनौती बन गया।

कुछ विशेषज्ञों, अर्थशास्त्रियों और नीति निर्माताओं के अनुसार ये कुछ प्रभाव हो सकते है :

- केस डाउन शटर के रूप में आर्थिक गतिविधि का नुकसान
- लोगों को नौकरी खोने के कारण आय का नुकसान
- वैश्विक बंद के कारण निर्यात में गिरावट
- कई क्षेत्रों में उत्पादन में व्यवधान (disrupation)
- FY21 की जीडीपी वृद्धि में 1 प्रतिशत की कमी आ सकती है

डन एंड ब्रैडस्ट्रीटए के नवीनतम अर्थव्यवस्था पूर्णानुमान के अनुसार, मंदी की स्थिति में आने वाले देशों और दिवालिया होने वाली कंपनियों में प्रवेश करने की संभावना बढ़ गई है और भारत वैश्विक मंदी से 'विघटित' रहने की संभावना नहीं है।

अरुण सिंह, मुख्य अर्थशास्त्री डन और ब्रैडस्ट्रीट इंडिया ने कहा, चीन के अलावा, अन्य वैश्विक विनिर्माण केंद्रों में भी तालेबंदी की जा रही है, जिससे वैश्विक आपूर्ति श्रृंखला और वैश्विक विकास में कमजोरी बढ़ सकती है'।

भारत की आर्थिक वृद्धि पर सिंह ने कहा, 'भारत में 21 दिनों के लॉकडाउन को देखते हुए, भारत की जीडीपी हमारे FY20 के लिए 5 प्रतिशत के पहले के अनुमान से आगे मध्यम रहने की उम्मीद है और FY21 के लिए विकास अत्यधिक अनिश्चित रहेगा'।

रिपोर्ट के अनुसार, वाणिज्यिक गतिविधियों और की सभाओं पर तालाबंदी और प्रतिबंध से वैश्विक और घरेलू विकास को जोरदार रूप से प्रभावित करने की संभावना है।

सिंह ने आगे कहा कि आर्थिक वृद्धि का स्टीक मात्रात्मक आवकन अलग-अलग होगा और संशोधित होने की उच्च संभावना है क्योंकि प्रकोप की गंभीरता और प्रसार अनिश्चत है।

मूल्य परिदृश्य पर, मांग और उत्पादन गतिविधियों में मंदी, कच्चे तेल की वैश्विक कीमत में तेज गिरावट और अन्य प्रमुख वस्तुओं जैसे ऊर्जा, आधार धातुओं और उर्वरकों में कीमत घट जाएगी, मुद्रास्फीति पर दबाव बढ़ने की उम्मीद है।

सरकार के प्रयास :

- केंद्र सरकार द्वारा **Covid -19** महामारी से प्रभावित अर्थव्यवस्था को गति प्रदान करने के लिए **आत्मनिर्भर भारत अभियान के** तहत आर्थिक पैकेज की घोषणा की गई, इसके तहत सरकार ने विभिन्न क्षेत्रों के लिये लगभग 20 लाख करोड़ रुपय जारी करने की रूपरेखा प्रस्तुत की गई।

- Covid -19 के कारण उत्पन्न हुई आर्थिक चुनौतियों को देखते हुए भारतीय रिजर्व बैंक (RBI) द्वारा 27 मार्च को बैंक ऋण के भुगतान का 90 दिनों (1मार्च से 31 मई तक) के अस्थायी स्थगन की घोषणा की थी, इस अवधि को बाद में 31 अगस्त तक बढ़ा दिया।

- केंद्र सरकार द्वारा Covid -19 के दौरान ग्रामीण अर्थव्यवस्था में तरलता को बनाए रखने के लिये **मनरेगा** (महात्मा गांधी राष्ट्रीय ग्रामीण रोजगार गारंटी अधिनियम) के बजट परिव्यय में 65% की वृद्धि की गई, इसके साथ ही सरकार द्वारा 'प्रधानमंत्री किसान सम्मान निधि या **पीएम किसान (PM Kisan) योजना** और 'प्रधानमंत्री गरीब कल्याण योजना' आदि के माध्यम से अतिरिक्त सहायता उपलब्ध कराई गई।

- इसके साथ औद्योगिक क्षेत्र की वित्ती चुनौतियों के देखते हुए सरकार ने 'दिवाला और शोधन अक्षमता सहिता (IBC) , 2016' में संशोधन करते हुए (IBC) की प्रकिया शुरू करने हेतु डीफाल्ट की सीमा को 1 लाख से बढ़ा कर 1 करोड़ कर दिया गया था।

चुनौतिया :

- हाल के दिनों में कई क्षेत्रों से आर्थिक सुधार के संकेत मिलने के बावजूद भी देश की अर्थव्यवस्था में निरंतर आर्थिक सूधार आने वाले दिनो में खपत, निवेश और निर्यात में वृद्धि पर निर्भर करेगा।

- अक्टूबर माह मे देश के निर्यात में 5.4% की गिरावट देखी गई, जबकि अप्रैल – अक्टूबर के दौरान इस क्षेत्र मे 19% की गिरावट और इसी अवधि के दौरान देश के आयात में 11.6% की गिरावट दर्ज की गई।

- देश के निर्यात में सूक्ष्म, लघु और मध्यम उद्यम (MSME) क्षेत्र की भूमिका बहुत ही महत्त्वपूर्ण (वित्तिय वर्ष 2018–19 में लगभग 48.10%) हैं, परन्तु पिछले कुछ समय से इस क्षेत्र में वित्तिय तरलता और मानव संसाधन की कमी के साथ मांग में हुई गिरावट से स्थितिया ओर अधिक चिंता जनक हो गई।

- हाल के कुछ वर्षों में निर्यात क्षेत्र में भारत के प्रदर्शन में गिरावट देखी गई है, जबकि बांग्लादेश और वियतनाम जैसे देश इस क्षेत्र में तेजी से आगे बढ़ रहे है।

- इसके अतिरिक्त निजी क्षेत्र के निवेश में गिरावट भी एक बड़ी चुनौति बनी हुई है, जून 2020 में सकल स्थाई पुंजी निर्माण और जीडीपी का अनुपात 19.5%

रहा जबकि जून 2018 में यह 29% था। ऐसे में इस चुनौति से निपट में निजी क्षेत्र की भूमिका बहुत ही सीमित रहेगी।
- पिछले कुछ वर्षों से देश का बैंकिंग क्षेत्र भी कई प्रकार की चुनौतियों का सामना कर रहा था परन्तु Covid -19 महामारी से उत्पन्न हुई वित्तिय चुनौतियों के कारण NPA के मामलों मे वृद्धि से यह समस्या और भी जटिल हो गई है।
- सरकार द्वारा लागु मौद्रिक नितियों से वित्तिय तरलता की चुनौतियों को कम करने और बैक ऋण में सुधार लाने में भले ही सफलता प्राप्त हुई हो परन्तु बैंकिंग क्षेत्र में व्याप्त जोखिम को नजरअंदाज नही किया जा सकजा है।

समाधान :
- देश की अर्थव्यवस्था को गति प्रदान करने में खपत और सार्वजनिक निवेश में वृद्धि की भूमिका बहुत ही महत्त्वपूर्ण हो गई।
- इस महामारी से सीख लेते हुए सरकार को स्वास्थ्य, सूचना प्रोधौगिकी आदि क्षेत्रों में आयात निर्भरता को कम करते हुए स्थानीय आपूर्ति श्रृंखला को मजबूत करने पर विशेष ध्यान देना होगा।
- Covid -19 महामारी के दौरान कृषि क्षेत्र में सबसे कम गिरावट देखने को मिली, हांलाकि इस क्षेत्र में रोजगार और आय में वृद्धि के लिए विशेष प्रयास किए जाने चाहिए जिससे इस का पुरा लाभ उठाया जा सकें, सरकार द्वारा कृषि अवसरचना कोष की स्थापना इस दिशा में सकारात्मक कदम है।
- Covid -19 महामारी के कारण अर्थव्यवस्था की क्षति को कम करने के लिए खपत-निवेश चक्र को जल्द से जल गति प्रदान करना बहुत ही आवश्यक होगा।
- साथ ही सार्वजनिक खपत और विवेकाधीन खर्च में वृद्धि से निजी क्षेत्र के निवेश को भी बढ़ाया जा सकता है।
- सहकार को असंगठित क्षेत्रों और विशेष कर सूक्ष्म श्रेणी से जुड़ें उघोगों की वित्तिय चुनौतियों को दूर करने के लिए विशेष तथा लक्षित योजनाओं की शुरूवात पर विचार करना चाहिए।
- वर्तमान मे अर्थव्यवस्था में सुधार के सकेंतो के बीच विश्व के विभिन्न हिसों में Covid -19 के मामलों में वृद्धि के आकडें एक बड़ी चिंता का कारण हैं, परन्तु सरकार को इस नई सामान्य स्थिति में विकास के नए अवसर उत्पन्न करने होंगें।

निष्कर्ष :

Covid -19 महामारी ने वैश्विक अर्थव्यवस्था को गंभीर रूप से प्रभावित किया है। इस महामारी के दौरान आपूर्ति श्रृंखलाओं के बाधित होने, श्रमिकों के पालयन और वित्तिय तरलता की चुनौतियों साथ इस के किसी प्रमाणिक उपचार

के अभाव में उत्पन्न हुई अनिश्चितता से अन्य सभी क्षेत्रों के साथ आर्थिक क्षेत्र को अभूत पूर्व क्षति हुई है। देश के अधिकांश हिसों से लॉकडाउन के हटने के बाद पिछले कुछ महिनों में स्थितियों में कुछ सुधार हुआ है। हांलाकि देश की अर्थव्यवस्था को पुनः गति प्रदान करने के लिए सरकार को सार्वजनिक निवेश के साथ स्थानीय आपूर्ति श्रृंखला को मजबूत करने, वित्तिय तरलता को बनाए रखने तथा सार्वजनिक खपत को प्रोत्साहित करने पर विशेष ध्यान देने होगा।

References

- Chaddha, N, A Das, S Gangopadhyay and N Mehta (2017), 'Reassessing the Impact of Demonetisation on Agriculture and Informal Sector', India Development Foundation (IDF), New Delhi, January.
- Duflo, Esther, Abhijit Banerjee (2020), "A prescription for action: Nine steps after the next 21 days", Indian Express, March 29, 2020.
- FAO (2020), "Covid-19 Pandemic: Impact on Food and Agriculture", Food and Agricultural Organisation, Rome, http://www.fao.org/2019-ncov/q-and-a/en/
- Kapur, Dev and Subramanian, Arvind (2020), "How coronavirus crisis can be converted to opportunity to
- fundamentally strengthen Indian economy", Indian Express, April 3, 2020.
- Khera, Reetika (2020) "Covid-19: What can be done immediately to help vulnerable population", Ideas for India. https://www.ideasforindia.in/topics/poverty-inequality/covid-19-what-can-be-done-immediately-tohelp-vulnerable-population.html
- Narayanan, Sudha (2020), "Food and agriculture during a pandemic: Managing the consequence",
- https://www.ideasforindia.in/topics/agriculture/food-and-agriculture-during-a-pandemic-managing-theconsequences.html\
- Rangarajan, C. and S. Mahendra Dev (2020), "A Safety net: Post-Covid", Indian Express, July 3, 2020.
- Ray, Debraj and S. Subramanian (2020), "India's lockdown: An interim report", Working Paper Series,

- National Bureau of Economic Research (NBER), No. 27282, May 2020.
- RBI (2020), Monetary Policy Report, Reserve Bank of India, April 2020.

सहायक आचार्य (अर्थशास्त्र),
राजकीय महाविद्यालय, लूणी,
जोधपुर

9. Legal Aspects of Environmental Proction
(A Study of Environmental Policy and Laws)

Dr Madhuri Gupta

Introdution

The problem of environmental pollution is as old as the evolution of homo sapiens on this planet. Kautilya, the Prime Minister of Magadh, during the regime of Chandra Gupta Maurya, 300 B.C. in his *Arthashastra* exhaustibly deals with the question of environment protection. He laid down the rules for the protection and upgradation of environment minutely.

The Earth's atmosphere is a common heritage. The environmental issues take into account the human being, and not the state as a unit. Thus, it has become necessary to regulate behaviour and social transactions with new laws, designed to suit the changing conditions and values. As a result a new branch of law, called the Environmental law, grew at this stage in order to manage and face the myriad challenges of such a system. The environmental laws are of a much recent origin. The Environmental (Protection) Act, 1986, defines environment which includes water, air and land and the inter-relationship which exists between them on the one hand, and human beings on the other hand, and human beings, other living creatures, plants, micro-organisms and property, on the other. Environmental laws involve conversation of natural resources for their better use by the present day society as well as by future generations and it also govern the inter-relationship between natural resources and human beings. Its domain also extends to the relationship between natural resources and other living creatures.

Constitutional Directives for Environmental Protection

Article 21 of the Constitution guarantees the right to life, a life of dignity, to be lived in a proper environment free of danger of disease and infection. In *T. Damodaran Rao v. Municipal Corporation*, Hyderabad case, the court held that "The enjoyment of life and its attainment and fulfilment guaranteed by Art. 21, of the Constitution embraces the protection and preservation of natures gift without which life cannot be enjoyed". In Delhi Gas Leak Case the Supreme Court has given the judgment by way of expanding the ambit of Article 21 of the Constitution interpreted that the right to life includes the right to life in a healthy environment. Under Article 48A of the Indian Constitution, it is the fundamental duty of the state "to protect and improve environment and to safeguard the forest and wildlife of the country." Under this Article, the state may not only adopt the protectionist policy but also provide the improvement of polluted environment.

Besides the state obligation towards the society at large, the individual member of the society themselves also owe a fundamental duty "to protect and improve the natural environment including forests, lakes, rivers and wildlife and to have compassion for living creatures." in Article 51A (g). The Article specifically deals with the fundamental duty of the citizen with respect to the environment. Article 47 of the Constitution declares the raising of the level of nutrition and standard of living of its people and improvement of public health as one of the primary duties of the state.

The Constitution makes twofold provisions. On the one hand, it gives directives to the state for the protection and improvement of environment and on the other hand, it casts a duty on the citizen to help in the preservation of natural environment. The Code of Criminal Procedure, 1973 authorizes the District Magistrate and SDM to control and remove all pollution. Indian Penal Code makes various acts affecting environment as offence as under:

- Fouling of water of public spring or reservoirs rendering it less fit for the purpose for which it is ordinarily used.
- Making atmosphere noxious to health.

After 1972, The Parliament has enacted a number of laws directly relating to pollution and environment i.e. National Forest Policy, 1988 The Forest (Conservation) Act, 1980, The Wild Life (Protection) Act, 1972, The Wild Life (Protection Amendment) Act, 1986, The Water (Prevention and Control of Pollution) Act, 1974, The Air (Prevention and Control of Pollution) Act, 1981, and The Environment (Protection) Act, 1986. In addition to these, State

Government has enacted a number of special laws which can be evoked for protecting and improving environment.

The 73 Amendment Act, 1992 of the Constitution on panchayats adds the eleventh schedule to the Constitution which includes soil conservation, water management, watershed development, social and farm forestry, drinking water, non- conventional energy sources and maintenance of Community assets which are significant for environment management. By way of the 74th amendment, a state legislature can enact legislation on 'urban forestry, protection of the environment and promotion of ecological aspects.'

Conclusion

For this strict enforcement of the legislation, special Environmental Courts must be established under the Act, which shall be assisted by experts of various disciplines, including persons having special knowledge and experience. Judges should be given a special training in the environmental laws. It may be concluded that mere framing of legislation will not solve such a gigantic problem but public opinion has to be built up. Voluntary action groups 'should be formed to cope with the situation.

Associate Professor in Politica Science
SPNKS Govt. PG College, Dausa (Raj)
email : madhurigupta3569@gmail.com

10. Palladium Nanoparticles Synthesis and their Catalytic Application on Oxidation of Arginine in Aqueous Acidic Medium

Dhanraj[1]
Rashmi Gupta[2]
M. B. Yadav[3]

Abstract

The paper describes the preparation of Palladium nanoparticle (Pd np) through chemical reduction method using palladium chloride ($PdCl_2$) and stabilizer PVP (Poly vinyl pyrrolidone). Characterization of the palladium nanoparticle was done by UV-VIS Spectrometer and TEM. The range of the particle size was from 1 to 100 nm. Palladium nanoparticles of various shapes and sizes have been obtained by reduction in ethanol with HCl catalyst addition. The synthesized palladium nanoparticles are used as a catalyst for the oxidation of basic amino acid, arginine by N- bromosuccinimide in aqueous medium. These nanoparticles showed better catalytic activity as compared to equal amount of palladium precursor.

Keywords : Oxidation, Nanoparticle, Palladium, Arginine, Acidic medium.

Introduction

Nanoparticles prepared from noble metal have valuable importance due their distinctive physical–chemical properties such as catalytic, electronic, magnetic and optical properties and uses in the different fields of catalysts, medicine, electronics, chemical synthesis, fuel cell and oil refining processes. The size, shape and size distribution of metal nanoparticles constitute the major role. So concentration is focused on the preparation of noble metal nanoparticles with well-controlled morphology[1-6]. Compared to PGM (Platinum group metals), Palladium is attractive because of its lower cost and high activity towards oxygen reduction reactions[7]. Palladium(Pd) is interesting material for research due to its hydrogen storage preparation[8].

The role of nanoparticle has increased in the fields of chemical, nanotechnology and physics. Their properties are different when compared with those of bulk metals. Both homogenous and heterogenous catalysis has grown during the last many years. The major property making it very efficient is excess surface to volume ratio.

Many studies about the Pd catalysed oxidation of amino acid have been reported [9-11] but with the development of metal nanoparticles having high stability, their use as catalyst for bio chemical reactions are well documented in recent years [12-14]. Palladium nanoparticles can be prepared through different method such as ion exchange/ adsorbtion[15], microwave plasma[16], sonochemical reduction[17], sol–gel process[18] etc. All these methods are complex and costly, so metal nanoparticle can be made by simply loading some liquid polymeric matrices.

Amino acids are the building blocks of essential biomolecules such as proteins, hormones, enzymes[19-20] etc. Amino acids are basically derived from protein in diet or degradation intracellular proteins. **They lose their amino group through transamination or oxidative deamination. L-Arginine plays** important role in metabolism of any organism as it is precursor for synthesis of protein and other important biological molecule. For young organism it should be provided in the diet for optimal growth and proper development. For adults it is essential in case of trauma, burn injury and renal failure. L-Arginine improves the immune and digestive functions and plays crucial role in carcinogenesis and tumour growth.

In this manuscript, we present a one–step polyol method for synthesis of Pd monodispersed and good-shaped nanoparticles using ethanol as reducing agent and PVP(Poly vinyl pyrrolidone) as the capping agent and their application on the oxidation of amino acid Arginine by N- bromosuccinimide in aqueous medium

Experimental

Materials : Palladium (II) chloride ($PdCl_2$ 99.9%) were purchased from Johnson Matthey and PVP (Poly vinyl pyrrolidone), Mw- 400000 used as stabilizer. NBS (E-Merck), Arginine (E. Merck) and ethanol was of AR grade used as solvent and reducing agent and was used as received without further purification. All glassware was cleaned using aquaregia, subsequently rinsed with double distilled water and dried before use. Fresh solutions of NBS, KI, Hypo and Starch were prepared before the experimental set up. For Palladium nanoparticles synthesis, chemical reduction method was used.

Synthesis of Palladium nanoparticle

Typically 0.0887 gm of $PdCl_2$, 6 ml of 0.2 M HCl and 250 ml of distilled water were mixed to get 2mM concentration of H_2PdCl_4 solution. Then 15 ml of 2mM H_2PdCl_4, 21 ml of doubly deionized water, 0.0667 gm of PVP and 4 drops of 1 M HCL were mixed together in a reflux condenser assembly. As the solution began to reflux, add 14 ml of ethanol. Reflux the solution for 3 hours which results in a dark brown solution, so H_2PdCl_4 reduction occurs by ethanol. (Solvent and reducing agent both).

UV-Visible spectrum of palladium nanoparticles and TEM Analysis

UV-Visible spectral analyses were carried out on a double beam spectrophotometer-2203(systronics). The formation of Pd nps was monitored in 220-600 nm range. The reaction mixture changes gradually from pale yellow to dark brown due to surface plasmon vibrations. Fig.-1 shows the absorption peaks at 310 and 410 nm that attribute to $[PdCl_4]^{2-}$, while the peak at 256 nm and 315 nm corresponds to PVP-stabilised Pd NPs using ethanol as reductant.. This is ascribed to ligand (Cl⁻) → metal (Pd^{+2}) charge transfer transition of Pd (II) ions[21-22]. The disappearance of the absorption peak after 15 minute is due to complete reduction of metal ions (Pd^{+2}). The colour intensity of the reaction mixture changes leading to increase in the absorbance of the solution.

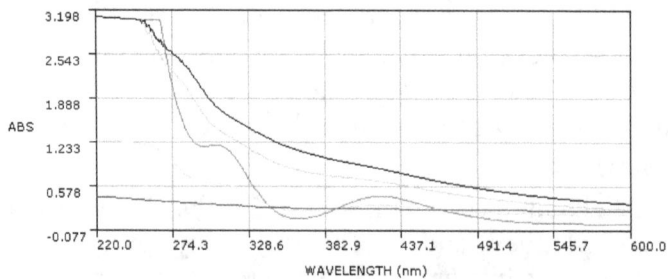

Figure-1. UV–vis spectra of PVP-protected Pd NPs in the range 220–600 nm

The morphological study of the palladium nano particle was carried out with scanning of Transmission electron microscope by employing JEOL-JEM-2010XII TEM at 200 kV. TEM images were recorded to confirm size and shape of newly synthesized palladium nanoparticles.

The influence of precursor concentration and metal/ PVP ratio

At a given temperature, the size of the palladium nanoparticles (Pd np) can be arranged optimally by changing the H_2PdCl_4 concentration from 1 to 4 mM . Similarly the PVP amount added was changed from 1: 5 (metal / PVP) to 1:20 .So the size of nanoparticles could be changed by changing the metal precursor concentration and PVP/ metal ratio. PVP act as efficient stabilizer and protecting agent which prevents the aggregation of particles. The optical precursor concentration taken was 2mM and PVP / metal ratio 1:10.

PVP also helps in the reduction of metal in ethanol speeding up the rate of particle formation. PVP and Palladium nanoparticles (Pd np) complexes by coordinate bond between N and O atoms of PVP and surface sites of Palladium nanoparticle (Pdnp) which causes reduction in the free metal nanoparticles concentration decreasing the electrode reduction potential of Pd ion and then increased the rate of reduction of metal ions during process of the growth of particle[23]. The increase in concentration of PVP minimizes the diffusion of Palladium nanoparticles leading to aggregation ie increasing the Pdnp size.

According to spectroscopic studies, PVP–Pd interaction occurs through the carbonyl group of the pyrrolidone ring. In our synthesis process, Pd NPs in the size range 1–100 nm in diameter have been obtained from aqueous solutions of $PdCl_2$ in the presence of PVP. The major outcome is that most of the large sized Pd NPs with spherical, tetrahedral, octahedral twinned decahedral icosahedral and cubic shapes have been found due to the aggregation of the smaller seeds of spherical Pd NPs that are proved. Noble metals have a face-centred cubic (fcc) lattice with different surface energies for different crystal planes, such as the combinations of the low-index and/or high-index {1 1 1}, {1 0 0} and {1 1 0} planes[24-26].

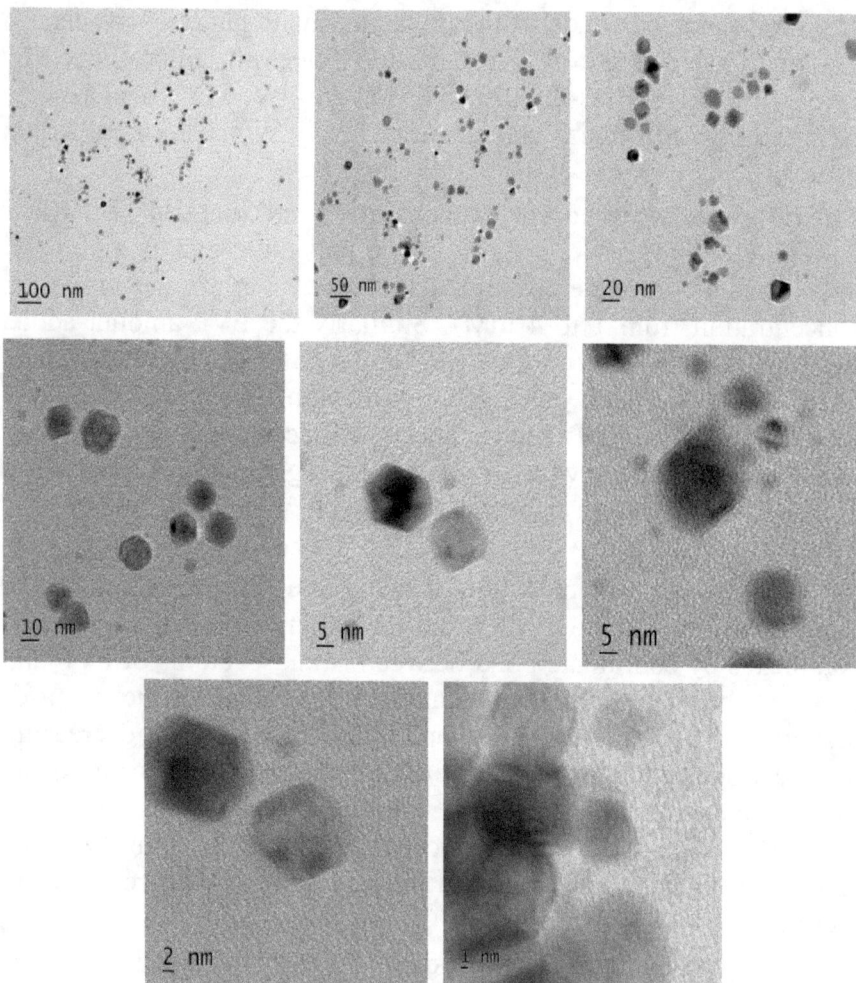

Figure-2. TEM images of major shapes and various sizes of Pd nanoparticles. TEM images of Pd nanoparticles with scale bars: (a) 100 nm, (b) 50 nm, (c) 20 nm, (d) 10 nm, (e, f) 5 nm, (g) 2 nm and (h) 1 nm

Kinetic Measurements

Appropriate amount of Arginine in acidic form, catalyst mercuric acetate, $NaClO_4$ (Ionic Strength), Pdnp and water (to keep the volume constant) were taken in the Erlenmeyer flask. The temperature was maintained at 30°C by circulating thermostated water. NBS solution kept in the thermostat separately was added to start the reaction. The progress of the solution was monitored by iodometric determination of the unreacted NBS in a measured weight of the reaction mixture at different intervals of time[27]. The rate constants were computed from the linear plots of log (NBS) against time.

Stoichiometry of the reaction

Different sets of reaction mixtures containing amino acid (arginine) and an excess of NBS were left to stand for 48 h at 303K. After completion of reaction it showed that one mole of amino acid (arginine) consumes two moles of NBS as shown in stoichiometry equation given below. The oxidation reaction product was identified by qualitative test. Ammonia was identified by Nessler's reagent and carbon dioxide was qualitatively detected by passing the gas into lime water.

$$RCH(NH_2)COOH + 2NBS + H_2O \xrightarrow{Pd(II)/H^+} RCHO + 2NHS + CO_2 + Br_2 + NH_3$$

R= -CH_2- CH_2- CH_2-NH-C(NH_2)=NH

Effect of NBS concentration

The concentration of NBS was varied from 1×10^{-3} to 5×10^{-3} mol dm^{-3} at fixed concentration of [Arginine] = 3×10^{-2} mol dm^{-3}, [Pdnps] = 3×10^{-5} mol dm^{-3}, [H^+] = 0.1 M and temperature 303 K. Pseudo first order rate constants (k_{obs}) were calculated from the slope of log (a-x) versus time plots and were found to be independent of initial concentration of NBS indicatinf first order w.r.t NBS(Table -1).

Effect of Pd nano catalyst

The concentration of Pd nano catalyst was varied from 1×10^{-5} to 7×10^{-5} mol dm^{-3} at fixed concentration of all reactants [NBS] = 3×10^{-3} mol dm^{-3}, [arginine] = 3×10^{-2} mol dm^{-3}, [H^+] = 0.1 M, at 303 K. The rate of reaction increases with increasing concentration of palladium nanoparticles (Fig.3). A plot of concentration of Pd nano catalyst versus rate constant shows the catalytic activity of palladium nano catalyst. The straight line indicated that the rate of reaction directly depends on concentration of palladium nanoparticles (Fig.-3). The straight line does not pass through the origin, so it is evident that the unanalysed oxidation of arginine by NBS is also possible.

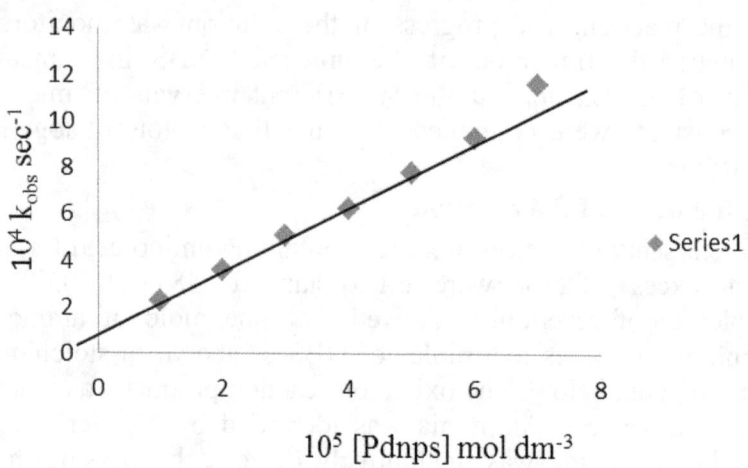

Figure- 3 Variation of [Pdnps]

Temp. = 308 K, [NBS] = 3 ×10^{-3} mol dm^{-3}, [Arginine] = 3×10^{-2} mol dm^{-3}, [H^+] = 0.1 M.

Effect of [H^+]

Hydrogen ion concentration was varied from 0.1 to 0.5 mol dm^{-3} at fixed concentration of all other reactants. The rate constants k_{obs} decreased with the increase in [H^+] concentration (Fig.-4). The plot of log k_{obs} versus log [H^+] is linear with a fractional slope.

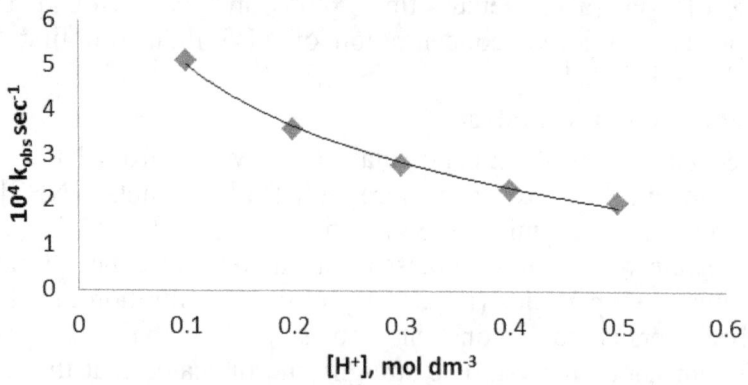

Figure-4 Variation of hydrogen ion
[NBS] = 3 ×10^{-3} mol dm^{-3}, [Arginine] = 3 ×10^{-2} mol dm^{-3}, [Pdnps] = 3 ×10^{-5} mol dm^{-3}, Temp. = 303K.

Table-1 Effect of [NBS], Arginine, Pd nano catalyst and H^+ on oxidation of arginine by NBS in perchloric acid medium in the presence of Pd nano catalyst

10^3[NBS] mol dm^{-3}	10^2[Arginine] mol dm^{-3}	10^5[Pdnp] mol dm^{-3}	[H^+] mol dm^{-3}	10^4 k_{obs} sec^{-1}
1	3	3	0.1	5.17
2	3	3	0.1	5.12
3	3	3	0.1	5.10
4	3	3	0.1	5.16
5	3	3	0.1	5.13
3	1	3	0.1	2.20
3	2	3	0.1	3.40
3	3	3	0.1	5.10
3	4	3	0.1	6.30
3	5	3	0.1	7.60
3	6	3	0.1	7.85
3	7	3	0.1	7.95
3	3	1	0.1	1.67
3	3	2	0.1	3.24
3	3	3	0.1	5.10
3	3	4	0.1	6.25
3	3	5	0.1	7.78
3	3	6	0.1	9.63
3	3	7	0.1	11.58
3	3	3	0.1	5.10
3	3	3	0.2	3.59
3	3	3	0.3	2.78
3	3	3	0.4	2.26
3	3	3	0.5	1.97

Effect of Arginine

The concentration of arginine was varied from 1×10^{-3} to 7×10^{-3} mol dm^{-3} at constant [NBS], [H^+], [Pdnps] and temp., the kinetic runs were carried out with initial concentration of arginine. A plot of (a-

x) versus arginine shows first order dependence of the reaction on arginine at low concentration, which shifts towards zero order at its higher concentration (Table-1). The plot of log k_{obs} versus log [arginine] was straight line with fractional slope confirming fractional order with respect to arginine.

Mechanism

Palladium nanoparticles are prepared in homogenous medium so definite mechanism of metal nanoparticles catalyzed oxidation is not clear. Although we identify the formation of transition species through certain physical measurements but it is very difficult to isolate and characterize from homogeneous mixture. In the oxidation of arginine by NBS in the presence of palladium nano particles, deamination of the amino group to NH_3 occurs, while NBS changes to succinimide. The plausible mechanism in support of the observed kinetics is given in scheme-1.

$$2NBS + Pd^0 + H_2O \rightarrow 2NHS + Pd^{+2} + O^{-2} + Br_2$$
$$Pd^{+2} + O^{-2} + R\text{-}CH(NH_2)COOH \rightarrow RCHO + NH_3 + CO_2 + Pd^0$$

$$2NBS + R\text{-}CH(NH_2)COOH + H_2O \rightarrow RCHO + 2NHS + NH_3 + CO_2 + Br_2$$

Where R= $-CH_2\text{-} CH_2\text{-} CH_2\text{-}NH\text{-}C(NH_2)=NH$

Conclusion

Palladium nanoparticles were synthesized successfully by reduction of H_2PdCl_4 using ethanol as reducing agent in presence of PVP polymer. In this paper we investigated the catalytic effect of synthesized palladium nano catalyst through the oxidation of arginine in aqueous acidic medium. The results of the study showed fractional first order kinetics with respect to arginine and first order with respect to palladium nano particles. The study will be helpful in the biochemical and medical fields.

References

1. Rioux, R. M., Song, H., Grass, M., Habas, S., Niesz, K., Hoefelmeyer, J. D., & Somorjai, G. A. (2006). Monodisperse platinum nanoparticles of well-defined shape: synthesis,

characterization, catalytic properties and future prospects. *Topics in Catalysis*, *39*(3), 167-174.
2. Zhang, Y., Grass, M. E., Habas, S. E., Tao, F., Zhang, T., Yang, P., & Somorjai, G. A. (2007). One-step polyol synthesis and Langmuir−Blodgett monolayer formation of size-tunable monodisperse Rhodium nanocrystals with catalytically active (111) surface structures. *The Journal of Physical Chemistry C*, *111*(33), 12243-12253.
3. Xiong, Y., McLellan, J. M., Yin, Y., & Xia, Y. (2007). Synthesis of palladium icosahedra with twinned structure by blocking oxidative etching with citric acid or citrate ions. *Angewandte Chemie International Edition*, *46*(5), 790-794.
4. Xu, S., & Yang, Q. (2008). Well-dispersed water-soluble Pd nanocrystals: Facile reducing synthesis and application in catalyzing organic reactions in aqueous media. *The Journal of Physical Chemistry C*, *112*(35), 13419-13425.
5. Stowell, C. A., & Korgel, B. A. (2005). Iridium nanocrystal synthesis and surface coating-dependent catalytic activity. *Nano Letters*, *5*(7), 1203-1207.
6. Wiley, B., Sun, Y., & Xia, Y. (2007). Synthesis of silver nanostructures with controlled shapes and properties. *Accounts of chemical research*, *40*(10), 1067-1076.
7. Mukherjee, S., Carmo, M., Kumar, G., Sekol, R. C., Taylor, A. D., & Schroers, J. (2012). Palladium nanostructures from multi-component metallic glass. *Electrochimica Acta*, *74*, 145-150.
8. Adams, B. D., & Chen, A. (2011). The role of palladium in a hydrogen economy. *Materials today*, *14*(6), 282-289.
9. Singh, P. (2011). Kinetic Investigations on Pd (II) Catalyzed Oxidation of Some Amino Acids by Acid Bromate. *SINET: Ethiopian Journal of Science*, *34*(2), 133-138.
10. Fawzy, A. (2016). Palladium (II)-catalyzed oxidation of L-tryptophan by hexacyanoferrate (III) in perchloric acid medium: a kinetic and mechanistic approach. *Journal of Chemical Sciences*, *128*(2), 247-256.
11. Singh, R. A., Srivastava, V. K., Verma, J., & Kumar, M. (2007). Kinetics and mechanism of Pd (II) catalyzed oxidation of valine

and leucine by acidic solution of chloramine-T. *Asian Journal of Chemistry*, *19*(2), 1482.
12. Piermatti, O. (2021). Green Synthesis of Pd Nanoparticles for Sustainable and Environmentally Benign Processes. *Catalysts*, *11*(11), 1258.
13. Gawande, M. B., Goswami, A., Felpin, F. X., Asefa, T., Huang, X., Silva, R., ... & Varma, R. S. (2016). Cu and Cu-based nanoparticles: synthesis and applications in catalysis. *Chemical reviews*, *116*(6), 3722-3811.
14. Mohammadi, P., Heravi, M., & Daraie, M. (2021). Ag nanoparticles immobilized on new magnetic alginate halloysite as a recoverable catalyst for reduction of nitroaromatics in aqueous media. *Scientific Reports*, *11*(1), 1-10.
15. Korovchenko, P., Renken, A., & Kiwi-Minsker, L. (2005). Microwave plasma assisted preparation of Pd-nanoparticles with controlled dispersion on woven activated carbon fibres. *Catalysis today*, *102*, 133-141.
16. Shim, H., Phillips, J., Fonseca, I. M., & Carabinerio, S. (2002). Plasma generation of supported metal catalysts. *Applied Catalysis A: General*, *237*(1-2), 41-51.
17. Chen, W., Cai, W., Lei, Y., & Zhang, L. (2001). A sonochemical approach to the confined synthesis of palladium nanoparticles in mesoporous silica. *Materials Letters*, *50*(2-3), 53-56.
18. Wu, Y., Zhang, L., Li, G., Liang, C., Huang, X., Zhang, Y., & Zhixiang, C. (2001). Synthesis and characterization of nanocomposites with palladium embedded in mesoporous silica. *Materials research bulletin*, *36*(1-2), 253-263.
19. Lopez, M. J., & Mohiuddin, S. S. (2020). Biochemistry, essential amino acids.
20. Barrett, G. C., & Elmore, D. T. (1998). *Amino acids and peptides*. Cambridge University Press.
21. Teranishi, T., & Miyake, M. (1998). Size control of palladium nanoparticles and their crystal structures. *Chemistry of materials*, *10*(2), 594-600.
22. Nemamcha, A., Rehspringer, J. L., & Khatmi, D. (2006). Synthesis of palladium nanoparticles by sonochemical reduction

of palladium (II) nitrate in aqueous solution. *The Journal of Physical Chemistry B, 110*(1), 383-387.
23. Bonet, F., Delmas, V., & Grugeon, S. (1999). R. Herrera Urbina RH, Silvert P. Y and Tekaia-Elhsissen K. *NanoStructured Materials, 11*(8), 1277-1284.
24. Song, H., Kim, F., Connor, S., Somorjai, G. A., & Yang, P. (2005). Pt nanocrystals: shape control and Langmuir- blodgett monolayer formation. *The Journal of Physical Chemistry B, 109*(1), 188-193.
25. Wang, Z. L. (2000). Transmission electron microscopy of shape-controlled nanocrystals and their assemblies. *The Journal of Physical Chemistry B, 104*(6), 1153-1175.
26. Montejano-Carrizales, J. M., Rodrguez-Lpez, J. L., Gutierrez-Wing, C., Miki-Yoshida, M., & Jos-Yacaman, M. (2004). Crystallography and shape of nanoparticles and clusters. In *Encyclopedia of Nanoscience and Nanotechnology* (Vol. 2, No. 282, pp. 237-282). American Scientific Publishers.
27. Khalid, M. A., & Kheir, A. M. (2008). Kinetics and Mechanisms of α-Amino Acids-Peroxodisulphate Reaction, Part I. *Sudan J. Basic Sci, 15*, 69-83.

[1]**Assistant Professor,
Department of Chemistry,
Government College, Kota, (Raj.)
danrajchem01@gmail.com**
[2]**Research Scholar,
Department of Chemistry,
Government College, Kota, (Raj.)
guptamegha151@gmail.com**
[3]**AssociateProfessor,
Department of Chemistry,
Government College, Kota, (Raj.)
mbyadav898@gmail.com**

11. Effects of Air Pollution on Human Health and Control Measures of Air Pollution : A Bibliometric Analysis

Rutuja Chothe[1]
Akanksha Botre[2]
Divya Patil[3]
Rohan Sawant[4]

Abstract

Gases, dust particles, fumes (or smoke), or odours are introduced into the atmosphere in a way that is damaging to humans, animals, and plants, this is referred to as air pollution. The health of people and all living organisms on our planet is jeopardized by air pollution. It generates smog and acid rain, leads to cancer and respiratory disorders, depletes the ozone layer, and contributes to global warming. Air pollution is a public health problem, particularly in metropolitan areas, since it has a negative impact on the health, survival, and activities of humans and other living organisms. Particle pollution, ground level ozone, carbon monoxide, sulphur oxides, nitrogen oxides, and lead are the six primary air pollutants, according to the World Health Organization. Air pollution cannot be totally removed in our modern age, but actions may be made to lessen it. In an effort to manage air pollution, the government has produced and continues to develop recommend-dations for air quality and regulations to limit emissions. We analyze globally-published literature in outdoor air pollution – related respiratory health. Outdoor air pollution documents related to respiratory health were retrieved from Scopus database. Mapping of author keywords was carried out using VOSviewer 1.6.6 and an h-index of 137. The most frequently encountered author keywords were: air pollution (835 occurrences), asthma (502 occurrences), particulate matter (198 occurrences), and children (203 occurrences). The United States of America ranked first (1082; 29.8%) followed by the United Kingdom (279; 7.7%) and Italy (198; 5.4%) for publications related to outdoor air pollution – related respiratory health. There was a dramatic increase in the number of publications in the last decade of the study period. Analysis of regional distribution of publications indicated that Mediterranean, African, and South-East Asia regions had the least contribution.

Keywords : Air Pollution, Pollutants, Environment, Human Health

Introduction :

Air pollution has become a major issue in recent decades, with substantial toxicological consequences for human health and the environment. Pollution sources range from tiny units of cigarettes and natural sources such as volcanic activity to massive volumes of emission from automotive motor engines and industrial operations [1, 2]. The long-term consequences of air pollution on the beginning of illnesses such as respiratory infections and inflammations, cardiovascular dysfunctions, and cancer are well acknowledged [3-6], and as a result, air pollution is associated with millions of deaths worldwide each year. [7-9] a new study found a link between male infertility and air pollution. [10] Primary pollutants are chemicals that are directly created by a process, such as volcanic ash or carbon monoxide gas from automobile exhaust. Solar radiation and heat in the lower atmosphere can convert primary pollutants into secondary pollutants such as ozone (O3) and other photochemical pollutants. An air pollutant is a chemical in the air that can be harmful to humans and the environment. Pollutants might be solid particles, liquid droplets, or gases. They can either be natural or man-made. Pollutants are divided into two types: primary and secondary. Typically, primary pollutants are directly created by a process, such as volcanic ash, carbon monoxide gas from automobile exhaust, or sulphur dioxide discharged by manufacturers. Secondary pollutants are not directly released. Rather, they arise in the air as a result of main contaminants reacting or interacting. Ground level ozone is an important example of a secondary pollutant, and it is one of the numerous secondary pollutants that contribute to photochemical smog. Some pollutants are both primary and secondary, meaning they are released directly and generated by other primary pollutants.

Air Pollution

Air pollution is defined as any harmful consequences of any source that contribute to atmospheric pollution and/or ecological damage. Human involvement and/or natural processes both contribute to air pollution. It consists of a wide range of contaminants, including elements in solid, liquid, and gas forms [11].

"Air quality index (AQI) is defined as a measure of the state of air relative to the requirements of one or more biotic species or to any human need," write Johnson et al. [12] The AQI is split into ranges, which are numbered and labelled with colour codes. It assigns a value ranging from a healthy standard level of zero to a very hazardous level of greater than 300 to reflect the level of health risk associated with air quality.

Sources of Air Pollution:
1. Natural sources
2. Human-made sources

1. Natural Sources :
Particulate matter (PM) is naturally occurring material that includes dust from the earth's surface (crustal material), sea salt in coastal locations, and biological material in the form of pollen, spores, or plant and animal detritus [1]. Volcanic eruptions may release large amounts of gases and particles into the atmosphere. On an average day, the Etna volcano generates 3,000 tonnes of sulphur dioxide (SO_2) and up to 10,000 tonnes during periods of high activity. During the Tambora catastrophic eruptions in 1815 in Indonesia, 100 billion tonnes of volcanic products were blasted into the sky, 300 million tonnes of which reached the stratosphere, resulting in a 0.7°C drop in mean global temperature. Periodic forest fires emit substantial levels of PM in certain rural regions. Thunderbolts, which emit substantial amounts of nitrogen oxides (NOx); algae on the ocean's surface, which emit hydrogen sulphide (H_2S); wind erosion, which transfers particles into the atmosphere; and humid zones, such as swamps, peat bogs, or small deep lakes, which emit methane (CH_4). Low quantities of O_3 exist naturally at ground level, generated by interactions between NOx and volatile organic molecules in the presence of sunshine (VOCs).

2. Human-Made Sources :
The majority of air pollution in cities is caused by man-made causes. These sources can be classed as mobile (cars, trucks, aeroplanes, marine engines, and so on) or point sources (factories, electric power plants, etc.). Road traffic is currently the most significant cause of air pollution in the world's largest cities. Carbon monoxide

(CO) and hydrocarbons are produced during the incomplete combustion of carbon-based fuels (coal, fuel oil, wood, natural gas). NOx is produced by the mixture of air, nitrogen, and oxygen produced by the high-temperature burning of fossil fuels included in motor fuel. Human activities have increased the quantity of VOCs produced by the petroleum, chemical, and transportation sectors, as well as NOx produced by combustion in power plants and cars. As a result, O3 concentrations rise and smog levels rise in heavily inhabited and industrial areas. Total ambient PM is influenced by human activities. Particles in urban areas are primarily produced by combustion from mobile and stationary sources. SO2 is formed when coal and sulphur from fuel oils oxidise. These are the fuels that are utilised to move, warm up, and provide energy to numerous industrial operations. Furthermore, the business generates waste pollutants such as fluorine derivatives and aluminium. Ore processing produces "heavy" metals such as cadmium, zinc, and lead. Domestic waste incineration emits mercury. Agriculture, via the use of nitrogen fertilisers, produces nitric oxide (N2O), a greenhouse effect gas, and ammonia (NH3), both of which contribute to acidification processes. CH4, another greenhouse gas, is mostly generated by the digestion and excretion of farm animals [16].

Types of Air Pollution :
1. Indoor air pollution
2. Outdoor air pollution

1. Indoor Air Pollution :
Indoor air pollution is described as the presence of contaminants in a confined area's atmosphere. For cooking, almost half of the world's population (households) utilise conventional fuels such as firewood, animal dung, coke, and so on. Particulate matter, oxides of sulphur, oxides of nitrogen, carbon monoxide, hydrocarbons, and organic pollutant and odour causing pollutant are the most common pollutants that cause indoor air pollution problems due to fuel combustion. In our country, over 80% of housewives spend their time indoors, with 4-6 hours spent in kitchens for the purpose of cooking. A normal individual needed 1 m3/hr of fresh air to breathe. It is difficult to disperse indoor air contaminants or include fresh air during periods of calm weather and low breezes. Globally, 4.3

million people die prematurely from illnesses caused by home air pollution caused by inefficient use of solid fuel for cooking.

2. Outdoor Air Pollution :

Outdoor air pollution is a serious environmental health issue that affects people in low-, middle-, and high-income nations alike. In 2016, ambient (outside) air pollution was predicted to cause 4.2 million premature deaths globally owing to exposure to fine particulate matter of 2.5 millimetres or less in diameter (PM2.5), which causes cardiovascular and respiratory disorders, as well as malignancies. People in low- and middle-income countries bear a disproportionate share of the burden of outdoor air pollution, accounting for 91 percent (of the 4.2 million premature deaths) and bearing the biggest burden in the WHO South-East Asia and Western Pacific areas. The most recent burden estimates highlight the critical impact that air pollution plays in cardiovascular disease and mortality. Evidence confirming the links between ambient air pollution and the risk of cardiovascular disease is becoming increasingly available, including research from extremely polluted locations [15].

Types of Pollutant :

Air pollutant refers to particulate matter (both liquid and solid) and certain gases that are present in high quantities and will harm the environment directly or indirectly.

Table No 1. Classification of air pollutant

Natural Contaminants	Particulates	Gases
Natural fog	Dust	SO_2, SO_3, H_2S
Pollen grain	Smoke	NO, NO_2, NH_3
Bacteria	Mist	O_3, CO, CO_2
Product of volcanic eruption	Fog	HF, HCl
	Fumes	Hydrocarbon

Air pollutant are also classified as:

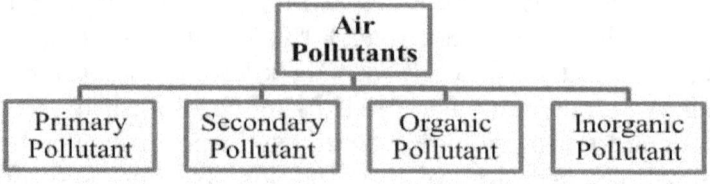

1. Primary pollutants :
Pollutants which are emitted directly from the source into the atmosphere and present in their original form are called as primary pollutant.

Examples of primary air pollutants :
1. Oxides of Nitrogen (NOx)
2. Oxides of Sulphur (SOx)
3. Carbon monoxide (CO)
4. Fine particles (less than 100 micron in diameter)
5. Coarse particles (greater than 100 micron in diameter)
6. Halogen compounds
7. Organic Compounds
8. Radioactive Compounds

2. Secondary Pollutants :
Secondary air pollutants are those which are form in the atmosphere by reacting two or more primary pollutants.

Examples of secondary air pollutants :
1. Ozone (O_3)
2. Formaldehyde
3. PAN (peroxyl acetyl nitrate)
4. Photochemical Smoke
5. Acid Rain ($SO_2 + O_2 + H_2O$)

3. Organic Pollutants:
- Organic pollutants include carbon and hydrogen, as well as nitrogen, sulphur, oxygen, and phosphorus.
- Hydrogen compounds are organic molecules that simply contain carbon and hydrogen.
- Aldehyde and ketone are composed of hydrogen, carbon, and oxygen.

4. Inorganic Pollutants:
Inorganic pollutants consists of carbon monoxide, sulphur dioxide, carbonates, ozone, hydrogen fluoride, hydrogen chloride, hydrogen sulphide etc.

Table No. 2 Sources of Air Pollution

Source	Pollutants
Oceans	Sea water spray containing dissolved salt, CO_2, H_2S, CH_4.
Volcanoes	Solid Particles, SO_2, H_2S, HCl, CO_2, CO, NH_3.
Decaying Vegetables	CO, CH_4, CO_2, H_2S, NH_3.
Deserts	Solid Particles
Forest fire	CO, CO_2, aldehyde, soots, etc.
Lightning	Nox and O_3

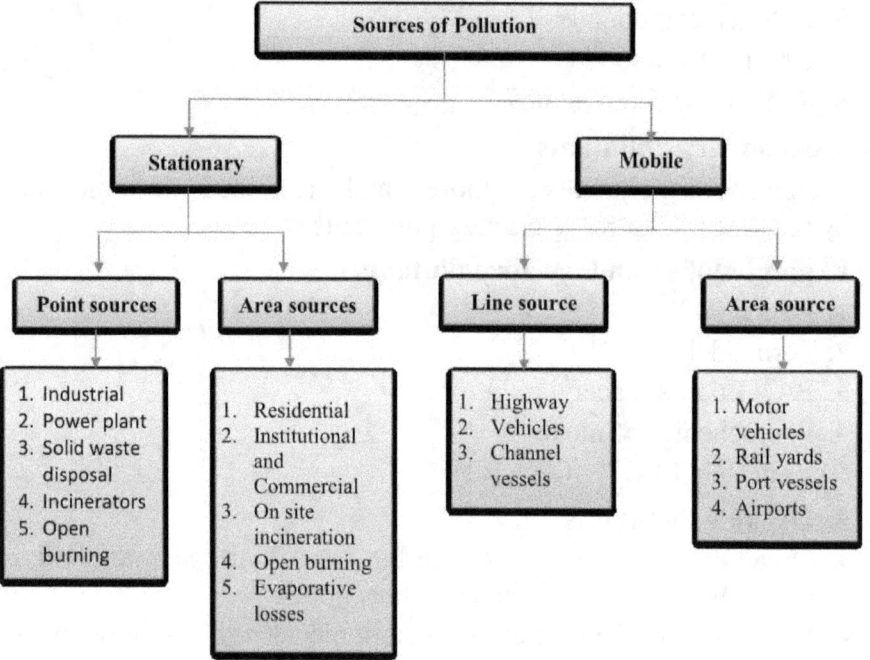

Effects of air pollution :

The impact of air pollution on human health is now being contested in both scientific and political circles. However, natural causes of air pollution have always existed. For the first time, Plinius the Younger recorded a deadly respiratory condition caused by natural air pollution: the patient was Plinius the Elder, who had travelled to Pompei (Italy) to see Mount Vesuvius' eruption in the year 73 AD and had breathed air pollutants released by the volcano [8]. Despite the fact that in his book On Asthma: Its Pathology and Treatment, published in London in 1860 [9], Henry Hyde Salter associated "impure air" with asthma. With the outbreaks of black fog in London in the 1950s, people became aware of the health implications of air pollution. Indeed, in 1952, air pollution induced by coal burning for heating killed 4,000 people in London [10].

The effects of the main air pollution indicators on health

Air pollutants can cause health issues either directly when they enter the body or indirectly through environmental alteration. Pollutants enter the body via three main pathways. 1) Inhalation: Every day, man breaths 15 m3 of polluted air. 2) Ingestion: Some air pollutants can settle on soil or surface water, where they are absorbed by plants and consumed by animals, eventually entering the food chain[13]. 3) Skin contact: This is a less common sort of interaction, unless in cases of accidental contamination or violent engagements. Air pollution can cause major health issues such as asthma, lung irritation, bronchitis, pneumonia, and lower resistance to respiratory infections, as well as allergies, unfavourable neurological, reproductive, and developmental impacts, cancer, and even premature mortality. Several reviews have fully documented on the health impacts.

The effects of the main air pollution indicators on the environment

Table No.3 summarises the main health and environmental impacts of typical air pollutants. Some pollutants are also responsible for environmental conditions like acid rain and climate change, notably global warming. Temperature increases may have a number of consequences, including an increase in heat-related sickness, more extreme weather events, such as floods and droughts, and the associated damage, and an increase in incidences of vector-borne and water-borne sea level [13].

Table No. 3 Main air pollution indicators and their effects on the environment and health

Pollutants	Health Effects	Environmental Effects
NO_2	It causes respiratory irritation. It may	NOx oxidises in the atmosphere to become

	aggravate pre-existing respiratory illnesses. In asthmatic patients, it may cause bronchial hyperresponsiveness and a reduction in lung function.	nitric acid, a major component of acid rain It combines with VOC to form O_3
SO_2	It causes respiratory irritation. It may aggravate pre-existing respiratory illnesses, such as asthma episodes in asthmatic people. It exacerbates adult respiratory symptoms such as coughing. It affects the lung function of youngsters.	It oxidises in the atmosphere to become sulphuric acid, a major component of acid rain
Lead	This metal builds up in the body. It damages the brain and nerve system, particularly in youngsters (lead poisoning), as well as the renal system.	
PM	The impacts of particles on health are proportional to their size. PM10 causes include: Irritation of the nose and throat Damage to the lungs Bronchitis The possibility of cardiac arrest If they contain hazardous substances, they can cause cancer. Death occurs early.	Smoke and dust can dirty and discolour structures.
CO	It binds to the oxygen-carrying spot on haemoglobin, reducing O2	It oxidises in the atmosphere to become CO_2, a greenhouse effect

	transport throughout the body. It is extremely poisonous at high quantities, producing headaches, nausea, impaired thinking, and even death.	gas It can combine with other gases to form O_3.
VOC	They have different impacts based on the chemical component. They have been linked to cancer, as well as negative neurological, reproductive, and developmental impacts.	They can combine with NOx to form O_3.
O3	It has the potential to irritate the eyes. It has the potential to irritate the respiratory tract. It causes violent coughing, shortness of breath, and lung discomfort. It makes you more susceptible to respiratory infections like bronchitis and pneumonia. It worsens asthma attacks.	It damages plants and trees It induces reduction of visibility.

Economical Effects

The economic impact of air pollution may be indirect. In layman's terms, the economy flourishes when people are healthy and businesses that rely on farmed raw materials and natural resources operate at peak performance. Every year, air pollution decreases agricultural crop and commercial forest outputs by billions of dollars. This, along with people missing work for health reasons, may have a significant impact on the economy.

Control: Measures to reduce Air Pollution

Pollution-reduction measures are always a major issue. As a result, preventative efforts are always preferable to reducing air pollution.

These preventative techniques might originate from the government (laws) or from individuals. Monitoring equipment has been put at various sites throughout numerous large cities. Authorities read them on a regular basis to assess the air quality. Prevention at the government (or community) level [12].

- Governments all around the world have already taken measures to combat air pollution by using green energy. Some countries are investing in wind energy, solar energy, and other renewable energy to reduce the use of fossil fuels, which generate significant air pollution.
- Governments are also requiring corporations to be more responsible with their production operations, so that while pollution is still produced, it is much more managed.
- Car manufacturers are also producing more energy-efficient vehicles that emit less pollution than previously.

Individual Level Prevention

- Encourage your family to commute by bus, rail, or bicycle. There will be fewer automobiles on the road and less pollution if we all do this.
- Use energy intelligently (light, water, boiler, kettle, and firewood). This is due to the fact that many fossil fuels are used to generate power, and if we can reduce our consumption, we will also reduce the quantity of pollution we produce. [14]
- Recycle and repurpose items. This will reduce the need to create new products. Remember that manufacturing businesses produce a lot of pollution, therefore reusing items like shopping plastic bags, clothing, paper, and bottles might help.

Control devices

The following things are often employed by industry as pollution control equipment or transportation devices. They can either eliminate or remove impurities from an exhaust stream before they are released into the atmosphere.

1. **Mechanical collectors** (dust cyclones, multi-cyclones)
2. **Electrostatic precipitators :** An electrostatic precipitator (ESP) or electrostatic air cleaner is a particulate collecting device that uses the force of an induced electrostatic charge to remove particles from

a moving gas (such as air). Electrostatic precipitators are very efficient filtering devices that can quickly remove tiny particles such as dust and smoke from the air stream while obstructing the passage of gases through the device. [11].

3. Bag houses : A dust collector, which is designed to manage large dust loads, is made up of a blower, a dust filter, a filter-cleaning system, and a dust receptacle or dust removal system (distinguished from air cleaners which utilise disposable filters to remove the dust).

4. Particulate scrubbers : Wet scrubber technology is a type of pollution control technique. The phrase refers to a wide range of devices that employ contaminants from furnace exhaust gas or other gas streams. The dirty gas stream is brought into contact with the scrubbing liquid in a wet scrubber by spraying it with the liquid, driving it through a pool of liquid, or by some other contact method to remove the pollutants.

Particulate Pollutants Removal :
1. Settling Chamber
2. Cyclone
3. Fabric Filter
4. Electrostatic precipittator
5. Scrubber or Wet Collector
6. Inertial separator

Gaseous Pollutants Removal:
1. Wet absorption
2. Dry absorption
3. Combustion
4. Catalytic incineration

Table No. 4 Control of Indoor Air Pollution by using Plants

Sr. No.	Name of Plants	Description
1.	Aloe vera (Aloe barbadensis)	Aloe vera is a succulent, perennial plant that has the ability to filter benzene and formaldehyde. It is easy to grow and required lots of sunlight.

Greener Living

2.	Spider plant (Chlorohytum comosum)	It is one of the best indoor plants to remove formaldehyde from air. It can also remove benzene, carbon monoxide and xylene. Can neglect this plant but its resilience keeps it alive.
3.	Snake Plant (Sansdvieria trifasciata 'Lavrenil')	Its other names are mother-in-law's tongue and bedroom plant. The biggest advantage of this plant is that it coverts carbon dioxide into oxygen in the night also. To arrange clean air, put 6 plants upto height of 3 feet. It is used to remove formaldehyde and nitrogen dioxide.
4.	Golden pathos (Scindapsus aures)	This fast growing plant is create at removing formaldehyde. It grows in any type of light (bulb or tube light). It is toxic if consumed. So, if you have kids running around indoors, this one is not useful. It can eliminate carbon monoxide and carbon dioxide.
5.	Bamboo palm (Chamaedorea sefritzii)	This plant is natural humidifier which can be beneficial areas with dry air. It helps in eliminating carbon monoxide, xylene, benzene and formaldehyde. It often produce small flowers and berries.
6.	Money pant (Epipremnum Aureum)	Many people think about this plant that if you put this plant in the room, the flow of money and sources of income will increase. But factually it is not true. This is indirectly true, because this plant cleans the chemical toxins from the air

		and release fresh air into the atmosphere which keeps us healthy and reduces medical expenses.
7.	Red-edged dracaena (Dracaena marginnata)	It is slow growing and add colour to the environment. It is poisonous.

Some Facts and Statistics about Air Pollution
- Children are more affected by air pollution than adults because they have larger concentrations of contaminated air in their systems per body size.
- The country with the worst air quality in the world is India.
- If air pollution mortality were reduced, the European Union would save 161 billion Euros per year.
- In major cities, automobiles, buses, motorbikes, and other vehicles on the road account for more than 80% of deadly pollutants that cause lung disease.
- According to the World Health Organization, there are as many fatalities from air pollution (1.3 million per year) as there are from automobile accidents.
- The typical adult breaths 3,000 litres of air every day.
- The Great Smog of London in 1952 was one of the worst air pollution disasters in history, resulting in the deaths of almost 8,000 people. [12]
- Road traffic is the leading driver of air pollution in Europe, with over 5,000 people dying each year from lung cancer and heart attacks caused by car exhaust emissions.

Result and Discussion
Analysis of Author Keyword Co-Occurrence :
In bibliometric research, topic mapping is critical. Figure 1 illustrates all of the issue categories related to the keywords of scientific literacy in general. In the bibliometric analysis, VOSviewer may give six unique mapping visualisations. The thickness of the connecting line represented the strength of a pair of topic areas or keywords.

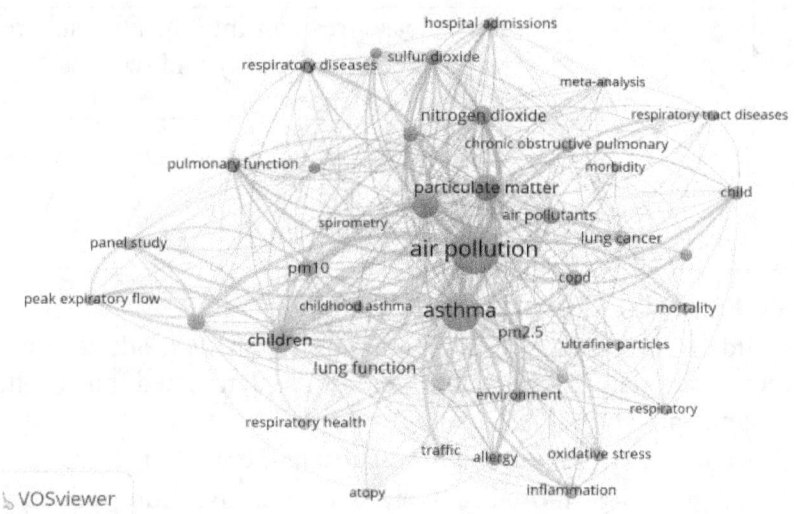

Fig. 1 The Network Visualization of Literacy Topic Area

5.2 In terms of country, co-authorship is as follows :

Countries having an emphasis on scientific literacy research are depicted in Figure 2. The United States and India have the most scientific literacy research studies, followed by Canada, Australia, and Turkey, according to the data. Meanwhile, as the VOSviewer mapping results reveal, scientific literacy research in Indonesia is still in its infancy.

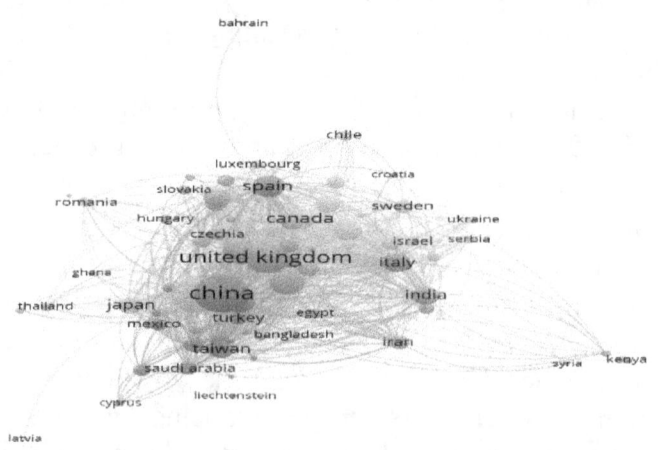

Fig. 2 The Visualization of Countries Related to Scientific LiteracyResearch

5.3 Co-authorship in terms of Authors :

This analytical parameter is considered with 04 additional parameters. This parameter considers the word, authors, organisations, and countries. This research does not include documents with a large number of authors. This number is considered to be 13. For the author's minimum number of documents, the barrier is set at 4. It should be highlighted that 328 of the 1549 writers met the requirements from the scopus and web of science databases.

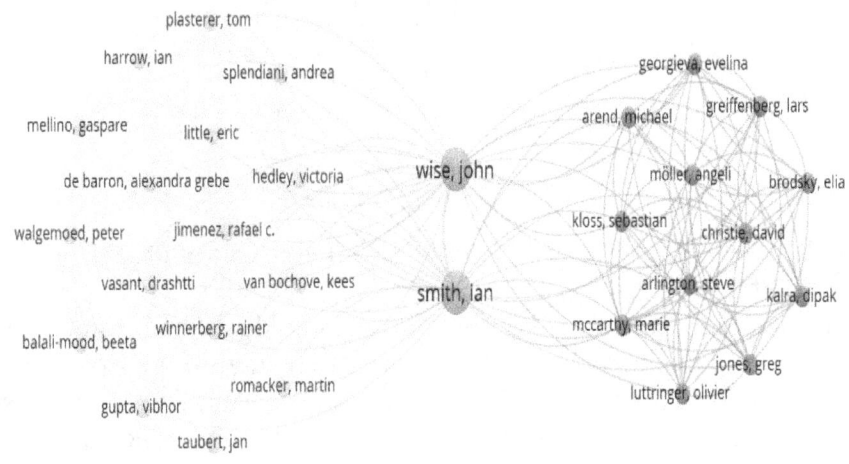

Fig. 3 Network Analysis of Co-authorship in terms of authors

5.4 CO-authorship in terms of Organizations :

Co-authorship in the unit of organisations is calculated by disregarding the citation of at least two publications in organisations; 45 organisations meet the condition out of the total of 1426 displayed in the image. Stony Brook University (SBU),NY,United States has the highest link strength of 5 and the highest number of citations of 154. (with 2 documents).

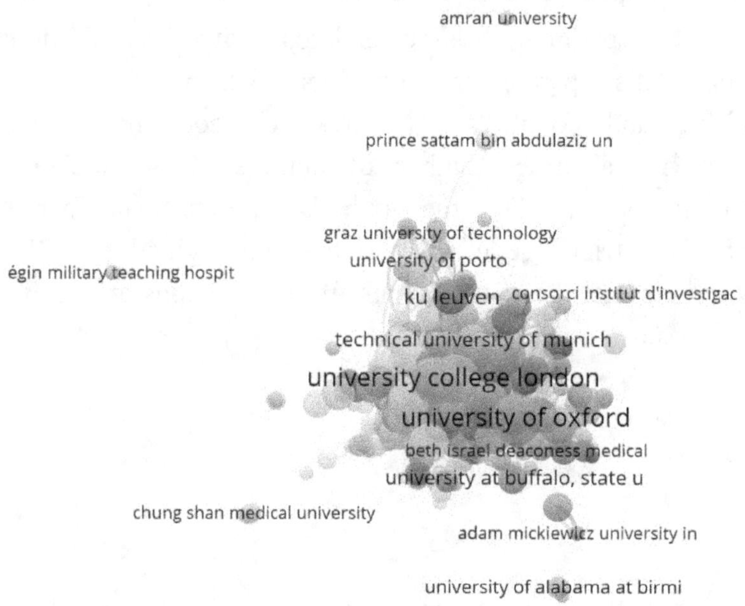

amran university

prince sattam bin abdulaziz un

graz university of technology
university of porto
égin military teaching hospit
ku leuven   consorci institut d'investigac
technical university of munich
university college london
university of oxford
beth israel deaconess medical
university at buffalo, state u
chung shan medical university
adam mickiewicz university in
university of alabama at birmi

Fig. 4 Network Analysis of Co-authorship in terms of organizations

Conclusion :

Air pollution can only be avoided if individuals and companies cease using the hazardous substances that create it in the first place. This would necessitate the halt of all fossil-fuel-burning operations, from industrial manufacturing to domestic air conditioner use. Air pollution has a significant influence on human health, activating and inducing various diseases that result in high morbidity and mortality, particularly in developing nations such as Iran. As a result, air pollution control is critical and should be at the top of the government's priority list. These countries' policymakers and lawmakers must update all air pollution laws and regulations.

According to the Scopus database, the second presents a bibliographical and collaborative network analysis, as well as keywords, of the documents published in the journal from 2016 to 2022.

- The maximum number of papers published under the category of article is 547, while the maximum number of papers published

under the category Conference Paper is 516. There are 89 reviews and 3 chapters in the book.
- In Scopus, under the category Bibliometric, 1294 items were retrieved, with the most articles contributed in 2021 and the fewest in 2016.
- The highest papers, Jayaraman, R. ranks first with a total of 12 articles contributed, followed by wise john with 11 articles and smith jan. on 10th Rank with 6 articles published.
- A subject-by-subject analysis reveals that the most contributions, 753, were made in Environment Science.
- China has highest number of paper published
- University College London has lot of research work on air pollution sector

References:
1. Robinson DL. Air pollution in Australia: Review of costs, sources and potential solutions. Health Promot J Austr 2005;16:213-20.
2. Habre R, Coull B, Moshier E, Godbold J, Grunin A, Nath A, et al. Sources of indoor air pollution in New York city residences of asthmatic children. J Expo Sci Environ Epidemiol 2014;24:269-78.
3. Rumana HS, Sharma RC, Beniwal V, Sharma AK. A retrospective approach to assess human health risks associated with growing air pollution in urbanized area of Thar Desert, Western Rajasthan, India. J Environ Health Sci Eng 2014;12:23.
4. Yamamoto SS, Phalkey R, Malik AA. A systematic review of air pollution as a risk factor for cardiovascular disease in South Asia: Limited evidence from India and Pakistan. Int J Hyg Environ Health 2014;217:133-44.
5. Zhang W, Qian CN, Zeng YX. Air pollution: A smoking gun for cancer. Chin J Cancer 2014;33:173-5.
6. Brucker N, Charão MF, Moro AM, Ferrari P, Bubols G, Sauer E, et al. Atherosclerotic process in taxi drivers occupationally exposed to air pollution and co-morbidities. Environ Res 2014;131:31-8.

7. Biggeri A, Bellini P, Terracini B. Meta-analysis of the Italian studies on short-term effects of air pollution – MISA 1996-2002. Epidemiol Prev 2004;28 4-5 Suppl: 4-100.
8. Vermaelen K, Brusselle G. Exposing a deadly alliance: Novel insights into the biological links between COPD and lung cancer. Pulm Pharmacol Ther 2013;26:544-54.
9. Kan H, Chen B, Zhao N, London SJ, Song G, Chen G, et al. Part 1. A time-series study of ambient air pollution and daily mortality in Shanghai, China. Res Rep Health Eff Inst 2010;(154):17-78.
10. Zhou N, Cui Z, Yang S, Han X, Chen G, Zhou Z, et al. Air pollution and decreased semen quality: A comparative study of Chongqing urban and rural areas. Environ Pollut 2014;187:145-52.
11. Vallero D. Fundamentals of Air Pollution. 4th ed. California, USA: Academic Press; 2007
12. 12.Johnson D, Ambrose S, Bassett T, Bowen M, Crummey D, Isaacson J, et al. Meanings of environmental terms. J Environ Qual 1997;26:581-9
13. http://en.wikipedia.org/wiki/Air_pollution
14. http://eschooltoday.com/pollution/air-pollution
15. http://www.who.int/topics/air_pollution
16. http://www.nrdc.org/air/
17. Air Pollution, M N Rao & H V N Rao, Tata McGraw-Hill, 2007

[1,2,3] **UG Student,**
Department of Civil Engineering,
Dr. D. Y. Patil Institute of Technology Pimpri, Pune
[4] **Assistant Professor,**
Department of Civil Engineering,
Dr. D. Y. Patil Institute of Technology Pimpri, Pune

12. Studies of Electrical output in Photogalvanic Cell for Energy Conversion and Storage

Sushil Kumar Yadav

Abstract

Devices for converting and storing solar energy based on dye-sensitized solutions are called photogalvanic (PG) cells. To get fresh insights into how to create PG cells that are comparatively more affordable, cleaner, and ecologically acceptable, the photogalvanic of Bismarck Brown (BB) as a dye sensitizer with different reductants such as Ascorbic Acid (AA), EDTA, and Glucose (Glu.) have been examined. This study used PG cells to evaluate three systems: BB-AA, BB-EDTA, and BB-Glu. These systems produced photocurrents of 915 mV, 810 mV, and 720 mV, respectively, and photo potential of 155 A, 135 A, and 120 A, respectively. The fill factors for the BB - AA, BB - EDTA, and BB - Glu systems were 0.54 percent, 0.48 percent, and 0.40 percent, respectively. The conversion efficiencies for the BB - AA, BB - EDTA, and BB - Glu systems were 0.899 percent, 0.614 percent, and 0.405 percent, and the storage capacities for the BB - AA, BB - EDTA. A mechanism for the creation of photocurrent in PG cells has also been proposed, as well as the impact of various conditions on the electrical outputs of the cell.

Keywords : Glucose, EDTA, Ascorbic Acid, Conversion Efficiencies, Fill Factor.

1. Introduction

Today's world places a significant demand on the development of technologies for creating renewable energy.To meet the rising worldwide need for power without causing environmental damage, we face a problem.The entire energy used by the earth in a year is less than the quantity of sunlight that hits the Earth in an hour.A solar focused cell is the best device for turning solar energy into electrical energy.Research on solar-based cells aims to increase sunlight conversion efficiency while simultaneously addressing the demand for a workable power source.

There are five photoprocesses that involve the basic carbanion, including ring opening, isomerization anionradical creation, reductive alkylation, and electron transfer with anodic current production, as observed by Fox, Kabir-Ud-Din, and Singletary [1979]. This suggests that carnations go through photoinduced chemical reactions. It will require new endeavours to improve the efficiency with which incoming photons are gathered by employing safranine-o as a photosensitizer, as reported by Baranham, Mazzer, and Clive [2006]. The resulting photopotential and photocurrent were 790.0 mV and 185.0 A, respectively. The photogalvanic cell's power at power point was 15.28 W while the measured conversion efficiency was 0.1469 percent, the fill factor was 0.08, and the cell's greatest power was 146.15 W.

For the conversion and storage of solar energy in D-Xylose-NaLS systems, Gangotri, Regar, Lal, Genwa, Kalla, and Meena [1997,2011] studied a comparison of photogalvanic cell performance with various photosensitizers using Methyl Orange, Rose Bengal, Toluidine Blue, and Brilliant Cresyl Blue, as well as D-Xylose as a reductant and Sodium Lauryl Sulphate. M. Chadra and T. Shree [2019] If we properly equip and utilise these technologies and possibilities, reported renewables have the potential to play a big role in rural electrification. One of the most crucial challenges is the conservation of energy. Therefore, new technology and energy efficiency are essential to addressing our problems with energy conservation and global warming. In a system with the dye Victoria Blue acting as a photosensitizer and the reducing agent Ascorbic acid, a photogalvanic effect has been seen.

Chandra[2021] Four systems, including Rh B-EDTA-Tween80, MB-DTA-NaLS, Rh 6G-EDTA-CTAB, and Safranine-EDTA-ALS in PG cells, were studied. Additionally, it was said that by the year 2050, it is anticipated that the world's emerging areas' energy demand will increase quickly and fall short of their basic needs. Koli(2021) noted that Sudan-I dye (photosensitizer), fructose (reductant), and sodium lauryl sulphate (surfactant) photogalvanics have been investigated in alkaline medium at low and artificial sun intensity with the aim of finding a relatively better combination of chemicals such as photosensitizer, reductant, and surfactant for further enhancing the efficiency of these cells.

2. Materials and Methods

As a photogalvanic cell, an H-shaped cell was utilised with a known amount of photosensitizers, sodium hydroxide, reductant, distilled water and the total volume was adjusted to 25 ml. The H type cell's one arm was submerged in a saturated calomel electrode while the other arm was immersed in a platinum electrode.Alkali solution was employed to keep the pH of the fluid in the photogalvanic cell stable when needed. Standard oxalic acid used to standardise the alkali solution, and a digital pH metre (Systronics model 802) was utilised to measure the pH though solution.At a predetermined time period, an electronic pH metre was utilised to monitor the system's fluctuation in potential difference. To achieve a steady potential, the device was first maintained in the dark. This stable potential became the dark potential when the platinum electrode was lit via the window generated in the H type cell's arm. A 200W tungsten filament lamp was used as a light source. After illuminating the system for a length of time, a steady potential is obtained. The photopotential is calculated by subtracting the dark potential from the stable potential obtained after lighting (mV).The current generated in the photochemical system was measured using a micro-ammeter (New Tech, India).

After achieving a stable photopotential under illumination, the current was measured. In the same system, changes in current with respect to time, maximum photocurrent, and current at equilibrium were observed.The system's current-voltage (i-V) experiments were conducted utilising an inside the circuit an external load (log 470K) determine the power point, which is defined as the point at which the multiplication of potential and current is greatest.Conversion Efficiency in Cells was determined using current and potential values at the power point, as well as light intensity.The formula was as follows:

$$\text{Conversion Efficiency} = \frac{V_{pp} \times i_{pp}}{10.4 mWcm^{-2}} \times 100 \ \%,$$

Photopotential and photocurrent at point of power are denoted by V_{pp} and i_{pp}.

3. Discussions and Findings
3.1 Potential Variation during Time
The platinum electrode of the photogalvanic cell was exposed to light after it had remained in the dark until it reached a stable potential. It had been shown that potential changed as light increased and finally reached its maximum value over time. The cell's potential decreased when the light source was withdrawn, and after some time, a stable potential was attained. After establishing a steady potential by keeping the system dark, it grew with illumination and reached its peak, or open circuit voltage (Voc), before the light source was turned off and the cell's potential was reduced. The BB-AA System had the highest open circuit voltage, whereas the BB-Glu. System had the lowest. The BB-AA System had the highest voltage at power point, while the BB-Glu. System had the lowest. In the BB-AA System, BB-EDTA System, BB-Glu. System, the rate of change in potential on illumination was 6.02, 5.28, and 4.48 mV min-1, respectively. In the BB-AA System, BB-EDTA System, BB-Glu. System, the rate of change in potential after removing the source of light was 2.23, 2.11, and 1.86 min-1, respectively. V_{oc} and V for BB-AA system =1110.0 mV and 915.0 mV, V_{oc} and V for BB-EDTA system =980.0 mV and 810.0 mV and V_{oc} and V for BB-Glu. system=870.0 mV and 720.0 mV. As a result of the following the photogalvanic cell is most efficient with the BB-AA System and least efficient with the BB-Glu. System, according to the overall results.

3.2 Current Variation during Time
The current in all three systems rapidly increases after a few minutes of illumination, reaching maximum value (i_{max}) of 198.0, 180.0, and 170.0 A in the BB-AA System, BB-EDTA System, and BB-Glu. System, respectively, and rates of the first generation of current are in the order of 19.2, 15.3, and 13.4, A min-1 in BB-Glu. System, respectively. In the BB-AA System, the short circuit current (i_{sc}) (i_{eq}) was measured at 155.0 A, 135.0 A in the BB-EDTA System, and 120.0 A in the BB-Glu. System.

3.3 Variation in pH's Effect

All three systems with photosensitizers (dye) were found to work efficiently in the strong alkaline range. pH=12.7 to 13.0 was the working range for this study.The photopotential of the system was observed to grow as the pH was raised, reaching a maximum value for a certain pH, and then falling as the pH was raised further.The needed pH was found to be larger than the reductant'spKa values in every example tested in this investigation (i)Enhanced dye solubility and lowered dye aggregation at higher pH ranges result in increased dye diffusion in the liquid electrolyte, (ii) enhanced solubility and lowered dye aggregation at higher pH ranges result in enhanced dye diffusion in the electrolyte solution, and (iii) enhanced solubility and lowered dye aggregation at higher pH ranges result in higher dye diffusion in the electrolyte solution, and (iv) the fact that dye reduction and full solubilization need a pH range of 12.7–13. At pH greater than 13 (which implies a very high concentration of OH), the drop in current and power can be ascribed to an obstruction in the regeneration of the reductant original state due to a higher chance of OH ions recombination with the oxidised state of the reductant.

3.4 Variability's Effect of Reductant

When the concentration of three reducing agents was increased, it was discovered that Ascorbic Acid, EDTA, and Glucose was increased in different systems with Bismarck Brown as the photosensitizer, the output of these cells increased, reached In all cases, the maximum value was reached and then declined when the concentration of reduction agent was raised further. The dye-to-reductant ratio was maintained at 1:105-101 in these systems.The lower the reductant concentration, the lower the electrical output, The dye molecule travels slowly towards the electrode because there are less molecules available for electron donation, and the higher the reduction agent concentration, the fewer molecules accessible for electron donation. Graph 4shows the effect of varying the concentrations of three reductant, Ascorbic Acid, EDTA, and Glucose, with Bismarck Brown as the photosensitizer.At decreasing reduction agent concentrations, the number of accessible reductant molecules decreases, resulting in a decrease in the number of colour sensitizer molecules. As a result, the number of dye sensitizer molecules that can conduct electrons to the platinum electrode may be restricted, resulting in low cell power

3.5 Variability's Effect of Photosensitizer (Dye)

When concentration of photosensitizer was increased, the photopotential and photocurrent increased as well. The level of photosensitizer (Dye) was controlled between 2.410-6 and 5.610-6 M for effective results in electrical output.There will be a limited number of photosensitizer molecules to absorb solar light in the cell at the lower end of the photosensitizer concentration range, resulting in low electrical output, whereas higher photosensitizer concentrations will prevent the desired intensity of light from reaching the photosensitizer molecules near the electrodes, resulting in the rapid drop in electrical output. This might be due to a scarcity of dye photosensitizer molecules at lower dosages than the sensitizer's ideal concentration for collecting photons and transferring electrons to the illuminated chamber's anodic platinum electrode. Only dye sensitizer molecules that have been photo-excited and are near to the platinum electrode can reach the platinum electrode. Higher sensitizer concentrations do not enable enough photons to reach the platinum electrode, resulting in photo-excitation of fewer dye sensitizer molecules and decreased cell output.

3.6 The Cell's i-V Characteristics, Performance, and Power Efficiency

A digital pH device used for measuring the circuit voltage in open (Voc), while a micro-ammeter was used to measure the circuit current in short (isc) (having the other circuit off).The electrical parameters between these two extreme values (Voc and isc) were computed using a carbon pot (log 470K) linked in the circuit of a micro-ammeter via which an external load was provided. For all three systems, Graph 6 shows the equivalent potential value in relation to current values.In i-V curves were found to differ from their expected regular rectangular forms in all systems.The point of power (the point on the curve where the potential and current is higher) and factor of fill of i-V curves were determined. BB-A A system strength at point of power and factor of fill = 93.50 W and

0.54 percent, BB-EDTA system strength at point of power and factor of fill = 63.90 W and 0.48 percent, and BB-Glu. System strength at point of power and factor of fill= 42.16 W and 0.40 percent.

The systems were also exposed to light (under ideal conditions). These systems efficiency of conversion and sunlight conversion data are presented (1)Power, efficiency of conversion and $t_{1/2}$ for BB-AA system = 93.5 µW, 0.899 and 40.0 min., (2) Power, efficiencyof conversion and $t_{1/2}$ for BB-EDTA system = 63.9 µW, 0.614 and 34.0 min. and (3) Power, efficiencyof conversion and $t_{1/2}$ for BB-Glu. system= 42.1 µW. 0.405 and 31.0 min. Table-1 summarises the key findings from several systems, Considering the current research's overall findings and illustrating the significance of these cells in relation to the sun energy storage

Table 1. Summary of solar energy storage for different reducing agents using Bismarck Brown (BB) as photosensitizer

Observations	**BB - AASystem**	**BB - EDTA System**	**BB - GluSystem**
	Values	**Values**	**Values**
Open Circuit voltage (V_{oc})	1110.0 mV	980.0 mV	870.0 mV
Photopotential (V)	915.0 mV	810.0 mV	720.0 mV
Photocurrent of Equilibrium (i_{eq})	155.0 µA	135.0 µA	120.0 µA
Maximum Photocurrent (i_{max})	198.0 µA	180.0 µA	170.0 µA
Short circuit current (i_{sc})	155.0 µA	135.0 µA	120.0 µA
Current at power point (i_{pp})	110.0 µA	90.0 µA	80.0 µA
Potential at	850.0 µA	710.0 µA	527.0 µA

power point (V_{pp})			
Power at power point	93.50 μ W	63.9 μ W	42.16 μ W
Rate of Generation	19.2 μ A min^{-1}	15.3 μ A min^{-1}	13.4 μ A min^{-1}
Conversion Efficiency	0.8990 %	0.6144 %	0.4053 %
Charging Time	190.0 min.	180.0 min.	180.0 min.
$t_{1/2}$	40 min.	34 min.	31 min.
Factor of fill (n)	0.54 %	0. 48%	0.40 %

According to the data, Bismarck Brown-Glucose System has the lowest i-V Characteristics of the Cell, Performance, and Conversion Efficiency, whereas Bismarck Brown-Ascorbic Acid (BB-AA) System has the greatest.

4. Conclusions

The objective of the study is to convert solar energy to electrical energy in the photogalvanic with the aid of redox processes since solar energy is currently extremely expensive in absolute terms compared to other energy sources, such as a non-renewable source. Water is soluble photosensitizer dye known as Bismarck Brown. These characteristics make the dye an appropriate light-absorbing option for dye-sensitizer PG cells. Observational evidence suggests that there is still room for growth in the conversion and storage of solar energy. It's possible to create more systems with increased electrical output, cell performance, and cell storage capacity.

Acknowledgment

The Author is grateful to U.G.C. (MRP), New Delhi for financial assistances and Principal, Govt. Dungar College, Bikaner (Raj.) for providing the necessary laboratory facilities.

References
1. Fox, M.A., Kabir-Ud-Din, M., and Singletary, N.J. (1979). Energy storage and electron transfer by carbanion photolysis. Sun II, 1,102-106.
2. Baranham, K.W.J., Mazzer, M., and Clive, B. (2006). Resolving the energy crisis. Nuclearorphotovoltaics, Nat. Mater., 5, 161-164.
3. Gangotri, K.M., Regar, O.P., Lal, C., Genwa, K.R., Kalla, P. and Meena, R. (1997).Use of Micelles in Photogalvanic Cell for solar energy conversion and storage Toluidine Blue-Glucose-CetylPyridinium Chloride System. Arabian J. Sc. Eng., 22,115-118.
4. Bhimwal, M.K., and Gangotri K.M. (2011). A comparative study on the performance ofphotogalvanic cells with different ,photosensitizers for solar energy conversion andstorage:D-Xylose-NaLSsystems.Energy, 36(2), 1324–1331.
5. Chadra, M., and Shree, T. (2019). Chemistry -An-Eco-Friendly-Technology for Solar Energy Conversion and Storage in Electrical Energy. Int. J. New In. Eng. Tech. 12,76-82.
6. Chandra, M., (2021). Photochemical Study of Surfactant in Solar Cell for Solar EnergyConversionand Storagein Electrical Energy. Annals of R.S.C.B., 25, 4517-4522.
7. Chandra, M., (2021). Use of Solar Cell for Solar Energy Conversion inElectrical. Eu. J. Mol. clinic medicine, 08, 680-686.
8. Koli, P., (2021). Sudan-IdyeandFructosechemicalsbasedphotogalvaniccellsforelectrochemicalsolarenergyconversion andstorageat lowand artificialsunintensity. Arabian Journal of chemistry, 14, 1-6.

**Solar Photochemistry Research Lab,
P.G. Department of Chemistry,
Govt. Dungar College (Three times 'A' Grade),
M. G. S. University Bikaner 334001, India
email : suashil@gmail.com**

13. Political Governance and Covid -19

Dr. Ranjana Garg

Abstract

During times of COVID-19, Governments around the world must act quickly and decisively, even in the face of limited information. During crises Governments are facing issues of emergency management, continuity of operations, and citizen engagement and care. Cognitive assistants and self-service tools can help agencies provide services to help citizens maintain physical and mental health. The Indian government has so far followed a step-by-step model and been on the front foot with early <u>screening</u> at airports from mid-January onwards, initiating travel <u>restrictions</u> and in collaboration with states, applying <u>restrictions</u> on events and on places of social gathering including restaurants, theatres and gyms. Such a response ensured that there was no panic among the citizens and avoided inconvenience to the extent possible. The Indian government has also evacuated more than <u>1400</u> of its citizens and those of its neighbors from high-risk countries, including China, Japan, Iran and Italy. This is not the first time that India has evacuated its citizens and those of other countries during such crises to ensure their safety and security.

Keywords : Governance, Cognitive, corona virus disease, mass media, health sector, prevention programme, social behavioral changes

Corona virus disease (COVID-19) is an infectious disease caused by a newly discovered coronavirus.Most people infected with the COVID-19 virus will experience mild to moderate respiratory illness and recover without requiring special treatment. Older people and those with underlying medical problems like cardiovascular disease, diabetes, chronic respiratory disease, and cancer are more likely to develop serious illness. COVID-19 is a disease caused by a new strain of corona virus. 'CO' stands for corona, 'VI' for virus, and 'D' for disease.

Various time period of COVID-19 pandemic lockdown:
- Phase 1: 25 March 2020 – 14 April 2020 (21 days)
- Phase 2: 15 April 2020 – 3 May 2020 (19 days)

- Phase 3: 4 May 2020 – 17 May 2020 (14 days)
- Phase 4: 18 May 2020 – 31 May 2020 (14 days)
- Phase 5: Unlock phase 1, from 1 June to 30 June.

Role of communication sector for war against covid-19 :
- Media don't just help us pass the time; they keep us informed. Increasingly, media create shared cultural moments and reflect who we are as people. The industry needs financial models that work to be able to keep fulfilling these functions, which appear ever-more important during times of COVID-19.
- Media is playing an important role in the COVID-19 response, even as it poses challenges to the industry.
- New research shows between 80% and 90% of people consume news and entertainment for an average of almost 24 hours during a typical week.
- In India after 25 march most of people in lockdown and it is but natural that to see outer world all people use media although it is print media or mass media platforms for COVID-19-related information, but what is provided is far from factual and does not further a critical rational discourse. Rather, the media has become a tool of propaganda and sensationalism. Media houses spreading fake news to increase sensation and the TRP of the channel.

Efforts done by Indian Govt. to subsidize covid-19 for Indian people :

Reforms for agriculture equipments and product :
- PM kisan scheme
- Rs. 13,855 crore has gone towards payment of PM-KISAN.
- Marketing reforms will be taken for farmers to sell their agricultural product at prices of their choice under 20 lakh crore rahat.
- Package one lakh crore rs. Are to be given to agricultural cooperative societies, farmer producer organization and start ups for boosting farm gate.
- Under PM Matsya Sampada yojana 20,000 crore has been allocated for fishermen.
- For boost up of animal husbandry rs. 15,000 crore has been given.

Reforms For daily wages :
- According to MGNREGA scheme daily wages to be hiked to rs.180 to 202.
- Govt provided paid leave to domestic workers.
- Some key provisions given in labour laws relating to health and safety of workers.
- Several states which include UP, MP, GUJRAT, MAHARASHTRA, ODISA and GOA have undertaken steps to ease labour laws .employers have been given the flexibility to increase work-shifts up to 72 hours a week with overtime for workers.
- Ministry of labour and employment take decision that EPF fund should be decrease 12% to 10 %.

Reforms for Industry :
- NITI Aayog CEO Amitabh Kant said- the proposed reforms were aimed at attracting global in investments protecting and creating job in industry across the states.
- Govt emphasis stress on supply chain management system.

Common reforms :
- The package will focus on land, labour, liquidity and laws. It will cater to various sections, including cottage industry, MSMEs, laborers, middle class, and industries.
- To develop digital payment infrastructure the government gave Rs 34,800 crore financial assistance were provided to about 39 crore beneficiaries.
- Pradhan Mantri Garib Kalyan Ann Yojana 67.65 lakh MT of food grains have been lifted by 36 states/UTs for April 2020. Around 16 LMT of food grains have been distributed, covering 60.33crore beneficiaries by 36 states/UTs for April 2020.
- Select tax payments for some sectors, reduction in import and export duties, relaxation in payment of dues and fees and additional interest subvention for exports.
- The government said it plans to set up a chain of 20 lakh retail shops called 'Suraksha Stores' across India which will provide daily essentials to citizens while maintaining stringent safety norms, news agency PTI reported.

Greener Living

- Under the National Social Assistance Programme, Rs 1,400 crore has been disbursed to about 2.82 crore old age people, widows and disabled people.
- The last date for filing Income tax returns for the financial year 2018-19 has been extended to June 30, 2020. The interest rate on delayed income tax payment has been decreased to 12% from 9%.
- Nearly 20 crore women Jan Dhan account holders received Rs 500 each in their account. The total disbursement under the head was 9,930 crore, the finance ministry said.
- Deadline for linking Aadhaar with PAN card has also been extended from March 31 to June 30, 2020.
- The government is also providing medical insurance cover of Rs 50 lakh per person to health worker fighting the corona virus pandemic.
- Govt. declares a package focus on land, labour. Liquidity and loans.
- For poor. Household using 5 kg cooking gas cylinders and he or she will entitled to eight free refills in three months. The number of free refills will be limited using 14.2 kg cylinders.

Key tricks to fight against corona :
Socio and Physical : Social distancing is an effort to stop the transmission of corona virus in large crowds in meetings, movie halls, weddings and public transport. To enforce the importance of social distancing, schools, colleges, malls and movie halls are now closed across states. People are being advised to work remotely and reduce interaction with other people to a minimum. As advised by the WHO, a six-foot distance is ideal to stop the spread of the disease It is important to remember to maintain a six-foot distance between you and others to contain the spread of the disease.

- **Mask Compulsory to All :** the CDC is recommending that everyone wear a cloth mask when they go out in public. There are two types of masks which are recommended for various categories of personnel working in hospital or community settings, depending upon the work environment: 1. Triple layer medical mask 2. N-95 Respirator mask.

- **Section 144 :** Section 144 of Criminal Procedure Code (CrPC) imposes power to executive magistrate to restrict particular or a group of persons residing in a particular area while visiting a certain place or area. This move was implemented to prevent a danger to human life health and safety and to ultimately slow down the spread of COVID-19.
- **PPE Kit for Doctors and Medical Staff :** Personal Protective Equipments (PPEs) are protective gears designed to safeguard the health of workers by minimizing the exposure to a biological agent. Components of PPE are goggles, face-shield, mask, gloves, coverall/gowns (with or without aprons), head cover and shoe cover.
- **Aarogyasetu App :** Aarogya Setu is the Indian COVID-19 tracking mobile application developed by the National Informatics Centre and that comes under the government Ministry of Electronics and Information Technology. Aarogya Setu is designed to keep track of other app users that a person came in contact with. It then alerts app users if any of the contacts tests positive for COVID-19.
- **Sanitize Hands and All Things We Use :** During a global pandemic, one of the cheapest, easiest, and most important ways to prevent the spread of a virus is to wash your hands frequently with soap, water and sanitizers.

Methods to Protect Covid-19 given by Govt. of India :
- Closure of all educational establishments (schools, universities etc), gyms, museums, cultural and social centers, swimming pools and theatres. Students should be advised to stay at home. Online education to be promoted.
- Possibility of postponing exams may be explored. Ongoing exams to be conducted only after ensuring physical distance of one meter amongst students.
- Encourage private sector organizations/employers to allow employees to work from home wherever feasible.
- Meetings, as far as feasible, shall be done through video conferences. Minimize or reschedule meetings involving large number of people unless necessary.
- Restaurants to ensure hand washing protocol and proper cleanliness of frequently touched surfaces. Ensure physical

distancing (minimum 1metre) between tables; encourage open air seating where practical with adequate distancing.
- Keep already planned weddings to a limited gathering; postpone all non-essential social and cultural gatherings.
- Local authorities to have a dialogue with organizers of sporting events and competitions involving large gatherings and they may be advised to postpone such events.
- Local authorities to have a dialogue with opinion leaders and religious leaders to regulate mass gatherings and should ensure no overcrowding/at least one metre distance between people.
- Local authorities to have meeting with traders associations and other stakeholders to regulate hours, exhibit Do's and Don'ts and take up a communication drive in market places like sabzi mandi, anaj mandi, bus depots, railway stations, post-offices etc., where essential services are provided.
- All commercial activities must keep a distance of one meter between customers. Measures to reduce peak hour crowding in markets.
- Non-essential travel should be avoided. Buses, Trains and aero planes to maximize social distancing in public transport besides ensuring regular and proper disinfection of surfaces.
- Hospitals to follow necessary protocol related with COVID-19 management as prescribed and restrict family/friends/children visiting patients in hospitals.
- Hygiene and physical distancing has to be maintained. Shaking hands and hugging as a matter of greeting to be avoided.
- Special protective measures for delivery men/ women working in online ordering services.
- Keep communities informed consistently and constantly.

Conclusion :
In my opinion among all world India performed most generously and positively against corona. Indian government was first to take seriously step by his countrywide lockdown since various faces from 25 march 2020 to till now. Government agencies have quickly incorporated with state government to slow down and/or prevent the further spread of the COVID-19.Indian Prime Minister Mr., Modi

gives 20 lack crore relief packages to every sectors and every face of economy poorer, laborers to fight against corona. Last but not the least "Stay home stay safe".

References:
- Bulletin world health organization, volume-98, May 2020.
- Killer by ME, Biggs HM, Haynes A, Dahl RM, et al. <u>Human corona virus circulation</u>, Vol 101; 2018 Apr; 101:52-6.
- www.mygov.in/covid-19
- The Indian Journal of Medical Research (IJMR) [ISSN 0971-5916]
- The Indian express, sat. May 16 2020.the editorial page.

Associate Professor in Political Science
Govt. PG College, Dausa (Rajasthan)
email : <u>drranjana76@gmail.com</u>

14. पर्यावरण संवर्धन एवं सतत् विकास
(ऐतिहासिक परिप्रेक्ष्य)

मधु कुमावत

संकेताक्षर : सतत्, पर्यावरण, जैव-विविधता, पारिस्थितिकी, पारितंत्र.

सामान्य शब्दों में कहे तो -" सतत् विकास वह विकास है जो भविष्य की पीढ़ियों की अपनी जरूरतों को पूरा करने की क्षमता से समझौता किए बिना वर्तमान की जरूरतों को पूरा करता है। 'सतत् विकास' की संकल्पना का वास्तविक विकास 1987 में "हमारा साझा भविष्य" नामक रिपोर्ट, जिसे 'द ब्रंटलैंड रिपोर्ट' के नाम से भी जाना जाता है, के आने के बाद हुआ एवं तभी से इस शब्द का व्यापक रूप से प्रयोग किया जाने लगा। संयुक्त राष्ट्र संघ का मानव विकास संबंधी अंतर्राष्ट्रीय सम्मेलन वर्ष 1972 में स्टॉकहोम में आयोजित किया गया था। वर्ष 1974 में बेरी महोदय ने प्रसिद्ध पुस्तक "The Closing Circle" प्रकाशित की थी। सतत् विकास एक काफी पुरानी अवधारणा है; परंतु दूसरे महायुद्ध के पश्चात इसकी महत्ता पर विशेष बल दिया जा रहा है। विकास की ऐसी क्षमता जिससे पारितंत्र उत्पादन देता रहे तथा भविष्य के लिये स्वस्थ्य एवं टिकाऊ अवस्था में बना रहे, ऐसा विकास जिससे मानव जीवन सुखी बना रहे, प्राकृतिक संसाधनों का ऐसा सदुपयोग जिससे भविष्य की पीढ़ियों के लिये भी संसाधन उपलब्ध रहें और सबका जीवन सुखी बना रहे। सतत विकास प्राप्त करने के लिये निम्न पर ध्यान देना अति आवश्यक है: जैव-विविधता, ग्रीन हाउस गैसों का उत्सर्जन, खतरनाक कूड़े-करकट का प्रबंधन, उद्योगों से निकलने वाले बड़े-करकट का प्रबंधन, पारिस्थितिकी सुरक्षा। वैज्ञानिकों का विचार है कि विश्व के अधिकतर भागों में विकास करते समय पारिस्थितिकी के सिद्धांतों को ध्यान में नहीं रखा जा रहा है, जिसके कारण प्राकृतिक संसाधनों तथा पर्यावरण का तीव्रता से ह्रास हो रहा है। हममें से प्रत्येक व्यक्ति के प्रयास से भी पारितंत्र तथा पारिस्थितिकी की समुत्थान-शक्ति को सतत स्थिति में भारी सहायता मिल सकती है। बाइसिकिल का उपयोग करें, वाहन को आवश्यकता पड़ने पर थोड़ी दूरी तक ही चलाए। दैनिक जीवन में सरकारी वाहनों का इस्तेमाल करें। उत्तम प्रकार के बिजली के बल्ब तथा उपकरणों का प्रयोग करे। घरों की विद्युतरोधी उपकरणों की ठीक देख-रेख की जाए। ऊर्जा के विकल्प साधनों को खोजा जाए। भोजन ऐसे

Greener Living

प्रदेशों/क्षेत्रों से प्राप्त करने की कोशिश करनी चाहिए जहाँ गोबर तथा कंपोस्ट और हरी खाद का फसलों को उगाने में इस्तेमाल होता हो । रासायनिक खाद से उगाई फसलें सब्जियाँ तथा फल इत्यादि स्वास्थ्य के लिये हानिकारक होती हैं । सतत विकास वर्तमान की परम आवश्यकता है ताकि पारितंत्र की उत्पादकता को बनाये रखा जा सके । वास्तविकता यह है कि मानव जीवन का आधार पारितंत्र एवं पर्यावरण ही है । पारितंत्र एवं पर्यावरण को सतत बनाये रखने के लिये विभिन्न देशों में विभिन्न उपाय किये जा सकते हैं, फिर भी भारत जैसे विकासशील देश को विशेष उपायों पर बल देने की आवश्यकता है ।

सहायक आचार्य, इतिहास
श्री रंकपा राजकीय स्नातकोत्तर महाविद्यालय, किशनगढ़
मो. न. 9461208397
Email – madhukumawat289@gmail.com

15. Synthesis of Aluminium (III) and Gallium (III) Complexes with Biaoctive Schiff Bases and Their Spectral, Electrochemical and Biological Aspects

Dr. Sunita yadav,
Dr Neelam Gupta
Prof. R.V. Singh

Abstract

In Schiff base complexes of aluminium, the coordination environment at the metal center can be modified by attaching different substituents to the ligand, providing useful steric and electronic properties essential for the fine tuning of structures and reactivity. Aluminum is the third abundant element in the earth inferior to oxygen and silicon, and it is widely used as building materials, water purification, food additives and clinical drug Gallium plays an important role in pharmaceuticals and as antitumor, antiviral and anticoagulant agents and thallium as a probe for K^+ in biological systems. Biological important complexes of aluminium (III) and gallium(III) derived from biologically active sulfur donor ligands 2-hydroxy-N-phenyl benzothiazoline have been prepared and investigated using a combination of micro analytical analysis, melting point, electronic, IR, ^1H NMR and ^{13}C NMR spectral studies,. Aluminium and gallium isopropoxide interacts with the ligand in 1:1 and 2:3 molar ratios (metal: ligand) resulting in the formation of coloured products. On the basis of conductance and spectral evidences, a penta coordinated structure for aluminium (III) and gallium(III) complexes have been assigned. The ligand are coordinated to the aluminium(III) and gallium (III) via the azomethine nitrogen atom and the enolic oxygen atom.

Keywords : Schiff bases, X-ray powder diffraction studies, benzothiazoline, 2-hydroxy-N-phenylbenzamide.

1. Introduction :

Benzothiazolines are not themselves a Schiff bases, but are known to form the corresponding classical Schiff base complexes[1].The coordination chemistry of group 13 metal ions is of biochemical interest because of the potential use in the treatment and diagnosis of disease[2-5].Aluminum is the third abundant element in the earth inferior to oxygen and silicon, and it is widely used as building materials, water purification, food additives and clinical drug [6]. In Schiff base complexes of aluminium, the coordination environment at the metal center can be modified by attaching different substituents to the ligand, providing useful steric and electronic properties essential for the fine tuning of structures and reactivity[7]. Gallium plays an important role in pharmaceuticals[8] and as antitumor[9], antiviral[10] and anticoagulant agents and thallium as a probe for K^+ in biological systems[11].

2. Experimental
2.1 Synthesis of ligand

The ligand benzothiazoline of 2-hydroxy-N-phenyl benzamide was prepared by the condensation of 2-hydroxy-N-phenyl benzamide with 2-aminothiophenol in 1:1 molar ratio using ethanol. All the chemicals were dried and purified before use. The parent ligand exists in the tautomeric forms (benzothiazoline ring as well as Schiff base) depicted in Figure 1 & 2. The reaction mixture was stirred for 3–4 h, and the solid separated out was filtered, purified by recrystallization from ethanol, and dried *in vacuo*.

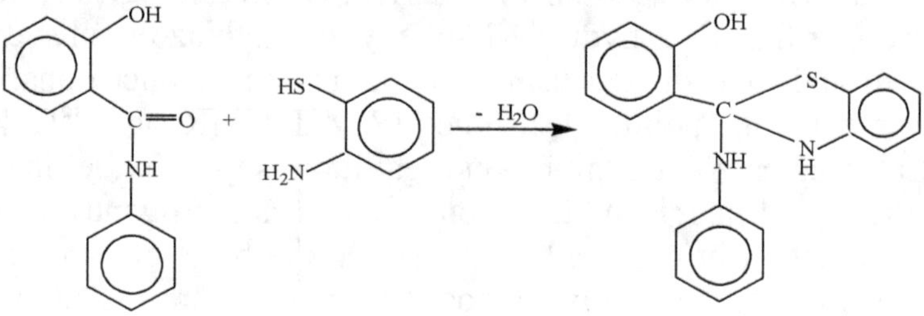

Fig.1.

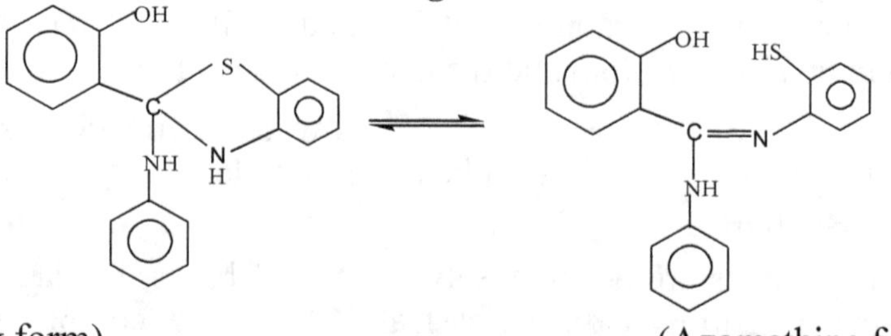

(Ring form)　　　　　　　　　　　　(Azomethine form)
Fig 2 Tautomeric structures of the ligand

2.2 Preparation of aluminium (III) and gallium (III) complexes

Aluminium (III) and gallium (III) isopropoxide and ligand were dissolved in dry benzene in 1:1 and 2:3 molar ratios. The resulting mixture was refluxed for 16-20 hours. The progress of the reaction was checked by measuring the amount of isopropanol in the azeotrope. After completion of the reaction the excess of the solvent was removed under reduced pressure and dried in vacuo. The physical properties and analytical data of these complexes are enlisted in **Table 1**.

2.3 Analytical methods and physical measurements

The molecular weights were determined by the Rast camphor method. IR spectra of the ligand and their metal complexes were recorded with the help of Nicolet Megna FT IR 550 spectrophotometer using KBr pellets. The purity of these ligand and their metal complexes was checked by the TLC on silica Gel-G using anhydrous dimethylsulphoxide and benzene (1:1) as solvent. Isopropanol in the azeotrope and isopropoxy in the complexes were estimated by an oxidimetric method.[12]

^{1}H NMR and ^{13}C NMR spectra were recorded in deuterated dimethylsulphoxide (DMSO-d_6) using tetramethylsilane (TMS) as standard on a JEOL AL 300 FT NMR spectrometer. Electronic spectra of the complexes were recorded in DMF on a UV-160 A Shimadzu spectrophotometer in the range 200-600 nm. Nitrogen and sulfur were estimated by the Kjeldahl's and Messenger's methods, respectively[13].

3. Results and Discussion

The reactions that led to formation of the metal (III) Schiff-base complexes and their adducts can be represented by equations 1 and 2.

$$2\text{ M (OPr}^i)_3 + 2\text{ HO}^{\frown}\text{N}^{\frown}\text{XH} \xrightarrow[\text{Dry Benzene}]{1:1} \{\text{M (OPr}^i)_2(\text{O}^{\frown}\text{N}^{\frown}\text{X})\}_2 + 4\text{Pr}^i\text{OH} \quad (1)$$

$$2\text{ M (OPr}^i)_3 + 3\text{ HO}^{\frown}\text{N}^{\frown}\text{XH} \xrightarrow[\text{Dry Benzene}]{2:3} \{\text{M}_2(\text{O}^{\frown}\text{N}^{\frown}\text{X})_3\} + 6\text{Pr}^i\text{OH} \quad (2)$$

(Where, M=Al or Ga and O$^{\frown}$N$^{\frown}$X represents the donor set of the ligand molecule and X = O).

The resulting products are coloured solids and soluble in DMF, DMSO, THF and methanol. The molecular weight determinations by the rast camphor method revealed the dimeric nature of metal derivatives.

The U.V. spectrum of the ligand consists of two broad bands centered at 260 nm and 310 nm characteristic of the cyclic form of the ligand. These bands arising out of ϕ-ϕ* and π-π* (benzenoid) transitions, respectively. A new band around 398 nm due to n-π* electronic transitions of the azomethine group is observed in the spectra of the complexes which remains absent in the free ligands and thus proves the benzothiazoline nature of this ligand.

In the IR spectrum of the ligand the absence of ν(SH) at 2610 cm^{-1} and ν(C=N) at 1640 cm^{-1} is the strong evidence for a ring structure. The bands at 960-925 cm^{-1} in the spectra of 1:1 complexes of bifunctional tridentata ligand are assignable to ν C–O vibrations of bridging isopropoxy groups. The complexes exhibit new bands in the region 760-612 cm^{-1}, 590-460 cm^{-1} and 430-300 cm^{-1} which may be attributed to the different vibrational modes of Al – O[14], Al $\leftarrow$N[15] and Al –S[16], respectively. The gallium complexes exhibit new bands in the region 660–600 cm^{-1}, 480–350 cm^{-1} and 320–280 cm^{-1} which may be attributed to the different vibrational modes of Ga– O, Ga$\leftarrow$N[17] and Ga-S[18], respectively.

The ^{1}H NMR spectra of LH$_2$ and their aluminium complexes are recorded in **Table 2**. The disappearance of the –NH resonance signal of the ligand from δ 11.24 ppm in the aluminium (III) complexes, indicates the deprotonation of the functional group during the complexation. The aromatic protons and amino protons signals remain at almost the same positions in the aluminium complexes indicating their non-involvement in the complexation.

The ^{13}C NMR spectral data also support the authenticity of the proposed structures. The considerable shifts in the positions of carbon atoms adjacent to the azomethine nitrogen (δ 167.15-174.36 ppm) and thiolic sulfur/enolic oxygen (δ 176.24-184.20 ppm) support the proposed coordination in the complexes. Thus the shifts in the position of carbon atoms adjacent to the coordinating atoms clearly suggest the bonding of the azomethine nitrogen and amido oxygen to the aluminium and gallium atoms. The signals for (OCH(CH$_3$)$_2$) and (OCH(CH$_3$)$_2$) carbons of isopropoxy group in the spectra of 1:1metal complexes have been observed in the region δ 73.16–75.15 and 23.24–24.92 ppm, respectively, and are not observed in the spectra of 2:3 complexes. Chemical shift values of all the complexes are listed in **Table 3.** ^{27}Al NMR spectra of these compounds have been recorded in CDCl$_3$ solution with reference to Al(NO$_3$)$_3$. The ^{27}Al NMR spectra of metal complexes have a sharp signal at δ 11.97–14.90 ppm assigned to five-coordinated aluminium complexes. The following pentacoordinated structures can be proposed for the aluminium and gallium complexes. These structures are given below:

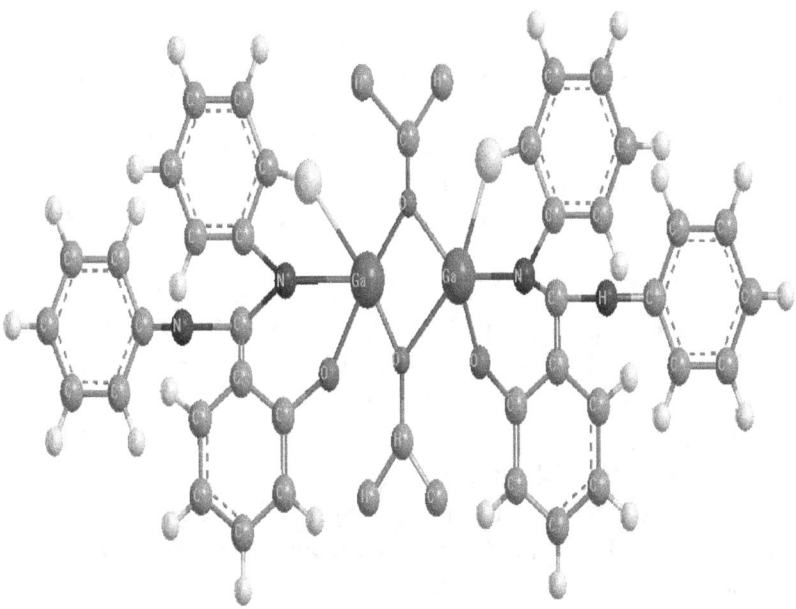

Fig. 3: Structure of the {Ga(OPr^i)(L)}$_2$, 1:1 complex

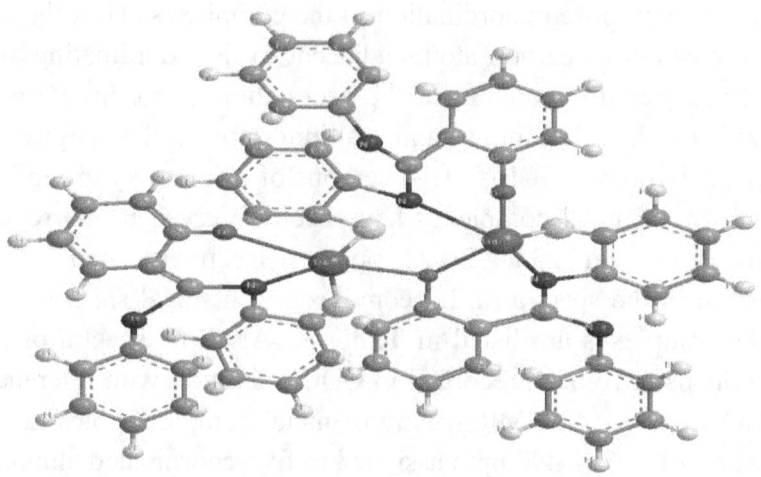

Fig. 4: Structure of the {Ga$_2$(L)$_3$} 2:3 complex

References :
1. M. Hossain, S. K. Chattopadhyay and S. Gosh, *Polyhedron*, **16** (1997) 143.
2. D.A. Moore, P.E. Fanwick, M.J. Welch, *Inorg. Chem.*, **28**, 1504 (1989).
3. S.M. Moerlin, M.J. Welch, K.N. Raymond, F.L. Weitl, *J. Nucl. Med.*, **22**, 710 (1981)
4. S. M. Moerlin, M. J. Welch, *Int. J. Nucl. Med. Biol.*, **8**, 277 (1981).
5. C.J. Mathias, Y. Sun, M.J. Welch, M.A. Green, J.A. Thomas, K.R. Wade, A.E. Martell, *Nucl. Med. Biol.*, **15**, 69 (1988).
6. J.-Q. Wang, L. Huang, L. Gao, J. H. Zhu, Y. Wang, X. Fan, Z. Zou, *Inorg. Chem. Comm.*, **11**, 203 (2008).
7. A. K. Jain, A. Gupta, R. Bohra, I.P. Lorenz, P. Mayer, *Polyhedron*, **25**, 654 (2006).
8. M.J. Welch, S.M. Moerlein, *ACS, Symp. Ser.*, **140**, 121 (1980).
9. B.J. Foster, B. Leyland-Jones, *Cancer Treat. Rep.*, **70**, 1311 (1986).
10. F. Kratz, B. Nuber, J. Weiss, B.K. Keppler, *Polyhedron*, **11**, 487 (1992).

11. B.G. Cox, J. STroka, I. Schneider, H. Scheider, *Inorg. Chim. Acta,* **147**, 9 (1988).
12. D.C. Bradley, F.M.A. Halim, W. Wardlaw. *J. Chem. Soc.,* 3450 (1950).
13. J.T. Makode, A.S. Aswar, *Indian J. Chem.,* **43(A)**, 2120 (2004).
14. R. Bohra, A. Dhammani, R.K. Sharma, R.C. Mehrotra, *Synth.React. Inorg. Met. Org. Chem.,* **36**, 681 (2001).
15. D.A. Atwood, J.A. Jegier, D. Rutherford, *Inorg. Chem.,* **35**, 63 (1996).
16. S. Sharma, R. K. Sharma, R. Sharma, A. Sharma, A.K. Rai, R.S. Gupta, Y.P. Singh, *Bioinorg. Chem. Appl.,* **1**, 215 (2003).
17. Y.Z. Shen, Y.Pan, L.Y. Wang, G.Dong, X.P. Jin, X.Y. Huang, H. Hu, *J. Organomet. Chem.,* **590**, 242 (1999).
18. N. Prasad, D.P. Dutta, V.K. Jain, *Main Group Met. Chem.,* **25(11)**, 677 (2002).

Table 1; Synthetic and analytical data of of the ligand and their aluminium(III) and gallium (III) complexes of benzothiazolines

S. No	Reactants (g)		Molar ratio	Product and Colour	M.P. (°C)	Analyses (%) Found/ (Calcd)					Mol. Wt. Found/ (Calcd.)
	Metal	Ligand				C	H	N	S	M	
1.	-	$C_{19}H_{16}N_2OS$ (LH$_2$) Benzothiazolines		Sandy brown	110	70.98 (71.22)	4.92 (5.03)	8.82 (8.74)	9.89 (10.01)		337.54 (320.41)
4.	Al(OPr^i)$_3$	LH$_2$	1:1	{Al(OPr^i)(L)}$_2$ Light green	168-170			6.82 (6.93)	7.82 (7.93)	6.54 (6.67)	814.52 (808.96)
5.	Al(OPr^i)$_3$	LH$_2$	2:3	{Al$_2$(L)$_3$} Light green	170-172			8.22 (8.35)	9.42 (9.54)	5.24 (5.35)	1014.42 (1009.14)
6	Ga(OPr^i)$_3$	LH$_2$	1:1	{Ga(OPr^i)(L)}$_2$ Chocolate	115-117			6.12 (6.26)	7.04 (7.17)	15.48 (15.59)	900.68 (894.40)
7	Ga(OPr^i)$_3$	LH$_2$	2:3	{Ga$_2$(L)$_3$} Chocolate	120-122			7.52 (7.68)	8.68 (8.79)	12.62 (12.74)	1101.42 (1094.63)

Table 2 : ^{1}H NMR spectral data (δ ppm) of the ligand and their aluminium (III) and gallium(III) complexes.

Compound	-OH (s)	-NH (bs)	-NH$_2$ (s)	-S-CH$_2$ (s)	φ-NH (s)	Aromatic protons (m)	Isopropoxy groups	
							Gem-dimethyl (d)	Methine (septet)
LH$_2$	12.11	5.20	-	-	10.63	6.92 - 8.12	-	-
{Al(OPr^i)(L)}$_2$	-	-	-	-	10.65	6.90 - 8.14	1.24 (bridging)	4.46 (bridging)
{Al$_2$(L)$_3$}	-	-	-	-	10.68	6.94 - 8.10	-	-
{Ga(OPr^i)(L)}$_2$	-	-	-	-	10.65	6.54 - 8.22	1.24 (bridging)	4.50 (bridging)
{Ga(L)$_2$}$_2$	-	-	-	-	10.67	6.48 - 8.25	-	-

Table 3 : ^{13}C NMR Spectral data (δ, ppm) of the ligand and their aluminium (III) and gallium(III) complexes.

Compound	Chemical shift values				
	>C=O / >C=S	>C=N	Aromatic carbons	Isopropoxy group	
LH$_2$	-	-	159.32, 137.03, 130.25, 130.46, 129.62, 128.56, 121.31, 120.86, 118.83, 118.74	-	-
{Al(OPr^i)(L)}$_2$	-	163.45	160.86, 138.99, 130.18, 129.79, 129.95, 125.58, 122.64, 120.68, 118.94, 119.99	73.27(bridging)	22.96(bridging)
{Al$_2$(L)$_3$}	-	162.24	160.86, 138.99, 130.18, 129.79, 129.95, 125.58, 122.64, 120.68, 118.94, 119.99	-	-
{Ga(OPr^i)(L)}$_2$	-	163.45	160.86, 138.99, 130.18, 129.79, 129.95, 125.58, 122.64, 120.68, 118.94, 119.99	73.27(bridging)	22.96(bridging)
{Ga(L)$_2$}$_2$	-	162.24	160.86, 138.99, 130.18, 129.79, 129.95, 125.58, 122.64, 120.68, 118.94, 119.99	-	-

Department of chemistry,
B. B. D. Govt. College Chimanpura, Shahpura,
University of Rajasthan, Jaipur (Rajasthan)
email : sunitaya1976@gmail.com,
neelamguptajpr@gmail.com

16. Health and Environment Impact of Air Pollution

Niharika Singh

Abstract

One of the largest problems facing us today is air pollution, which affects both public and individual health due to increased morbidity and mortality rates as well as its role in climate change. Numerous pollutants have a significant impact on human disease. Particulate matter (PM), which has particles of various but very small sizes, harms the reproductive, cardiovascular, and central neurological systems as well as causes cancer when inhaled. At ground level, ozone, which shields us from ultraviolet light in the stratosphere, is hazardous due to its negative effects on the respiratory and cardiovascular systems. Additionally, air pollutants that are harmful to people include nitrogen oxide, sulphur dioxide, volatile organic compounds (VOCs), dioxins, and polycyclic aromatic hydrocarbons (PAHs). When inhaled, carbon monoxide at high amounts can even be toxic immediately. When absorbed into the human body, heavy metals like lead can either result in acute poisoning or chronic intoxication, depending on the exposure. The principal disorders caused by the aforementioned compounds are chronic obstructive pulmonary disease (COPD), asthma, bronchiolitis, lung cancer, cardiovascular events, central nervous system dysfunctions, and skin diseases. Last but not least, climate change brought on by environmental degradation affects both natural disasters and the geographic distribution of many infectious diseases. The only way to solve this problem is by raising public awareness.

Keywords : Pollution, Climate, Contaminants, Pollutants, Diseases

Introduction :

Human activity seems to have a negative impact on the ecosystem by contaminating the water we drink, the air we breathe, and the soil where plants grow. The industrial revolution brought about the manufacturing of vast amounts of various pollutants that are damaging to human health and were released into the air, despite the fact that it was a major success in terms of technology, society, and the supply of numerous services. There is no question that there are many different aspects to the international public health problem of environmental pollution. This significant issue is connected to social, economic, administrative, and lifestyle behaviours. So it is obvious that in our time, urbanisation and industrialisation are reaching unprecedented and unsettling levels around the world. One of the major global public health threats is caused by anthropogenic air pollution. Anthropogenic air pollution causes nearly 9 million fatalities annually, it is one of the greatest global public health risks (WHO, 2019).

Air pollution is defined as "the introduction of chemicals, particles, or biological elements into the atmosphere that cause discomfort, disease, or death in humans, harm other living things such as food crops, or harm the built environment or the natural environment." An air pollutant is a material that can be harmful to both people and the environment. These contaminants could be gases, solid particles, or liquid droplets.

Causes of Air Pollution

Human and natural activities both can lead to air pollution. The sources of air pollution refer to the various locations, factors or activities, which are responsible for the releasing of pollutants into the atmosphere. It is widely known that human activities including the use of industrial machinery, power plants, combustion engines, and automobiles cause the bulk of environmental pollutants to be released on a huge scale. Since these activities are carried out on such a huge scale, they are by far the biggest sources of air pollution, with motor vehicles thought to be responsible for almost 80% of the pollution that exists today (Moller et al., 1994). Other human activities, such as field farming methods, petrol stations, fuel tank heaters, and transportation, are also having a small but noticeable impact on our environment. Other human activities, such as field cultivation methods, gas stations, fuel tank heaters, and cleaning practises, as well as a number of natural sources, including forest fires, volcanic eruptions, wind erosion, pollen dispersal, evaporation of organic compounds, and natural radioactivity, all are influencing our environment to a lesser extent (Jacobson and Jacobson, 2002).

Anthropogenic Sources
1. Various mobile sources include automobiles, ferries, aircraft, etc.
2. Stationary sources, such as furnaces and other fuel-burning heating appliances, as well as smokestacks from manufacturing plants, waste incinerators, and power plants. Burning traditional biomass, which includes wood, crop waste, and dung, is a major cause of air pollution in emerging and underdeveloped nations.
3. The use of chemicals, dust, and controlled fire techniques in forestry and agricultural management. A practice called controlled or prescribed burning is occasionally employed in farming, greenhouse gas reduction, and forest management. Foresters can use controlled fire as a tool because it is a natural component of both grassland and forest ecology. A controlled burn encourages the germination of some valuable forest trees, replenishing the forest.
4. Fumes, such as those generated by paint, varnish, aerosol sprays, hair spray and other solvents.
5. Military, such as nuclear weapons, gases pollutants, germ warfare and nuclear weapons.
6. The dumping of waste in landfills, which produces methane. Methane is highly flammable, it can combine explosively with air.

Non-Anthropogenic Sources (Natural)
1. Dust from natural sources, which are typically vast stretches of land with little to no vegetation.
2. Methane, which is released by the digestion of food by animals, like cattle.
3. Radon gas produced by radioactive decay in the crust of the Earth. Radium decay produces radon, a radioactive noble gas that is colourless, odourless, and naturally occurring. It's regarded as a health risk. Natural radon gas can build up in buildings, especially in small spaces like the basement, and it is the second most common cause of lung cancer after cigarette smoking.
4. Wildfire produces smoke and carbon monoxide.

5. Vegetation in some locations produces substantial levels of VOCs that are harmful to the environment on warmer days. A seasonal haze of secondary pollutants is created when these VOCs combine with primary anthropogenic pollutants, notably NO_x, SO_2, and anthropogenic organic carbon compounds.
6. Volcanic activity, which results in particles of sulfur, chlorine, and ash.

Although people frequently spend the majority of their time indoors, there is a concentration of air pollution due to a lack of ventilation. A carcinogen called radon (Rn) gas escapes from the earth in some areas and becomes trapped inside houses. Formaldehyde (H_2CO) gas is released by a variety of building materials, including carpet and plywood. As they dry, paint and solvents release volatile organic compounds (VOCs). Lead paint can break down into dust, which can then be inhaled. The usage of air fresheners, incense, and other scented goods causes intentional air pollution. Controlled wood burns in fireplaces and stoves can release a lot of smoke particles both indoors and outside. Use of pesticides and other chemical sprays indoors without adequate ventilation may result in fatalities due to indoor pollution. A common source of carbon monoxide (CO) poisoning and mortality is the indoor burning of charcoal or damaged vents and chimneys. Indoors, biological air pollution can also be detected in the form of gases and airborne particles.

Pets produce dander, people produce dust from minute skin flakes and decomposed hair; mold forms in walls and produces mycotoxins and spores; air conditioning systems can harbor legionnaires' disease and mold; and houseplants, soil, and nearby gardens can produce pollen, dust, and mold. Additionally, dust mites in bedding, carpeting, and furniture produce enzymes and micrometer-sized fecal droppings. These airborne contaminants can build up more than they would in nature indoors due to poor air circulation.

According to the type of pollutants, they can be divided into the following groups :

Primary Pollutants : These pollutants are those that are created as a direct result of a process, including sulphur dioxide discharged from industries, carbon monoxide gas from vehicle emissions, or volcanic eruption.

Secondary Pollutants : These pollutants are those that are not directly emitted. Instead, they develop in the air as a result of interactions between primary pollutants. One of the numerous secondary pollutants that contribute to photochemical smog is ground level ozone, which serves as an important example of a secondary pollutant.

Some pollutants can be both primary and secondary, which means they can both produced directly from other primary pollutants and emitted directly. World Health Organization (WHO) has published reports on six important air pollutants, including lead, carbon monoxide, sulfur oxides, nitrogen oxides, and ground-level ozone. As a result, all components of the environment, including groundwater, soil, and air, can be negatively affected by air pollution. Consequently, it seriously harm all organisms. In keeping with this, we are primarily interested in focusing on these pollutants because they are linked to more serious and extensive issues with human health and the environment, such as acid rain, global warming, the greenhouse effect, and climate changes, which have a significant ecological impact on air pollution (Manisalidis et al., 2016).

Primary Pollutants

1. Nitrogen Oxides (NOx) : These gases are naturally created during thunderstorms by electric discharge and are also released during high temperature combustion. It appears as a dome or plume of brown haze downwind of cities. The chemical compound known as Nitrogen oxide has the formula NO_2. It belongs to a diverse group of nitrogen oxides. The smell of this deadly reddish-brown gas is distinctively harsh and stinging. NO_2 is one of the most prominent air pollutants.

2. Carbon Monoxide (CO) : It is a poisonous gas that is colourless, odourless, and non-irritating. It is a byproduct of incomplete combustion of a fuel like wood, coal, or natural gas. A significant source of carbon monoxide is vehicle exhaust.

3. Sulphur Oxides (SOx) : The chemical molecule sulphur dioxide has the formula SO_2. Volcanoes and several industrial operations produce sulphur dioxide. Since sulphur compounds are frequently found in coal and gasoline, burning them releases sulphur dioxide. Acid rain is produced when SO2 is further oxidised, usually in the presence of a catalyst like NO2. This is a reason to be concerned about how using these fuels as a source of energy may affect the environment.

4. Ammonia (NH3) : It is an agricultural process byproduct. A compound with the chemical formula NH3 is ammonia. It typically manifests as a gas with a distinctively pungent smell. Many medications are synthesised using ammonia as a building block, either directly or indirectly. Ammonia is a caustic and dangerous substance while being widely used.

5. Particulate Matter (PM) : It is also known as particulates, atmospheric particulate materials, or fine particles, these tiny solid or liquid particles suspended in a gas. Contrarily, an aerosol is a mixture of gas and particle. Particulate sources can be both man-made and natural. Natural events such as volcanoes, dust storms, grassland and forest fires, living plants, and sea spray can all produce particles. Significant volumes of aerosols are also produced by human activities like the burning of fossil fuels in automobiles, power plants, and different industrial processes. Anthropogenic aerosols, or those produced by human activity, currently make up around 10% of all aerosols in our atmosphere on a global average. Higher concentrations of airborne fine particles are associated with health risks such heart disease, deteriorated lung function, and lung cancer.

6. Volatile Organic Compounds (VOCs) : Volatile organic compounds (VOCs) are a significant air pollutant found in outdoor air.They are frequently separated into the distinct groups of methane (CH4) and non- methane (NMVOCs) in this field.

Methane is a very effective greenhouse gas that enhance global warming. Due to their contribution to the formation of ozone and the maintenance of methane in the atmosphere, other hydrocarbon VOCs are also important greenhouse gases, but the impact varies depending on the local air quality. The aromatic compounds toluene, benzene, and xylene within NMVOCs are thought to be carcinogenic and may cause leukaemia if exposed for an extended period of time. Another hazardous substance that is frequently used in industries is 1, 3-butadiene.

7. Lead : A heavy metal used in several industrial facilities, lead is also released into the environment by some petrol engines, batteries, radiators, waste incinerators, and waste water. Lead exposure can happen by eating, inhalation, or skin absorption. When lead is inhaled, it is accumulated in the blood, soft tissue, liver, lungs, bones, cardiovascular, neurological, and reproductive systems. Adults also reported experiencing pain in their muscles and joints, as well as a loss of focus and memory. Increased lead levels in the environment are harmful to the growth of plants and crops. High lead levels have been linked to neurological consequences in vertebrates and animals (Manisalidis et al., 2020).

8. Chlorofluorocarbons (CFCs) : Chlorofluorocarbons (CFCs), which are currently prohibited from usage in products, are damaging to the ozone layer.

9. Toxic Metals : Lead, mercury, and their compounds are the two most toxic metals.

10. Radioactive Pollutants : It is produced by natural processes like radon's radioactive decay as well as nuclear explosions, nuclear accidents, and war explosives.

Secondary Pollutants

1. Ground level Ozone : Ozone (O3) is a gas created when oxygen is exposed to a high-voltage electric discharge. It arises in the stratosphere, but it can also start photochemical smog chain reactions in the troposphere. Nitrogen oxides and VOCs released from anthropogenically activities or naturally occurring sources interact chemically to produce ground-level ozone (GLO). As it reduces carbon assimilation, it becomes detrimental to cultures, forests, and vegetation. Ozone's antibacterial properties cause it to impact plant microflora, which in turn affects growth and yield. This is because ozone affects other natural habitats, including microflora. Ozone Ozone promotes cellular dysfunction and DNA damage in epidermal keratinocytes (McCarthy, et al 2013).

2. Particulates : It's created from compounds in photochemical smog's and gaseous primary pollutants. A kind of air pollution is smog, which is a combination of smoke and fog. Large-scale coal burning in an area results in a mixture of smoke and sulfur dioxide, which causes classic smog. Modern smog often originates from industrial and automobile emissions, which when exposed to the sun's ultraviolet rays create secondary pollutants that react with the original emissions to create photochemical smog.

Effects of Air pollution

Following are the effects of air pollution :

Effects on Health

According to the WHO, air pollution poses a serious risk for a number of diseases, including lung cancer, heart disease, and respiratory infections. Breathing problems, coughing, wheezing, asthma, and the aggravated state of pre-existing respiratory and cardiac disorders are only a few of the health repercussions of air pollution. These side effects may lead to increased pharmaceutical consumption and perhaps early mortality. Although the impacts of poor air quality on human health are extensive, the respiratory and cardiovascular systems of the body are primarily impacted. Individual responses to air pollutants are influenced by the kind of pollutant, the level of exposure, people's health, and genetics.

Particulate matter (PM), ground-level ozone, carbon monoxide, sulphur oxides, nitrogen oxides, and lead are some of the most common causes of air pollution. Over 3.3 million fatalities have been attributed to both indoor and outdoor air pollution worldwide. When it comes to the total number of deaths linked to both indoor and outdoor air pollution, children under the age of five who reside in poor nations are the most vulnerable. According to the World Health Organization, 1.5 million of the 2.4 million deaths per year that are directly linked to air pollution are caused by indoor air pollution.

The worst short term civilian pollution crisis in The Bhopal Gas Tragedy in 1984 was India's worst acute civic pollution crisis. Methyl isocynate (MIC) industrial vapours that leaked from the Union Carbide factory, owned by Union Carbide, Inc., U.S.A., killed over 25,000 people instantly and injured between 150,000 and 600,000. When the Great Smog of 1952 formed over London on December 4, the United Kingdom experienced its worst air pollution event. More than 4,000 people died in just six days, and 8,000 more died in the months that followed. Hundreds of civilian deaths are thought to have resulted from an accidental anthrax spore release from a biological weapons laboratory in the former USSR in 1979 close to Sverdlovsk (Rao and Rao, 2007).

Pneumonia, asthma, and other lower respiratory illnesses are more common in children worldwide who live in cities with high levels of air pollution. Children are particularly vulnerable to the risks of air pollution since they spend more time outside and have higher minute ventilation. In such cities, the risk of low birth weight is also increased.

Effects on Environment

Air pollution negatively impacts both the environment and human health. The following are the most significant types of air pollution and their effect on the environment:

(i) Acid Rain : It is precipitation that is either wet (rain, fog, snow) or dry (particulates and gas) that contains lethal levels of nitric and sulfuric acids. They have the ability to harm plants and trees, damage plantations and buildings, and even damage outdoor statues, constructions, and sculptures.

(ii) Eutrophication : It happens when high levels of nutrients, particularly nitrogen, encourage the blossoming of aquatic algae, which can disrupt the diversity of fish and result in their death.

(iii) Global Climate Change : It is a significant issue that affects mankind. The "greenhouse effect," as is well known, maintains the Earth's temperature. Unfortunately, anthropogenic activities have eliminated this protective temperature effect by producing significant amounts of greenhouse gases, and as a result, global warming is intensifying and having negative effects on human health, animal welfare, forests, wildlife, agriculture, and the water environment.

(iv) Haze : It is produced when fine airborne particles spread and reduce the air's transparency. It is caused by the gas emissions in the air from commercial buildings, power plants, vehicles, and automobiles.

(v) Ozone : It has been discussed previously; in contrast, ground-level ozone is harmful to human health and is a pollutant. Unfortunately, stratospheric ozone is gradually damaged by ozone-depleting substances (i.e., chemicals, pesticides, and aerosols). If this protecting stratospheric ozone layer is thinned, then UV radiation can reach our earth, with harmful effects for human life (skin cancer) and crops. In plants, ozone penetrates through the stomata, inducing them to close, which blocks CO_2 transfer and induces a reduction in photosynthesis (Singh, et al., 2011).

(vi) Wildlife : It is burdened by harmful pollutants that originate in the ecosystem's air, soil, or water, and as a result, animals that are exposed to excessive quantities of pollutants may experience health issues.

The survival of living things, including fish, and their capacity for productivity are also impacted by their effects on water bodies. When plants are exposed to ozone's effects, there are identified impairments in photosynthetic rhythm and metabolism (Zuhara and Isaifan, 2018).

Effects on Economical Values

Air pollution may have a detrimental impact on the economy. In simple language, the economy grows when people are healthy and businesses that depend on naturally occurring resources and cultivated raw materials are operating at full capacity. Each year, air pollution costs billions of dollars in lost agricultural crop and commercial forest outputs. 85% of overall damages are caused by health-related issues. Global damage costs are on the decline: from over 23% of Gross World Product (GWP) in 1900, it is anticipated that they will be below 3% of GWP by 2050. (Guy Hutton, 2011) In addition to this, people missing work due to illness can have a significant negative impact on the economy.

Prevention of Air Pollution

The following actions can reduce air pollution :

Measures to Reduce

A significant issue is always air pollution. This is why taking preventative measures is always a better strategy to reduce air pollution. These preventive measures may be implemented by the government (laws) or by individuals. There are monitoring devices put at various locations throughout several large cities. Authorities examine them frequently to assess the air's purity.

Governmental Preventative Action

Governments all around the world have already implemented green energy to combat air pollution. To reduce the use of fossil fuels, which result in significant air pollution, some governments are investing in wind and solar energy as well as other renewable energy sources. Governments are also putting pressure on businesses to be more responsible in their manufacturing processes so that even while pollution is still produced, it is much more under control.

Individual Level Prevention

Encourage your family to use the bus, train or bike when commuting. If we all do this, there will be fewer cars on road and less fumes.

Use energy such as light, water, boiler, kettle and fire woods wisely. This is because lots of fossil fuels are burned to generate electricity, and so if we can cut down the use, we will also cut down the amount of pollution we create.

Recycle and re-use things. This will minimize the dependence of producing new things. Remember manufacturing industries create a lot of pollution, so if we can re-use things like shopping plastic bags, clothing, paper and bottles, it can help.

Control Devices

The following things are frequently used by industrial or transporttation equipment as pollution control devices. Prior to being released into the atmosphere, they can either eliminate impurities or remove them from an exhaust stream.

(a) Mechanical Collectors : It is a multi-cyclone dust storm.

(b) Electrostatic Precipitators : An electrostatic precipitator, also known as an electrostatic air cleaner, is a particulate collecting device that collects particles from gases (such as air) by using the force of an electrostatic charge that has been induced. Electrostatic precipitators are extremely effective filtration devices that cause little to no resistance to the flow of gases through the device and are easily capable of removing tiny particulates from the air stream, such as dust and smoke.

(c) Bag Houses : A dust collector is a device made to manage large amounts of dust. It includes a blower, a dust filter, a mechanism for cleaning the filter, and a dust receptacle or dust removal system (distinguished from air cleaners which utilise disposable filters to remove the dust).

(d) Particulate Scrubbers: type of pollution control device is the wet scrubber. The phrase refers to a wide range of devices that employ contaminants from other gas streams or the flue gas from a furnace. In a wet scrubber, the polluted gas stream is forced through a pool of liquid, sprayed with the liquid, or exposed to another means of contact with the liquid in order to remove the pollutants.

Some Facts and Statistics about Air Pollution

1. Children are more affected by air pollution than adults because their systems contain higher levels of polluted air relative to their body sizes.
2. The world's worse air quality is found in India.
3. If air pollution-related mortality decreased, the European Union would save 161 billion Euros annually.
4. In big cities, more than 80% of the deadly toxins that harm lungs originate from cars, buses, motorcycles, and other moving vehicles.
5. According to the World Health Organization, air pollution causes 1.3 million more fatalities globally each year than automobile accidents.
6. An adult typically breathes 3,000 litres of air each day.
7. The Great Smog of London in 1952, which resulted in nearly 8,000 fatalities, was one of the worst air pollution incidents in recorded history.
8. With over 5,000 people every year passing away from heart attacks and lung cancer brought on by exhaust fumes from moving vehicles, road transportation is Europe's leading source of air pollution.

Thus, the only way to prevent air pollution is for people and businesses to stop using the hazardous compounds that are the cause of the problem. All processes that burn fossil fuels must stop, from residential air conditioner use to industrial manufacturing, in order to achieve this. Right now, this possibility seems implausible.

However, we need to establish laws that have strict guidelines for handling and manufacturing to industrial and power supplies. The rules are intended to further cut back on hazardous emissions into the atmosphere of the earth.

References :
- Choudhary MP, Garg V (2015). Causes consequences and control of air pollution; Research Gate 2015.
- Guy Hutton (2011). Air pollution global damage costs of air pollution from 1900 to 2050; Assessment Paper Copenhagen Consensus on Human Challenges (2011).
- Jacobson MZ, Jacobson PMZ (2002). Atmospheric pollution: History, Science, and Regulation; Cambridge University Press, p. 206.
- Manisalidis I, Stavropoulou E, Stavropoulos A, Bezirtzoglou E (2020). Environmental and Health Impacts of Air Pollution: A Review; Frontiers in Public Health, 2020 Vol 8.
- McCarthy JT, Pelle E, Dong K, Brahmbhatt K, Yarosh D and Pernodet N (2013). Effects of ozone in normal human epidermal keratinocytes; Exp Dermatol, 22:360-1.
- Möller L, Schuetzle D, Autrup H (1994). Future research needs associated with the assessment of potential human health risks from exposure to toxic ambient air pollutants; Environ Health Perspect, 102(Suppl. 4):193-210.
- Rao M N, Rao HVN (2007). Air Pollution; Tata McGraw-Hill, 2007.
- Singh E, Tiwari S, Agrawal M (2009). Effects of elevated ozone on photosynthesis and stomatal conductance of two soybean varieties: a case study to assess impacts of one component of predicted global climate change; Plant Biol Stuttg Ger, 11(Suppl.1):101-8.

- WHO (2018). First WHO Global Conference on Air Pollution and Health. Available online at: https://www.who.int/ airpollution/ events/conference/en/(accessed October 6, 2019).
- WHO (2019). Air Pollution; WHO. Available online at: http://www.who.int/ air pollution/en/ (accessed October 5, 2019).
- Zuhara S, Isaifan R (2018). The impact of criteria air pollutants on soil and water: a review, 278-84.

Assistant Professor,
Department of Zoology,
Agrawal P.G College, Jaipur (Rajasthan), India.
email: niharikas715@gmail.com

Greener Living

17. Floristic Diversity of Invasive Weeds in Shirpur Taluka of Dhule District, Maharashtra State, India

Rajni Kant Thakur[1,*] and Kumar Ambrish[2]

Abstract

The present study was aimed to document the floristic diversity of invasive weeds in the Shirpur and its adjacent area (Dhule, Nashik, Maharashtra, India). A total of 111 species of weeds belonging to 81 genera and 35 families was recorded in present study. Out of total recorded families, 31 were dicotyledons and 4 monocotyledons. Fabaceae was the dominant family followed by Convolvulaceae, Euphorbiaceae, Malvaceae, Amaranthaceae, Asteraceae, Poaceae, Commelinaceae, Cucurbitaceae, Solanaceae, Apocynaceae, and Boraginaceae. *Ipomoea* (with 8 species) was the largest genus followed by *Euphorbia* (5 species), *Indigofera, Phyllanthus, Sida* (3 species of each), *Alternanthera, Amaranthus, Boerhavia, Calotropis, Commelina, Cynotis, Leucas, Ludwigia, Oxalis, Physalis, Portulaca* and *Senna* (2 species each).

Keywords : Floristic diversity, Crop associated weeds, Invasive species, Nativity, Life-form.

Introduction

A weed is a plant that grows where it is not desired, vying for fertilizer, light, and other resources with cultivated plants. They have characteristic modifications that help in their perpetuation, multiplication, dissemination, stabilization, and overall adaptation (Vasic et al. 2012). The weeds are common dominant, unwanted, undesirable plant that compete with cultivated crop for water, nutrient and sunlight and another several reasons such as, high growth rate, high reproductive rate and produce harmful or beneficial allelopathical effect of cultivated crops (Qasem and Foy 2001). The view of weeds as invasive plants is increasingly shifting around the world as people begin to recognize their importance in broader habitats.

Invasive weed species have characteristics such as being "pioneer species" in different landscapes, being tolerant of a wide range of soil and weather conditions, being a generalist in distribution, producing copious amounts of seed that disperse easily, having aggressive root systems, having a short generation time, high dispersal rates, long flowering and fruiting periods, having a broad native range, and being abundant in their native range. When soil nutrients are lost due to wind and rain, it is these organisms that rapidly establish themselves as the first generation of tough plants in the natural growth of diverse habitats, reducing erosion by the presence of their roots. From the beginning of cultivation, weeds have been called a farmer's worst enemy. Farmers have been fighting them to save their crops for a long time. Invasive weeds inflict dramatic declines in farm, orchard, and grassland production based on their composition and severity. Invasive weeds are the most limiting factors in crop production (Buhler, 1992). Weed exposure is similar to gradual poisoning or disease, with symptoms appearing later in the crop cycle or after harvest. Not only productivity, but also ecological balance, human and animal wellbeing, architectural appeal, and overall economic aspects are all affected. Invasive weed species (IWS) pose a danger to ecosystems, plant species dispersion, and agricultural production.

Weeds, unlike other plants, may withstand severe edaphic, climatic, and biotic conditions. Invasive weed plant research also teaches us about their value, as some of them have a wide range of ethnobotanic applications and may be utilised to produce new pharmaceutical and food items. In other words, 'a weed could be defined a plant out of place or an unwanted plant, or a plant with a negative value, or plants which compete with man for the soil (Muzik, 1970). Many reports are available on the flora of Maharashtra (Singh and Karthikeyan 2000; Singh et al. 2001; Patil 2003, 2010; Sit *et al.*, 2007). No such report, however, is available on the diversity of weeds of Shirpur, Dhule district in Maharashtra. The primary goal of this research was to document the weed flora existing in the Shirpur as baseline information.

Materials and Methods
Study Area
Dhule is district of North Maharashtra (Khandesh area) situated in the lap of Satpura region. Satpura region is well known for its rich biodiversity. The Arunavati river and Tapi river are the rivers flows around the city and fulfill the needs of peoples of Shirpur. Shirpur (21.3496° N latitude; 74.8797° E longitude; 159 m asl altitude) is 50 km from the Dhule. The main profession of the people of the area is agriculture. The main food crops are wheat, barley, maize, finger millet and paddy while sugarcane, cotton, banana, papaya are common cash crops. Besides, the vegetable crops are also cultivated in this region including cucurbits, lady finger, gourd, capsicum, spinach, colocasia, potato, tomato, sugar beet, bean and brinjal.

Methodology
Intensive field studies were conducted to record the maximum number of weeds species in different habitats, i.e., agricultural lands, wastelands, protected areas, river banks and reserve forests of Shirpur during August, 2019 to December, 2022. Villages/ localities visited during the survey include Tarhadi, Shirpur, Warwade, Amode, Abhanpur, Tarhad, Boradi, Dahiwad, Aner, Anturli, Mukhed, Dabhapada, Vakwad, Thalner, Holnanthe and Ziranipada. Plant specimens were collected during the surveys and processed as per the standard method given by Jain and Rao (1976). Small herbs were collected as whole with intact root, stem, leave, flower, and fruit, whereas larger shrubs were sampled as twigs with leave, flower, and fruit. The collected plant specimens were identified with help of available literature, i.e., Hook.f. 1876; Singh and Karthikeyan (2000), Singh et al. (2001) and Patil (2003, 2010) while current nomenclature of plants was adopted from 'Plants of the World Online' database. The nativity of recorded weed species determined following authenticated literature and Plants of the World Online' (2022).

Results and Discussion
A total of 111 invasive weed species belonging to 81 genera and 35 families were recorded from the Shirpur Taluka of Dhule district

Greener Living

(Table 1).

Table 1: Invasive weeds in Shirpur taluka of Dhule district, Maharashtra state, India

Sr. No.	Name of the Plant	Family	Nativity	Life form	Habit	Mode of Introduction
1	*Abutilon indicum* (L.) Sweet	Malvaceae	Africa	Shrub	Perennial	Ornamental
2	*Acalypha indica* L.	Euphorbiaceae	Tropical & Subtropical Asia.	Herb	A	Un-intentional
3	*Achyranthes aspera* L.	Amaranthaceae	Tropical and sub-tropical Old world	Herb	A	Un-intentional
4	*Alternanthera philoxeroides* (Mart.) Griseb.	Amaranthaceae	Trop. America	Herb	A	Un-intentional
5	*Alternanthera sessilis* (L.) R.Br. ex DC.	Amaranthaceae	Trop. America	Herb	A	Un-intentional
6	*Amaranthus spinosus* L.	Amaranthaceae	Trop. America	Herb	A	Vegetable
7	*Amaranthus viridis* L.	Amaranthaceae	Trop. America	Herb	A	Vegetable
8	*Argemone mexicana* L.	Papaveraceae	S.America	Herb	A	Un-intentional
9	*Boerhavia diffusa* L.	Nyctaginaceae	Tropics & Subtropics.	Herb	Perennial	Medicinal
10	*Boerhavia erecta* L.	Nyctaginaceae	Tropical & Subtropical America.	Herb	Perennial	Un-intentional
11	*Brassica napus* L.	Brassicaceae	S. Europe.	Herb	A	Un-intentional
12	*Buglossoides arvensis* (L.) I.M.Johnst	Boraginaceae	Africa	Herb	A	Un-intentional
13	*Cajanus scarabaeoides* (L.) Thouars	Fabaceae	Asia	Climber	A	Un-intentional
14	*Calotropis gigantea* (L.) Dryand.	Apocynaceae	Trop. America	Shrub	A	Medicinal
15	*Calotropis procera* (Aiton) Dryand.	Apocynaceae	Trop. America	Shrub	A	Medicinal
16	*Celosia argentea* L.	Amaranthaceae	Trop. Africa	Herb	A	Ornamental
17	*Chrozophora plicata* (Vahl) A.Juss. ex Spreng.	Euphorbiaceae	Africa	Herb	A	Un-intentional
18	*Cleome viscosa* L.	Cleomaceae	Trop. America	Herb	A	Vegetable
19	*Coccinia grandis* (L.) Voigt	Cucurbitaceae	Africa	Climber	A	Vegetable
20	*Commelina benghalensis* L.	Commelinaceae	Tropical & Subtropical Old World	Herb	A	Un-intentional
21	*Commelina forskaolii* Vahl	Commelinaceae	Africa	Herb	A	Un-intentional
22	*Convolvulus arvensis* L.	Convolvulaceae	Temp. & Subtropical Old World	Climber	A	Un-intentional
23	*Corchorus olitorius* L.	Malvaceae	Tropical & Subtropical Old World.	Herb	A	Un-intentional
24	*Crotalaria medicaginea* Lam.	Fabaceae	Asia	Herb	A	Un-intentional
25	*Croton bonplandianus* Baill.	Euphorbiaceae	S.America	Herb	Perennial	Un-intentional
26	*Cuscuta reflexa* Roxb.	Cuscutaceae	Mediterranean	Climber	A	Un-intentional

Greener Living

27	*Cyanotis axillaris* (L.) D.Don ex Sweet	Commelinaceae	India to Australia	Herb	A	Un-intentional
28	*Cyanotis cristata* (L.) D.Don	Commelinaceae	NE	Herb	A	Un-intentional
29	*Cynodon dactylon* (L.) Pers.	Poaceae	Trop. America	Herb	Perennial	Un-intentional
30	*Cyperus rotundus* L.	Cyperaceae	Tropical & Subtropical Old World	Herb	A	Un-intentional
31	*Dactyloctenium aegyptium* (L.) Willd.	Poaceae	Tropical & Subtropical Old World.	Herb	A	Un-intentional
32	*Datura innoxia* Mill.	Solanaceae	Trop. America	Shrub	Perennial	Noxious
33	*Descurainia sophia* (L.) Webb ex Prantl	Brassicaceae	Temp. Eurasia	Herb	A	Un-intentional
34	*Digera muricata* (L.) Mart.	Amaranthaceae	SW Asia	Herb	A	Un-intentional
35	*Digitaria longiflora* (Retz.) Pers.	Poaceae	Tropical & Subtropical Old World	Herb	A	Un-intentional
36	*Diplocyclos palmatus* (L.) C.Jeffrey	Cucurbitaceae	Africa and Asia	Climber	A	Un-intentional
37	*Emilia sonchifolia* (L.) DC. ex DC.	Asteraceae	Trop. America	Herb	A	Un-intentional
38	*Euphorbia heterophylla* L.	Euphorbiaceae	Trop. America	Herb	A	Un-intentional
39	*Euphorbia hirta* L.	Euphorbiaceae	Trop. America	Herb	A	Un-intentional
40	*Euphorbia hypericifolia* L.	Euphorbiaceae	Tropical & Subtropical America	Herb	A	Un-intentional
41	*Euphorbia prostrata* Aiton	Euphorbiaceae	Tropical & Subtropical America	Herb	A	Un-intentional
42	*Euphorbia serpens* Kunth	Euphorbiaceae	Tropical & Subtropical America	Herb	A	Un-intentional
43	*Euphorbia thymifolia* L.	Euphorbiaceae	Trop. America	Herb	Perennial	Un-intentional
44	*Heliotropium indicum* L.	Boraginaceae	S.America	Herb	A	Un-intentional
45	*Hyptis suaveolens* (L.) Poit.	Lamiaceae	Trop. America	Shrub	A	Noxious
46	*Indigofera cordifolia* Roth	Fabaceae	Asia	Herb	A	Un-intentional
47	*Indigofera linnaei* Ali	Fabaceae	Trop. America	Shrub	A	Un-intentional
48	*Indigofera trita* L.f.	Fabaceae	Tropical & Subtropical Old World	Climber	A	Un-intentional
49	*Ipomoea triloba* L.	Convolvulaceae	Mexico to Brazil, Caribbean	Climber	A	Un-intentional
50	*Ipomoea cairica* (L.) Sweet	Convolvulaceae	Africa and Asia	Climber	A	Un-intentional
51	*Ipomoea carnea* Jacq.	Convolvulaceae	Trop. America	Shrub	Perennial	Un-intentional
52	*Ipomoea nil* (L.) Roth	Convolvulaceae	Tropical & Subtropical America	Climber	A	Un-intentional
53	*Ipomoea obscura* (L.) Ker-Gaw	Convolvulaceae	Trop. Africa	Climber	Perennial	Un-intentional
54	*Ipomoea pes-tigridis* L.	Convolvulaceae	Trop. East Africa	Climber	A	Un-intentional

55	*Ipomoea purpurea* (L.) Roth	Convolvulaceae	Tropical & Subtropical America	Climber	A	Un-intentional
56	*Ipomoea quamoclit* L.	Convolvulaceae	Trop. America	Climber	Perennial	Un-intentional
57	*Lantana camara* L.	Verbenaceae	Trop. America	Shrub	Perennial	Ornamental
58	*Launaea procumbens* (Roxb.) Ramayya & Rajagopal	Asteraceae	Egypt to Central Asia	Herb	A	Un-intentional
59	*Lepidagathis trinervis* Nees	Acanthaceae	Pakistan to India	Herb	A	Un-intentional
60	*Leucaena leucocephala* (Lam.) de Wit	Fabaceae	Trop. America	Tree	Perennial	Fuel
61	*Leucas aspera* (Willd.) Link	Lamiaceae	Asia	Herb	A	Un-intentional
62	*Leucas longifolia* Benth.	Lamiaceae	W. India, Sri Lanka	Herb	A	Un-intentional
63	*Lindenbergia muraria* (Roxburgh ex D. Don) Brühl	Plantaginaceae	Africa and Asia	Herb	A	Un-intentional
64	*Ludwigia octovalvis* (Jacq.) P.H.Raven	Onagraceae	Trop. America	Herb	A	Un-intentional
65	*Ludwigia perennis* L.	Onagraceae	Trop. America	Herb	A	Un-intentional
66	*Malvastrum coromandelianum* (L.) Garcke	Malvaceae	Trop. America	Herb	A	Un-intentional
67	*Martynia annua* L.	Martyniaceae	Trop. America	Herb	A	Un-intentional
68	*Melilotus officinalis* subsp. *alba* (Medik.) H.Ohashi & Tateishi	Fabaceae	Europe to China, N. Africa to Myanmar, Ethiopia to S. Africa	Herb	A	Un-intentional
69	*Merremia emarginata* (Burm. f.) Hallier f.	Convolvulaceae	Tropical Africa, S. China to Tropical Asia	Herb	A	Un-intentional
70	*Mirabilis jalapa* L.	Nyctaginaceae	Peru	Herb	A	Ornamental
71	*Cucumis maderaspatanus* L.	Cucurbitaceae	Tropical & Subtropical Old World	Climber	A	Un-intentional
72	*Oxalis corniculata* L.	Oxalidaceae	Europe	Herb	A	Medicinal
73	*Oxalis latifolia* Kunth	Oxalidaceae	Tropical & Subtropical America	Herb	A	Medicinal
74	*Parthenium hysterophorus* L.	Asteraceae	Trop. America	Climber	A	Un-intentional
75	*Passiflora foetida* L.	Passifloriaceae	Trop. S. America	Herb	A	Ornamental
76	*Pergularia daemia* (Forssk.) Chiov.	Apocynaceae	Africa and Asia	Climber	A	Ornamental
77	*Phyllanthus maderaspatensis* L.	Phyllanthaceae	Africa and Asia	Herb	A	Un-intentional
78	*Phyllanthus tenellus* Roxb.	Phyllanthaceae	Tanzania to Mozambique, SW. Arabian Peninsula, W. Indian Ocean	Herb	A	Un-intentional
79	*Phyllanthus urinaria* L.	Phyllanthaceae	Tropical & Subtropical Asia to N. Australia.	Herb	A	Medicinal

Greener Living

80	*Physalis angulata* L.	Solanaceae	Trop. America	Herb	A	Un-intentional
81	*Physalis pruinosa* L.	Solanaceae	Trop. America	Herb	A	Un-intentional
82	*Poa annua* L.	Poaceae	Temp. Old World to Tropical	Herb	A	Un-intentional
83	*Portulaca oleracea* L.	Portulacaceae	Trop. S. America	Herb	A	Vegetable
84	*Portulaca quadrifida* L	Portulacaceae	Trop. America	Herb	A	Un-intentional
85	*Prosopis juliflora* (Sw.) DC.	Fabaceae	Mexico	Shrub	Perennial	Un-intentional
86	*Rorippa dubia* (Pers.) H.Hara	Brassicaceae	Indian Subcontinent to China	Herb	A	Un-intentional
87	*Senna alata* (L.) Roxb.	Fabaceae	SW. Mexico to Tropical America	Shrub	Perennial	Ornamental
88	*Senna obtusifolia* (L.) H.S. Irwin &.Barneby	Fabaceae	Tropical & Subtropical America	Shrub	A	Un-intentional
89	*Setaria verticillata* (L.) P.Beauv.	Poaceae	Tropical & Subtropical Old World	Herb	A	Un-intentional
90	*Sida acuta* Burm.f.	Malvaceae	Trop. America	Herb	A	Un-intentional
91	*Sida cordifolia* L.	Malvaceae	Tropical & Subtropical Asia to N. Australia	Herb	A	Un-intentional
92	*Sida rhombifolia* L.	Malvaceae	Tropical & Subtropical Old World	Shrub	A	Un-intentional
93	*Solanum virginianum* L.	Solanaceae	Tropical Africa, Arabian Peninsula, S. Iran to S. Central China and Indo-China.	Herb	A	Un-intentional
94	*Sonchus asper* (L.) Hill	Asteraceae	Mediterranean	Herb	A	Un-intentional
95	*Spermacoce pusilla* Wall.	Rubiaceae	Indian Subcontinent to S. China and Philippines	Herb	A	Un-intentional
96	*Spigelia anthelmia* L.	Loganiaceae	Tropical & Subtropical America	Herb	A	Un-intentional
97	*Stachytarpheta jamaicensis* (L.) Vahl	Verbenaceae	SE. U.S.A. to Tropical America	Herb	A	Un-intentional
98	*Synedrella nodiflora* (L.) Gaertn.	Asteraceae	West Indies	Herb	A	Un-intentional
99	*Tephrosia purpurea* (L.) Pers.	Fabaceae	S. Egypt to Chad, Arabian Peninsula to NW. India	Shrub	A	Un-intentional
100	*Torenia fournieri* Linden ex E. Fourn.	Linderniaceae	India to S. China and Indo-China, Taiwan	Herb	A	Ornamental
101	*Trianthema portulacastrum* L.	Aizoaceae	Tropics & Subtropics	Herb	A	Un-intentional
102	*Tribulus terrestris* L.	Zygophyllaceae	Trop. America	Herb	A	Medicinal
103	*Trichodesma indicum* (L.) Lehm.	Boraginaceae	Trop. Central America	Herb	A	Un-intentional

104	*Trichosanthes cucumerina* L.	Cucurbitaceae	Asia	Climber	A	Un-intentional
105	*Tridax procumbens* (L.) L.	Asteraceae	Trop. America	Herb	A	Un-intentional
106	*Triumfetta rhomboidea* Jacq.	Malvaceae	Trop. America	Herb	A	Un-intentional
107	*Turnera ulmifolia* L.	Passifloraceae	Asia	Herb	A	Un-intentional
108	*Verbascum coromandelianum* (Vahl) Hub.-Mor.	Scrophulariaceae	Asia	Herb	A	Un-intentional
109	*Waltheria indica* L.	Malvaceae	Trop. America	Herb	A	Un-intentional
110	*Xanthium strumarium* L.	Asteraceae	Trop. America	Shrub	A	Un-intentional
111	*Zephyranthes citrina* Baker	Amaryllidaceae	Central America	Herb	A	Ornamental

Among 35 families, 31 belong to dicotyledon and 4 to onocotyledon. *Argemone mexicana* L., *Boerhavia diffusa* L., *Cleome viscose* L., *Croton bonplandianus* Baill., *Datura innoxia* Mill., *Euphorbia heterophylla* L., *Euphorbia serpens* Kunth, *Tribulus terrestris* L., *Turnera ulmifolia* L., *Tridax procumbens* (L.) L., *Amaranthus viridis* L., *Cyperus rotundus* L., *Digitari longiflora* (Retz.) Pers., *Cleome viscose* L., *Ludwigia octovalvis* (Jacq.) P.H. Raven, *Phyllanthus urinaria* L., *Senna obtusifolia* (L.) H.S. Irwin & Barneby, *Sonchus asper* (L.) Hill and *Xanthium strumarium* L. were the common weeds in the study area. Some of the plants photographs are shown in below **photoplate 1**(on next page). Weeds like *Parthenium hysterophorus* contain several allele chemicals that inhibit the seed germination and growth of other plants (Kumar and Varshney 2007).

Fabaceae is dominant family, followed by Convolvulaceae, Euphorbiaceae, Malvaceae, Amaranthaceae, Asteraceae, Poaceae, Commelinaceae, Cucurbitaceae, Solanaceae, Apocynaceae, Boraginaceae, Brassicaceae, Lamiaceae, Nyctaginaceae, Phyllanthaceae, Onagraceae, Oxalidaceae, Passifloriaceae, Portulacaceae, Verbenaceae, Acanthaceae, Aizoaceae, Amaryllidaceae, Cleomaceae,

Cuscutaceae, Cyperaceae, Linderniaceae, Loganiaceae, Martyniaceae, Papaveraceae, Plantaginaceae, Rubiaceae, Scrophulariaceae, Solanaceae and Zygophyllaceae.

Photoplate 1: Photos of Some Invasive Weeds (A-I) of Shirpur Taluka of Dhule District, Maharashtra.
A. *Abutilon indicum*(L.) Sweet   B. *Argemone mexicana* L.   C. *Calotropis gigantea* (L.) W.T.Aiton
D. *Croton bonplandianus* Baill.   E. *Datura metel* L.   F. *Euphorbia heterophylla* L.
G. *Ipomoea obscura* (L.) Ker Gawl.   H. *Passiflora foetida* L.   I. *Trichosanthes cucumerina* L.

The largest genera was *Ipomoea* represented by 8 species, followed by *Euphorbia* (5 species), *Indigofera, Phyllanthus, Sida* (3 species each), *Alternanthera, Amaranthus, Boerhavia, Calotropis, Commelina, Cynotis, Leucas, Ludwigia, Oxalis, Physalis, Portulaca* and *Senna* (2 species each).

Most of weeds were introduced un-intentionally, some introduced due their food values and ornamental purposes from Africa, America, Asia, Mediterranean, Australia, Egypt, Chad, Arabian Peninsula, West Indies, Peru, etc. (**Table 2**).

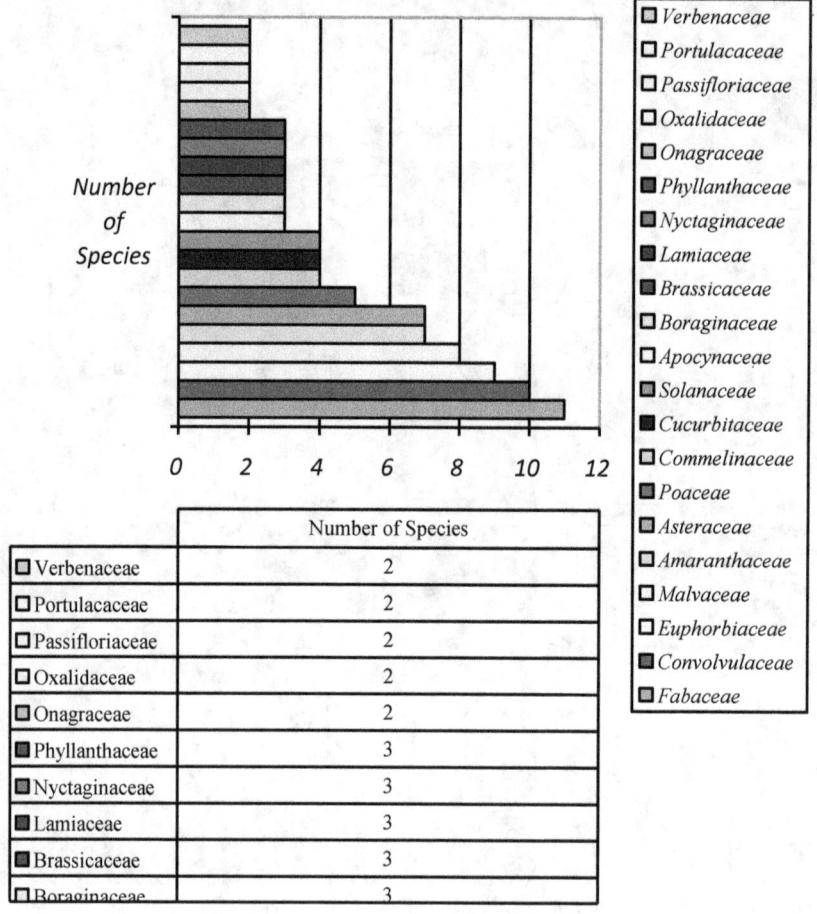

	Number of Species
☐ Verbenaceae	2
☐ Portulacaceae	2
☐ Passifloriaceae	2
☐ Oxalidaceae	2
■ Onagraceae	2
■ Phyllanthaceae	3
■ Nyctaginaceae	3
■ Lamiaceae	3
■ Brassicaceae	3
☐ Boraginaceae	3

Fig. 1. Comparative percentage of weed families of Tehsil Shirpur, District Dhule (Maharashtra), India.

Farmers have significant challenges in eliminating and managing invasive weeds in their agricultural systems. To remove weeds from agriculture farms, several chemical, biological, and mechanical approaches are used. Weed control can only be successful if the identification, characterisation, and life cycle of weeds are thoroughly understood. Many invasive plants are nevertheless appreciated by individuals who are unaware of their weedy characteristics. Others are identified as weeds, yet property owners do little to stop them from spreading. Some species do not become invasive until they have been ignored for an extended period of time. Invasive plants aren't all created equal. Identification of invasive weeds at the seedling stage is also critical for the successful implementation of an eradication campaign. Weeds' both detrimental and beneficial characteristics must be addressed in any eradication plan. Leguminous weeds, for example, can improve soil fertility by fixing atmospheric nitrogen with the help of some bacteria present in root nodules of these leguminous plants that is beneficial for the crops. Similarly, we must consider how to make appropriate use of weeds that have been removed for diverse purposes. Weeds having therapeutic qualities might be sold to pharmaceutical firms for further research and development. Farmers' income will be increased, either directly or indirectly.

Acknowledgements

The Director, Botanical Survey of India; Director, Shirpur Education Society and Principal, Amrishbhai R. Patel School are acknowledged for administrative help and facilities. We thank our colleague for their support and local people of the Shirpur area for their hospitality and assistance during the field work.

References

Buhler CD. 1992. Population dynamics and control of annual weeds in corn as influenced by tillage systems. *Weed Sci.* 40: 241-248.

Hooker, J. D. (1876). *The Flora of British India.* 2: 81-219. L. Reeve & Co., London.

Jain, S.K. & R.R. Rao (1976). *A Handbook of Field and Herbarium Methods*. Today and Tomorrow Printers & Publishers, New Delhi, India, 157pp.

Kumar, S. and Varshney J G., 2007. Biological control of Parthenium : present and future, National Research Centre for Weed Science, Jabalpur, India; pp-157.

Muzik, T.J.(1970). Weed Biology and Control. McGraw Hill Book Co., New York, USA.

Patil DA. 2010. Observations on marsh and aquatic crop Weeds in Khandesh region of Maharashtra. *Life sciences Leaflets*. 2010;10:273-279.

Patil, D.A.(2003). Flora of Dhule and Nandurbar Districts (Maharashtra). Bishen Singh Mahendra Pal Singh, Dehradun, India.

Plants of the World Online (2021) www.plantsoftheworldonline.org

Qasem JR and Foy CL. Weed Allelopathy, its ecological impacts and future prospects : a review. *J Crop Prod*. 2001;4:43-119

Singh N.P. and Karthikeyan S. (2000). Flora of Maharashtra State: Dicotyledons. Volume I. Botanical Survey of India.

Singh N.P., Lakshminarsimhan P., Karthikeyan S. and Prasanna P. V. (2001). Flora of Maharashtra State: Dicotyledons. Volume II. Botanical Survey of India.

Sit AKB. Malay S, Biswanath and Arnunachalam V. 2007. Weed floristic composition in palm gardens in Plains of Eastern Himalayan region of West Bengal. Indian Acad Sci current Sci. 2007;92(10)1434-1439.

Vasic, V., B. Konstantinovic & S. Orlovic (2012). Weeds in forestry and possibilities of their control. In: Price, A.J. (ed.). *Weed Control*.

[1]**Amrishbhai R. Patel School, Shirpur, Dhule, Maharashtra, India**
[2]**High Altitude Western Himalayan Regional Centre, Botanical Survey of India, Solan, Himachal Pradesh, India**
*email corresponding author: <u>thakurrkbsi@gmai.com</u>

18. Optical Properties of Polyvinylpyrrolidone / Polyvinylacetate Blend Films

A. Rawat[*],
A. K. Agrawal,
Shivali Chauhan
P. J. Singh

Abstract

Films of Polyvinylpyrrolidone, Polyvinylacetate and their blends were prepared using solution cast method and characterized using X-ray diffraction (XRD) and Fourier transform infrared (FTIR) spectro-scopy techniques. The dependence of the absorption coefficient (α) of the film samples on photon energy (hv) was determined in the spectral range 200 nm to 400 nm at room temperature. Optical band gap of the sample films has been calculated by using Tauc's relation and the variation in the values of optical band gap with the variation of composition in the blend films have been found from 4.78 eV to 5.01 eV. The tail width of the localized states has been calculated by using Urbach's relation. Absorption coefficient and extinction coefficient have been calculated at 250 nm wavelength at the fundamental edge. The optical band gap has been correlated with the number of carbon atoms per molecule.

Keywords : Blend, optical band gap, Absorption coefficient and extinction coefficient

1. Introduction

Polymer blending is a convenient route for the development of new polymeric materials, which combine the excellent properties of more than one existing polymer. This strategy is usually cheaper and less time consuming than the development of new monomers and/or new polymerization routes, as the basis for entirely new polymeric materials. Thus the financial risk inherent to the development of new materials is limited in case of polymer blends. An additional advantage of polymer blends is that a wide range of material properties is within reach by merely changing the blend composition. Properties of resulting materials may be tailored to meet requirements of customers or specific applications. Nevertheless, the market for polymer blend based materials has increased continuously during the past 2-3 decades, and is expected to increase in future. Polymer blends have been considerably studied in view of their wide potential application for novel system and devices[1-3]. Suitable addition of dopants, blends or copolymers to the polymer matrix, the optical and electrical properties of these materials could be selectively modified for particular properties in various applications[4-8]. Optical absorption studies are important to provide details of the electronic band structure, localized states and type of optical transitions, making these materials very attractive for chemical sensors in the detection of ionic species and for display panels[9-11].

Polymers have very diverse structure and applications ranging from domestic articles to sophisticated scientific and medical instruments. The modern era can definitely be called a polymer era, as polymers made revolutionary advancement in the field of medicine, with their help cripples could walk, heart valves can be repaired and damage human organs could be replaced. Now a days through proper selection of monomers and their combinations and adopting appropriate polymerization conditions and techniques, experts are able to construct polymer molecules of almost any desired size, shape, complexity and of any desired chemical structure suited to almost any contemplated end use.

Among many polymers, the polyvinylpyrrolidone (PVP) has good film forming adhesive behaviour and its formed films exhibit good optical quality (high transmission of visible range), and mechanical strength (easy processing) required for applications. The amorphous nature of PVP also provides a low scattering loss, which makes it as an ideal polymer for blending for different applications. PVP is easily soluble in water, so it is preferred to avoid phase separation in the reactions[12-14]. Polymer like polyvinylacetate (PVAc) is easily available in market. It has low cost and is mainly used in adhesives. The aim of present work is to prepare films of PVP, PVAc and their blends having different compositions. In this work we focused on the effect of different blend compositions on optical properties of

PVP, PVAc and their blends films through UV-Visible spectrophotometer at room temperature (35^0 C). Interesting effects of the blend contents were observed on the optical as absorption coefficient, optical band gap, absorption edge of the blend films showed blend content dependence.

2 Experimental Details

2.1 Sample Preparation

Solution cast method is an important commercial technique utilized to febricate thin layered films for diverse applications. This technique has good dimentional stability, clearity, flexibility and is fracture resistance. Solution cast method consists of dissolution of the film ingredients in a suitable solvent. The following are the advantages of solution cast method :

(i) Higher quality (uniformity) and thinner film
(ii) Freedom from pinholes and gel marks
(iii) Purity and clearity
(iv) Lack of residual stresses

PVP (MW: 40000 amu) supplied by CDH Pvt Ltd, New Delhi (India) and PVAc (MW: 40000 amu) supplied by HiMedia Laboratories Pvt. Ltd., Mumbai (India) were used as received for the film preparation by solution cast method[15-17]. For preparing blends of PVP and PVAc, both the polymers were disolved in a common solvent ethanol and the mixture was stirred thoroughly for a few hours in order to get proper mixing. The mixture was then poured in a Petri dish floating in mercury to ensure the uniform thickness of the film. The whole assembly was then placed in a dust free chamber for 1-2 days so that the solvent gets evaporated and the film is taken out of the Petri dish. The blend films of PVP and PVAc were prepared in the ratio 90/10, 80/20, 70/30, 60/40, 50/50, 40/60, 30/70, 20/80, 10/90. Two films of pure PVP and PVAc were also prepared by the same method. The thickness of the films was measured by micrometer (Mitutoyo, Japan) having least count of 1μm and was found of the order of 226 μm.

2.2 Optical Measurements

The variation of absorbance with the wavelength of light incident on the film samples has been recorded using Systronic double beem

UV-Visible spectrophotometer in the photon wavelength range 200-400 nm with a band width of 2 nm. The optical absorbance has great influence on the composition of the film. A sharp decrease in the absorption edge (between wavelengths 240 nm to 260 nm in figure 1) shows that the films are of a good compound. Using the fundamental relations of photon transmitance (T) and absorbance (A),

$$I_t = I_0 exp(-\alpha t) \quad \ldots\ldots(1)$$

Where I_t is the photon intensity at thickness (t) inside the material and I_0 is incident photon energy at the surface of material[18], and

$$A = log\left[\frac{I_0}{I_t}\right] \quad \ldots(2)$$

The absorption coefficient (α) has been evaluated from the measurement of optical absorbance (A) and the film thickness (t) using the relation

$$\alpha = 2.303\left[\frac{A}{t}\right] \quad \ldots\ldots(3)$$

The extinction coefficient (K) is related to the absorption coefficient (α) by the relation[19]

$$K = \frac{\alpha \lambda}{4\pi} \quad \ldots\ldots(4)$$

where λ is the incident photon wavelength. The absorption of radiation that leads to electronic transitions between the valence and conduction bands is direct or indirect transition. These transitions are described by the Tauc equation[20,21]

$$\alpha h\nu = \beta[h\nu - E_{op}]^r \quad \ldots\ldots(5)$$

where hν is the incident photon energy, E_{op} the optical band gap energy (Tauc energy) and the factor β depends on the transition probability and can be assumed to be constant within the optical frequency range and is related to the extent of the band tailing. The exponent r in the relation (5) takes the values (1/2, 3/2, 2, 3) depending on the material and the type of optical transition, whether it is direct or indirect. r = 1/2 & 3/2 for allowed direct and forbidden direct transitions respectively and r = 2 & 3 for allowed indirect and forbidden indirect transitions respectively. Plotting $(\alpha h\nu)^2$ against photon energy (hν) gives a straight line intercept on energy axis , equal to the optical energy band gap (E_{op}) for direct allowed transitions . The absorption edge is a sharp discontinuity in the absorption spectrum that occurs when the energy of the photon corresponds to the energy of an atomic shell. Each of the absorption edges in fig (1) exhibits different slopes and a saturation region for low energies. For the investigated samples the absorption edges were found to follow the Tauc power law (Eq 5) in the range over which the photon energy was higher than the optical band gap energy (E_{op}).

It is well known that the shape of the fundamental absorption edge in the exponential (Urbach) region yields information on the disorder effects[22]. With incident photon energy less than the band gap, the decrease in absorption coefficient is followed with an exponential decay of the density of states of localized into the gap[23] and the absorption edge is known as Urbach edge. The lack of crystalline long-range order in amorphous materials is associated with a tailing of density of states. At lower values of the absorption coefficient, the extent of the exponential tail of absorption edge characterized by the Urbach energy (E_u) is given by[24]

$$\alpha(v) = \alpha_0 exp\left[\frac{hv}{E_u}\right] \quad \ldots\ldots(6)$$

where α_o is a constant, E_u is the Urbach energy which indicates the width of the band tails of the localized states. The optical absorption coefficient just below the absorption edge shows exponential variation with photon energy indicating the presence of Urbach's tail. Plotting Ln α vs hv and taking the reciprocals of the slopes of the linear portion of these curves, E_u could be obtained. The history of film preparation also influences E_u values. The E_u values are related to the localized states induced by the polymer atomic structures. Possible structural defects, such as breaks, configurationally imperfections or torsions of the polymer chains, seem to be responsible for the energy described by Urbach tail energy (E_u). Moreover, large structural disorder and charged impurities may cause an increase in Urbach energy E_u.

3 Results and Discussion

3.1 Optical Response

The absorption of light energy by polymeric materials in the ultraviolet and visible regions involves promotion of electrons from the ground state to higher energy states. UV-Visible spectrophotometer has become an important tool for investigating the electronic transitions. It is used to estimate the value of optical band gap (E_{op}) in polymers. The comparative study of all film samples in the wavelength range 200 nm- 400 nm is presented in figures (1), (2a&b) & (3). Figure (1) represents the absorbance spectra of freshly prepared film samples. From the spectra it is observed that absorbance decreases with the increase in wavelength. A sharp fall in absorbance present at a particular wavelength indicates the presence of optical band gap in these samples. The Tauc relation as given in equation (5) is used for the determination of energy band gap as shown in fig (2a & 2b). The present polymers and their blend films, obey the rule of direct allowed transition. The variation in the values of optical band gap of all film samples is systematic. As PVAc concentration in the blend increases, the band gap for direct optical transition increases. This small variation is possibly due to amorphous nature of the films. This change in optical band gap can be explained in terms of the charge transfer complex formation between carbonyl groups or tertiary nitrogen atoms attached to the amide bond of PVP with the easter groups of PVAc, as it is evident by the shifting of optical absorption spectra. The formation of charge transfer complex is characterized by the shifting of the absorption band in addition to the broadening in the absorption band in UV-Visible region of spectra. The values of E_{op} so determined are listed in table (1). The value of E_{op} for PVP is 4.78 eV and for PVAc is 5.01 eV. The observed value of optical band gap for PVP is in good agreement with the values reported in litrature [17, 25].

The energy E_u reported in table (1) is linked with the absorption coefficient (α) in the lower energy region of the fundamental edge. Below the gap, in amorphous materials the transition from occupied extended states of the valence band to the empty tail states of the conduction band may occur. In a similar way transition from valance band tail states to the empty extended conduction band states are possible. Both types of transition should have similar matrix elements. During the deposition of amorphous film, unsaturated bonds are produced. These unsaturated bonds are responsible for the formation of some defects in the film. Such defects produce localized states. For the transition from localized to extended states (and from extended to localized states) with an exponential decay of the density of states of the localized states into the gap, one finds an exponential relation between absorption coefficient (α) and frequency (v) as given in eq (6). The Urbach energy (E_u) can be determined by plotting ln α vs hv and taking the inverse of the slope of the linear part of the graph (Fig 3). E_u is the energy which yields an indication of depth-of-tail levels extending into the forbidden energy gap below the absorption edge. As the Urbach energy parameter is a measure of the degree of disorder, the larger value of E is indicative of the greater compositional, tropological or structural disorder[26].

The relation between extinction coefficient (K) and absorption coefficient (α) is shown in eq (4). Both these parameters have been calculated at 250 nm wavelength for all samples. These parameters are presented in table (1). Further, the number of carbon atoms (M) in a cluster is correlated with the optical band gap (E_{op}) through the expression given by the relation[27]

$$E_{op} = \frac{34.3}{M^{\frac{1}{2}}} \quad \ldots\ldots\ldots\ldots(14)$$

Where M is the number of carbon atoms in carbonaceous cluster. The calculated values of M for film samples are presented in table (1). The value of M for PVAc is 47 and increases when PVP content in the blend is increased. Such an increase in the value of M can be correlated to the increased conjugation in monomer unit of PVAc matrix after blending with PVP.

3.2 XRD Analyses

Structural aspects of PVAc and PVAc/PVP blend films have been analyzed using X-ray diffraction technique. The XRD measurements were made on D8 Advance XRD machine by using monochromatic CuK_α (8.0478 KeV and λ = 0.15406 nm). The scanning angle (2θ) was set from 5^0 to 70^0 at a scanning rate of 1 step/sec i.e., 3^0 per min and the operating condition was 2.2 KW. The polymer film samples were mounted on a sample holder plate without using tape and the profiles of the spectra were obtained by the software. Figure (4) shows 10 different spectra of PVAc & PVAc/PVP blend films. The

XRD pattern confirms the amorphous nature of all the film samples. PVP film also has amorphous nature[17].

3.3 FTIR Measurements

Fourier transform infrared (FTIR) spectroscopy has been widely used by many researchers to study the information of polymeric blends. FTIR spectroscopy provides information regarding intermolecular interaction via analysis of FTIR spectra corresponding to stretching or blending vibrations of particular blends. The positions at which these peaks appear depend on the bond type (force constant and reduced mass). Hydrogen bonding or any other secondary interactions between chemical groups on different polymers usually cause a shift in peak position of the particular functional groups. Shift in peak positions will depend on the strength of interaction[28]. This kind of behaviour is exhibited by miscible blends that show extensive phase mixing. Xie et al.[29] studied the miscible and immiscible blends by FTIR spectroscopy and showed strong evidence of molecular interaction for miscible blends, whereas no interaction was detected for phase separated blends.

FTIR spectra of PVP, PVAc and their blend film samples are shown in Figures (5a) to (5f). Figure 5a shows the IR spectra of PVP film. The transmittance band related to C=0 stretching vibrations appeared at 1647 cm^{-1}. C–H asymmetric stretching vibrations of CH_2 bond appeared at 2953 cm^{-1}. The bonds at 933 cm^{-1}, 1280 cm^{-1} and 1454 cm^{-1} are attributed to C–C stretching, C–N stretching and C–H bending vibrations.

The FTIR spectrum of PVAc is shown in Fig. 5b. The peak in hydroxyl region appearing at 3457 cm^{-1} is assigned to O–H stretching vibrations, which may be due to the moisture content present in the film sample. The C–H stretching peak appeared at 2935 cm^{-1}. The peak due to C=O stretching vibrations present in the ester groups in PVAc is observed at 1735 cm^{-1}, whereas the peak assigned to C=O stretching vibrations in case of PVP, appeared at 1647 cm^{-1}. The C–H bending vibrations showed their existence at 1435 cm^{-1} and C–O stretching peak is located at 1107 cm^{-1}. The stretching vibrational peak due to C–C bond has been observed at

953 cm^{-1}. Some more peaks at 606 cm^{-1}, 632 cm^{-1} and 796 cm^{-1} (due to C–H rocking) are observed for PVAc and PVP/PVAc blend film samples but these peaks are absent in pure PVP sample (Fig. 5a). Also the C=O stretching peak of PVAc and that of PVP show their individual existence in the PVP/PVAc blend samples. No shift in the characteristic peaks of PVP and PVAc has been observed in the FTIR of PVP/PVAc blend film samples (Fig. 5c-5f). This indicates that the two polymers are immiscible. Khurma et al.[30] found no shift in the characteristic peaks of immiscible blends of polylacticacid and polyvinylbutyral. Hung et al.[31] found no evidence in FTIR spectrum for a specific interaction between PC and PMMA and characterized PMMA/PC blend as immiscible blend.

4. Conclusions

The optical results of PVAc, PVP and their blend films of various compositions exhibit compositional dependence at room temperature. Addition of PVP to the PVAc increases UV absorption coefficient and the localized states within the forbidden energy gap, consequently the optical energy band gap decreases.

Acknowledgement

One of the authors (A R) would like to thank UGC, Bhopal for awarding a teacher research fellowship. The authors are thankful to the Director, DAE-UGC consortium, Indore for providing XRD facility of the samples. The authors are also thankful to the Principal and Head, Department of Physics & Chemistry, M S J College, Bharatpur for providing experimental facilities.

Figure Captions

FIG (1) Absorbance vs photon wavelength
FIG (2 a&b) $(\alpha h\nu)^2$ vs photon energy
FIG (3) Ln α vs photon energy
FIG (4) XRD pattern of the film samples
FIG (5a) FTIR spectrum of PVP film
FIG (5b) FTIR spectrum of PVAc film
FIG (5c) FTIR spectrum of PVAc 80% + PVP 20% blend film
FIG (5d) FTIR spectrum of PVAc 60% + PVP 40% blend film
FIG (5e) FTIR spectrum of PVAc 40% + PVP 60% blend film
FIG (5f) FTIR spectrum of PVAc 20% + PVP 80% blend film

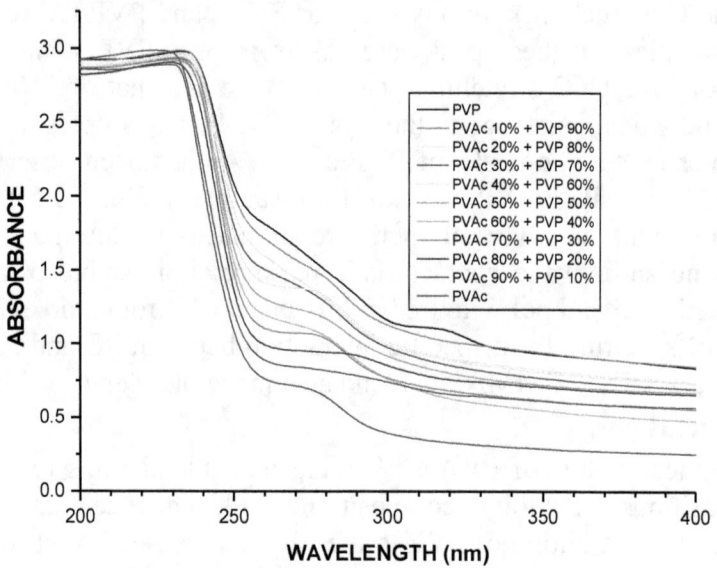

Figure 1:- Absorbance vs photon wavelength

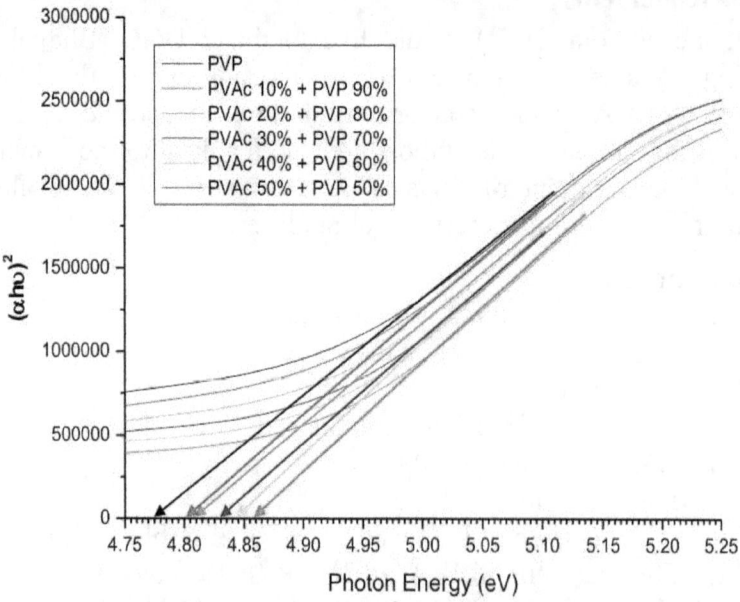

Figure 2(a):- $(\alpha h\nu)^2$ vs photon energy

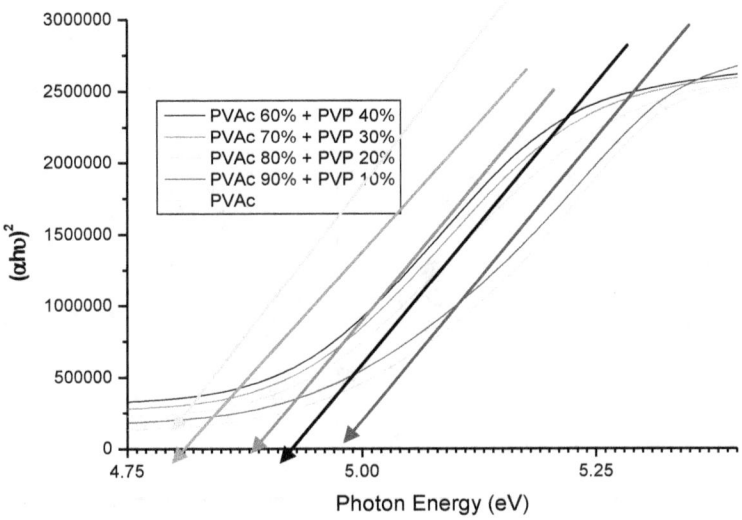

Figure 2(b):- $(\alpha h\nu)^2$ vs photon energy

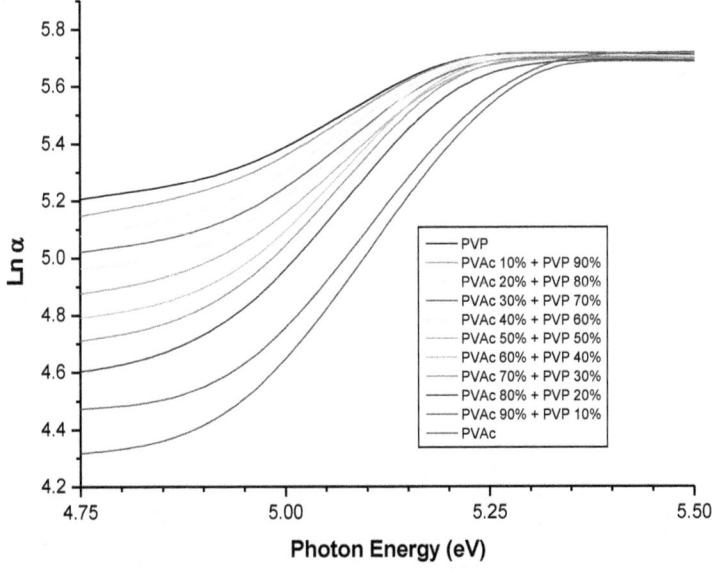

Figure 3:- Ln α vs photon energy

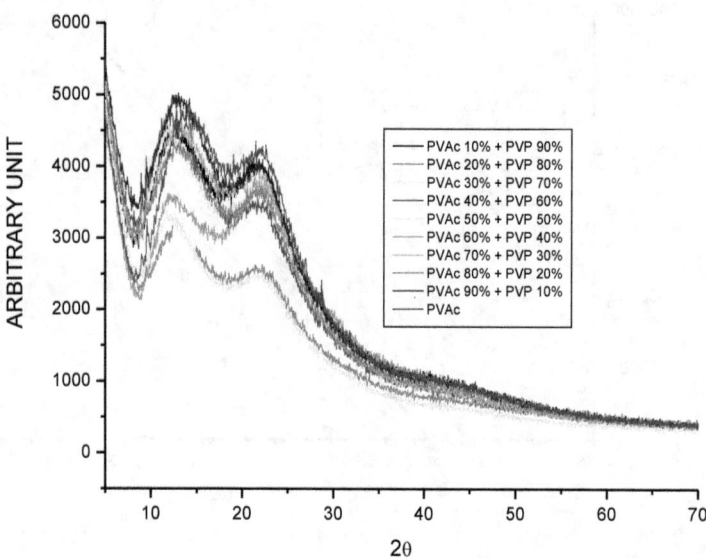

Figure 4:- XRD pattern of PVAc and PVP-PVAc blend film samples

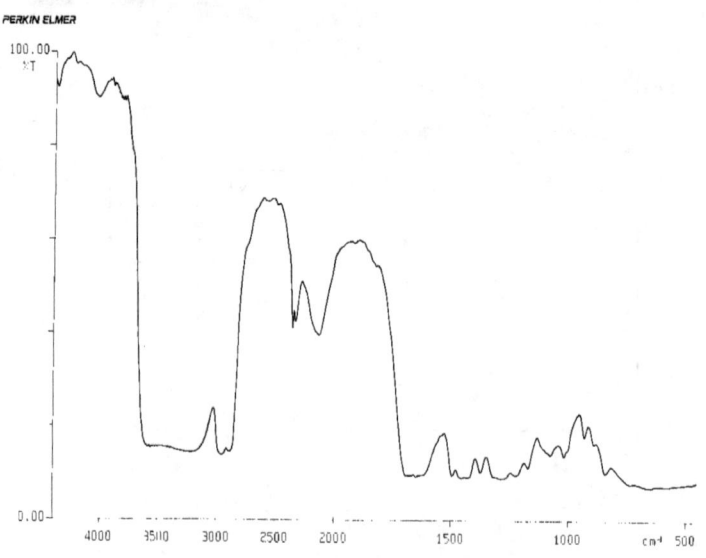

Figure 5a:- FTIR spectrum of PVP film

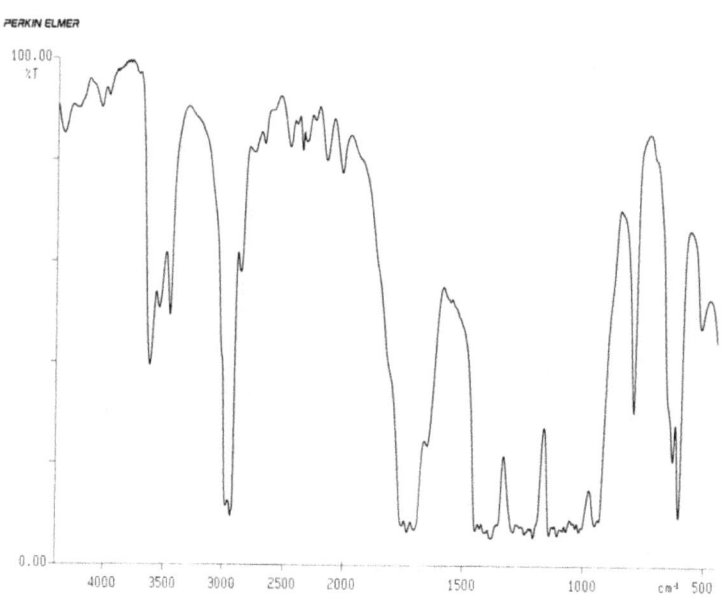

Figure 5b:- FTIR spectrum of PVAc film

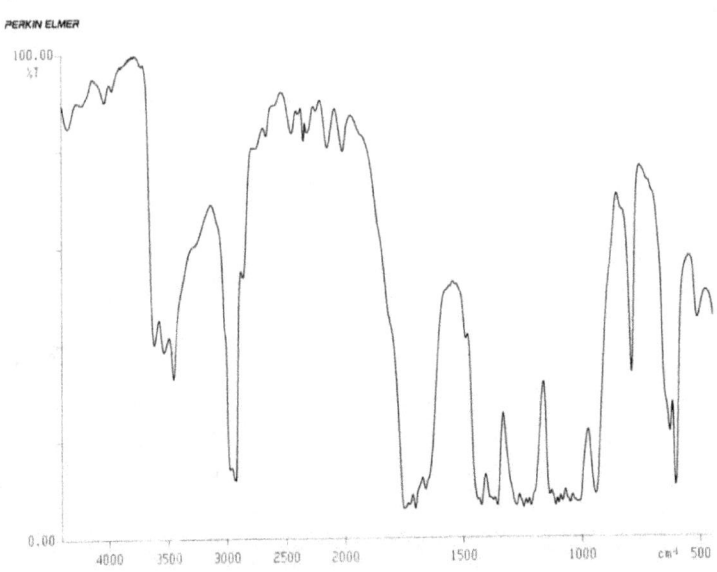

Figure 5c:- FTIR spectrum of PVAc 80% + PVP 20% blend film

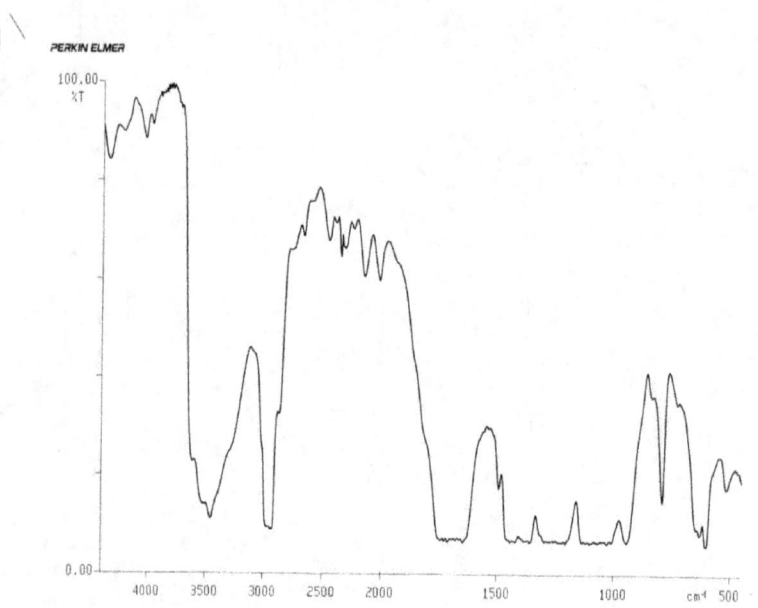

Figure 5d:- FTIR spectrum of PVAc 60% + PVP 40% blend film

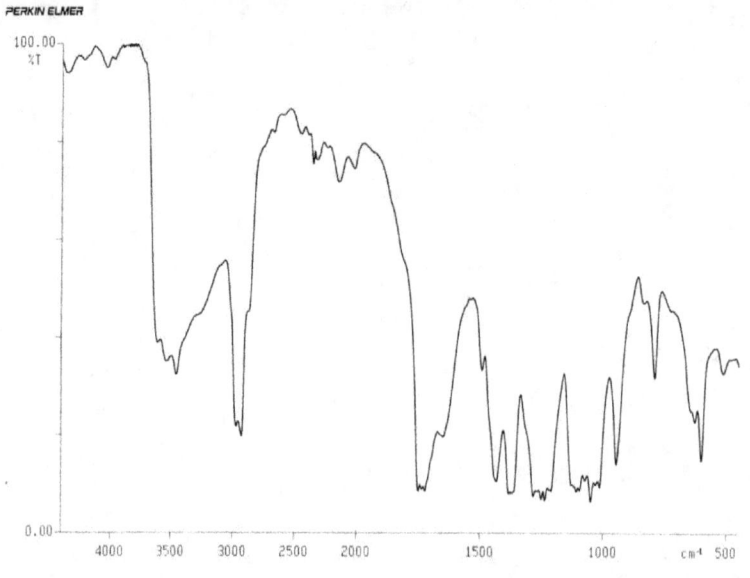

Figure 5e:- FTIR spectrum of PVAc 40% + PVP 60% blend film

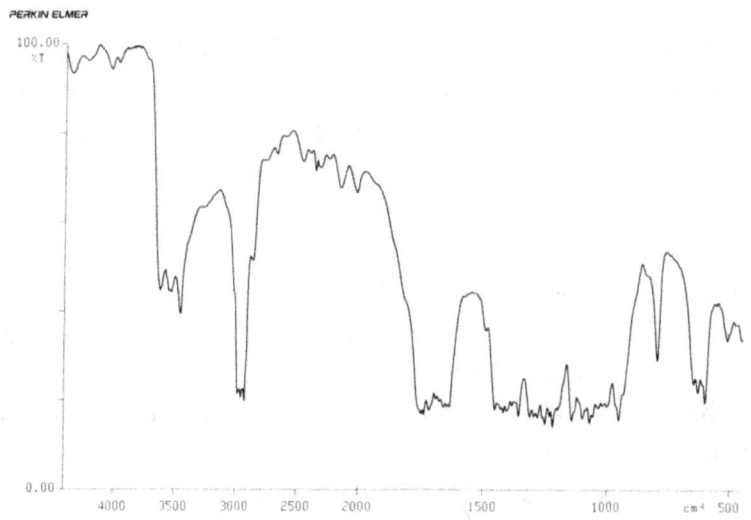

Figure 5f:- FTIR spectrum of PVAc 20% + PVP 80% blend film

Table 1- Optical data for PVP, PVAc and their blend films of various compositions

COMPOSITION	E_{op} (eV)	E_u (eV)	α (cm^{-1}) at 250 nm	K (x10^{-6}) at 250 nm	M
PURE PVP	4.78	0.488	196.88	391.52	52
PVAc 10% + PVP 90%	4.80	0.452	189.85	377.54	52
PVAc 20% + PVP 80%	4.81	0.401	176.70	351.40	51
PVAc 30% + PVP 70%	4.83	0.360	164.47	327.08	51
PVAc 40% + PVP 60%	4.84	0.329	157.54	313.30	51
PVAc 50% + PVP 50%	4.86	0.317	148.07	294.45	50
PVAc 60% + PVP 40%	4.88	0.266	134.41	267.30	50
PVAc 70% + PVP 30%	4.89	0.256	127.07	252.71	50
PVAc 80% + PVP 20%	4.90	0.245	116.07	230.82	49
PVAc 90% + PVP 10%	4.98	0.236	108.32	215.42	48
PURE PVAc	5.01	0.221	94.97	188.87	47

References

1. Preoneanu S, Torcu R, Brie M and Mihilesan G, "Electrochemical and optical studies of metallic ion insertion in polypyrrole film", *Mater.Sci. Forum*, 191(1995) 241-246, doi: 10.4028/ www.scientific.net /MSF.191.241
2. Armand M, "The history of polymer electrolytes", *Solid State Ionics*, 69(1994) 309-319
3. Koksbang R, Olsen I I & Shackle D, "Review of hybrid polymer electrolytes and rechargeable lithium batteries", *Solid State Ionics*, 69 (1994) 320-335
4. Abraham K M, & Alamgir M, "Li+-Conductive solid polymer electrolytes with liquid-like conductivity", *Journal of the Electrochemical Society*, 137,5 (1990) L1657–L1659
5. Reiche A, Tubke J, Siury K, Sander B, Fleischer G and Wartewig S, "Gel electrolytes with plasticizers of different polarity", *Solid State Ionics*, 85 (1996) 121-127
6. Reiche A, Steurich T, Sander B, Lobitz P and Fleischer G, "Characterization, mechanism and model Ion transport in gel electrolytes", *Electrochim. Acta*, 40 (1995) 2153-2157
7. Schartel B, Wending J and Wendorff J H, "Cellulose/poly (vinyl alcohol) blends. I. Influenceof miscibility and water content on relaxations", *Macromolecules* 29 (1996) 1521-1527
8. Huq R, Koksbang R, Tonder P E and Farrington G C, "Effect of plasticizers on the properties of new ambient temperature polymerelectrolyte", *Electrochim. Acta*, 37 (1992) 1681-1684
9. Aleshin A N, Mironkov N B, Suvarov A V, Conklin J A, Su J M and Kaner R B, "Transport Properties of ion-implanted andchemically doped Polyaniline Films", *Phys. Rev. B:Condens. Matter*, 54 (1996) 11638-11643
10. Ogura K, Saino T, Nakayama M and Shiigi H, "The humidity dependence of the electricalconductivity of a soluble Polyaniline-poly (vinylalcohol) composite film", *J. Mater. Chem.*, 7 (1997) 2363-2366

11. Devi C U, Sharma A K and Rao V V R N, "Electrical and optical properties of pure and silvernitrate-doped polyvinyl alcohol films", *Mater. Lett.*, 56 (2002) 167-174
12. Rui Z T, Ran L, Xin L L, Ying Z Y, Jin L T and Nian Y J, "Photochromic Polyoxotungstoeuropate K12 [Eu P5W30O110]/ Polyvinylpyrrolidone Nanocomposite Films", *Journal of Solid State Chemistry*, 172, 2 (2003) 458-463 doi:10.1016/S0022-4596(03)00036-7
13. Ramya C S, Selvasekarapandian S, Hirankumar G, Savitha T and Angelo P C, "Investigation Sonthe Effect of Complexation of NaFsalt with Polymerblend (PEO/PVP) Electroly Tesonionic Conductivity and Optical Energy-bandgaps," *Journal of Non-Crystal Solids*, 354 (2008) 1494-1502 doi:10.1016/ j. jnoncrysol. 2007.08.038
14. Zhang J, Liu H, Wang Z and Ming N, "Low-Tempera- ture Growth of ZnO with Controllable Shapes and Band Gaps", *Journal of Crystal Growth*, 310, 11 (2008) 2848-2853 doi:10.1016 /j.jcrysgro.2008.02.014
15. Tanwar A, Gupta K K, Singh P J & Vijay Y K, "Dielectric measurements on PWB materials at microwave frequencies", *Bull. Mater Sci,.* 29 (2006) 181-185
16. Awasthi K, Awasthi S, Srivastava A, Kamalakaran R, Talapatra S, Ajayan P M & Srivastava O N, "Synthesis and characterization of carbon nanotube–polyethylene oxide composites", *Nanotechno-logy* 17 (2006) 5417-5422
17. Rawat A, Mahavar H K, Chauhan S, Tanwar A & Singh P J, "Optical band gap of Polyvinylpyrolidone / Polyacrylamide blend thin films", *Indian J Pure and Appl. Phys,* 50 (2012) 100-104
18. Ezekoye B A, "Preparation and Optical Characterisation of Cd1-XZnXS Ternary Alloy Thin Films", *Journal of Science and Technology*, 23, 2 (2003) 41-47
19. Gumus C, Ozkendir O M, Kavak H & Ufuktepe Y, "Structural and optical properties of zinc oxide thin films prepared by spray

pyrolysis method", *J. Optoelectronics & Advanced Mater.*, 8, 1 (2006) 299-303
20. Tauc J, Grigorovici R & Vancu A, "Optical Properties and Electronic Structure of Amorphous Germanium", *Phys. Stat. Sol.*, 15 (1966) 627-637
21. Davis E A & Mott N F, "Conduction in non-crystalline systems V. Conductivity, optical absorption and photoconductivity in amorphous semiconductors", *Phil. Mag.*, 22 (1970) 903-922
22. Cody G D, Tiedje T, Abeles B, Brooks B & Goldstein Y, "Disorder and the optical absorption edge of hydrogenated amorphous silicon", *Phys. Rev. Lett.*, 47 (1981) 1480-1483
23. Abay B, Guder H S & Yogurtchu Y K, "Urbach-Martienssen's tails in layered semiconductor GaSe", *Solid State Communications*, 112 (1999) 489-494
24. Urbach F, "The long-wavelength edge of photographic sensitivity and electronic absorption of solids", *Phys. Rev. B*, 92 (1953) 1324-1326
25. Chahal R P, Mahendia S, Tomar A K & Kumar S, " Effect Of Ultraviolet Irradiation On The Optical And Structural Characteristics Of In-Situ Prepared Pvp-Ag Nanocomposites", *Digest J Nanomaterials & Biostructure*, 6, 1 (2011) 299-306
26. Mott N F & Davis E A, *Electronic Processes in Non-Crystalline Materials*, 2nd edn.(Clarendon Press, Oxford),1979, ISBN: 0198512880
27. Fink D, Chung W H, Klett R, Schmoldt A, Cardoso J, Montiel R, Vazquez M H, Wang L, Hosoi F, Omichi H & Goppelt-Langer P, "Carbonaceous Clusters in irradiated polymers as revealed by UV–Vis spectrometry", *Radiat. ED. Def.Solids*, 133 (1995) 193–208
28. Barsbay M & Guner A, , "Miscibility of dextran and poly(ethylene glycol) in solid state: effect of the solvent choice," *Carbohydrate Polymers*, 69, 2(2007) 214-223
29. Xie R, Yang B & Jiang B, "Phase behavior in mixtures of a homopolymer and a block copolymer 1. FTIR and DSC studies" *J. Polym. Sci., Part B: Polym. Phys.*, 33, 1(1995) 25-32

30. Khurma J R, Rohindra D R & Devi R, "Miscibility study of solution cast blends of poly(lactic acid) and poly(vinyl butyral)" *The South Pacific Journal of Natural Science*, 23, 1(2005) 22-25
31. Hung C C, Carson W G & Bohan S P, "Phase morphology of blends of polycarbonate with poly(methyl methacrylate-*co*-cyclohexyl methacrylate), and of polycarbonate with poly(methyl methacrylate) by solid state nuclear magnetic resonance, differential scanning calorimetry, and transmission electron microscopy" *J. Polym. Sci., Part B: Polym. Phys.*, 32, 1(1994) 141-148

Department of Physics,
M S J Govt. College, Bharatpur,
Rajasthan, India
email: anandmsj@gmail.com

19. Sustainable Development Goals (SDGs) in India : Achievements & Challenges

Mrs. Sumitra Devi Sahu

The idea of sustainable development would gain real momentum only if we are able to conserve resources and use them in a manner that they are sufficiently available for the coming generations as well . India's effort for sustainable development can be traced back to ancient times. In the 2022 Global Index of SDGs, India had ranked 121 out of the 163 countries. It had ranked 117 in 2020 and 120 in 2021. The trends indicate that the country is off-track, with eight years left to meet the global goals on sustainable development. This paper aims to focus on SDGs' Major Achievements in India. It also investigates the challenges associated with sustainable development goals SDGs with special reference to India. The Later part of the paper confers the sustainable development approaches and possible solutions to overcome these challenges. Various policies and programs, institutional arrangements, technological Solutions, frameworks and measurement systems for a better present and future, have also been discussed. There is a need for coordination between government agencies, NGOs and the public, for the proper management of environment quality and to achieve sustainable development goals in India.

Keywords : Sustainable development, Environment, Achievements, challenges, sustainability.

Introduction

There is a close relationship between economic development and environment of any economy .It is next to impossible to develop any country by neglecting its environmental problems .They have become serious in many parts of the country, and hence cannot be ignored. India's effort for sustainable development can be traced back since ancient period. The idea of environmental conservation gains real momentum if we are able to conserve resources and use them in a manner that they are sufficiently available for the coming generation as well or in other words sustainable development is needed. The United Nations defines sustainable development as "development that meets the needs of the present without compromising the ability of future generations to meet their own needs"..

In 2015, the UN General Assembly (UNGA) adopted the 2030 Agenda for Sustainable Development. 193 nations, including India, are committed to the 17 Sustainable Development Goals (SDGs). SDGs aimed to build a more prosperous, more equal, and more secure world by the year 2030 have been developed.

There is a significant departure from the Previous dialogues on sustainability to the new, which includes a "harmonising" of three elements: economic growth, social inclusion and environmental protection.

The Sustainable Development Goals

The Sustainable Development Goals (SDGs) which came into effect on 1 January, 2016 is an improvement on the Millennium Development Goals (MDGs) [1]. In India, as far as mdgs are concerned, considerable progress has been made in the field of basic universal education, gender equality in education, and global economic growth. However there was slow progress in the improvement of health indicators related to mortality, morbidity, and various environmental factors contributing to poor health conditions [2].With SDGs in place the Indian government is now trying to integrate the efforts taken towards achieving mdgs with SDGs. SDGs are wider in scope.

The 17 SDGs are as follows:

Fig 1

Sr.No.	Sustainable Development Goals
Goal 1	End poverty in all its forms everywhere
Goal 2	End hunger, achieve food security and improved nutrition and promote sustainable agriculture
Goal 3	Ensure healthy lives and promote well-being for all at all ages
Goal 4	Ensure inclusive and equitable quality education and promote lifelong learning opportunities for all
Goal 5	Achieve gender equality and empower all women and girls
Goal 6	Ensure availability and sustainable management of water and sanitation for all

Goal 7	Ensure access to affordable, reliable, sustainable and modern energy for all
Goal 8	Promote sustained, inclusive and sustainable economic growth, full and productive employment and decent work for all
Goal 9	Build resilient infrastructure, promote inclusive and sustainable industrialization and foster innovation
Goal 10	Reduce inequality within and among countries
Goal 11	Make cities and human settlements inclusive, safe, resilient and sustainable
Goal 12	Ensure sustainable consumption and production patterns
Goal 13	Take urgent action to combat climate change and its impacts*
Goal 14	Conserve and sustainably use the oceans, seas and marine resources for sustainable development
Goal 15	Protect, restore and promote sustainable use of terrestrial ecosystems, sustainably manage forests, combat desertification, and halt and reverse land degradation and halt biodiversity loss
Goal 16	Promote peaceful and inclusive societies for sustainable development, provide access to justice for all and build effective, accountable and inclusive institutions at all levels
Goal 17	Strengthen the means of implementation and revitalize the global partnership for sustainable development

Sustainable Development Goals

Source:www.un.org/sustainabledevelopment/sustainable-development-goals/

Sustainable Development Goals have been built on the universal principle of 'leave no one behind', As far as India is concerned, the national development goals of India, converge well with the SDGs and India is expected to play a leading role in determining the success of the SDGs, globally.

What are the broad challenges :

1. What to prioritize : There is a dilemma between, development and economic growth? Or, reduction of CO_2 emissions and sustainable development too. India's immediate priority is to provide livelihoods and employment to its population besides creating sustainable economic opportunities. India has to provide houses to millions, ensure food & nutritional security, and make health services accessible & affordable. For the sustainable inclusive growth, jobs have to be created. To push the economic growth further, India, plans to set up smart cities, construction of roads, railways, and other large infrastructure projects. Under 'Make in India's, it lays emphasis on manufacturing sector which will help create jobs. But, all these actions put together will increase India's cumulative as well as per capita Co2 emission rate which will potentially weaken India's global position on responses to climate change.

Although, prioritizing certain SDGs help with other SDGs as well- for example, decreasing poverty could have a positive impact on the good health and well-being of citizens- certain SDGs could be conflicted by their nature. The most notable potential trade-off exists between the second goal, which is ending world hunger, and the 15th goal, which calls for sustainable management of forest land and other terrestrial resources. The SDGs contains 17 main issues to be addressed, and which ones should governments respectively prioritize could be a tough question.

1. Defining Indicators : One of the major challenges for India is setting suitable and relevant indicators to effectively monitor the progress of SDGs and to measure outcomes. This was seen in the case of MDGs. Quality education has not successfully been defined. . India's myopic definition of "safe" drinking water has been misconstrued with the availability of hand pumps and tube wells and the official data suggested that 86% of Indians had access to safe drinking water and therefore were "on track" for the MDG goal on drinking water . But the number of waterborne diseases and deaths due to diarrhea are quite high in India.

2.Financing SDGs : In India, A new study estimates that implementing sdgs in India by 2030 would cost around US$14.4 billion.However India has only 5% of the required funding to implement SDGs. Given the recent cut in social sector schemes by the central government, there is likely to be a significant funding gap. According to the United Nations MDG 2014 report, despite high economic growth, India has the highest number of people (around one-third of the world's 1.2 billion extreme poor) living below international poverty line. At today's level of investment – public and private in SDG related sectors in developing countries, an average annual funding gap remains $2.5 trillion over 2015-2030. This gap can be bridged only through increased private sector investments, especially in infrastructure, food security and climate change mitigation sectors.

Fig. 2 Gap in funding sdgs in developing countries (in trillion $)

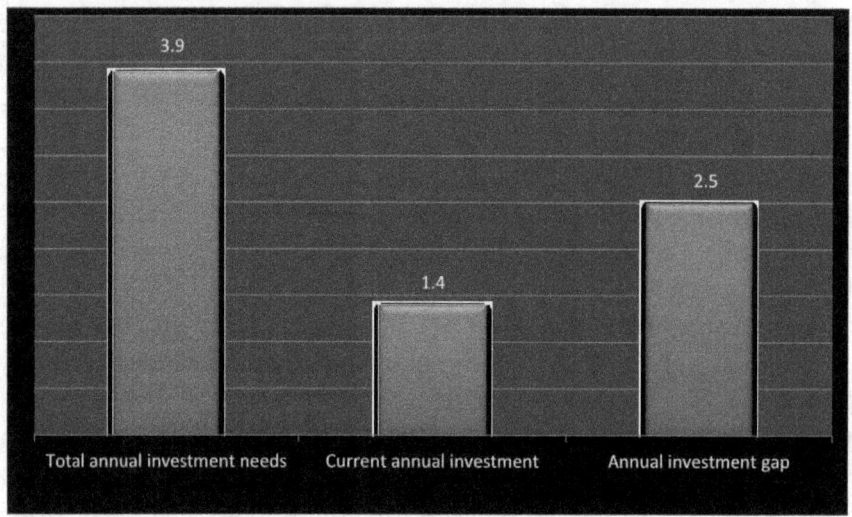

Source: unctad.org/en/pages/pressrelease.aspx?Originalversionid=194

3. Monitoring and Ownership : A third significant challenge is associated with implementing SDGs would be with respect to ownership. However, NITI Aayog is expected to play the lead role in tracking the progress of SDGs, its members have expressed reservations on being able to take on this mammoth task. Moreover, if states are expected to play a pivotal role (giving the devolution post 14th Finance Commission), it will require ownership not just nationally, but also at the state and local level.

4. Measuring Progress : Last but most important is the question of how to measure the progress or achievement of SDGs By   The Indian government it has been admitted that , the non-availability of data (particularly in respect to sub-national levels), periodicity issues and incomplete coverage of administrative data, have made accurate measuring progress of even MDGs virtually impossible.

5. Data Deprivation : For estimation, big data is useful only if it is collected intelligently and can be interpreted meaningfully. It is not possible to act effectively against poverty if we don't have data for number of people remains impoverished or data for groups that are most vulnerable to economic adversity. Further it cannot be determined how much progress been made over time, or which policies worked behind it. This is largest task for Sustainable Development Goals. It can be proved by the statement of World Bank's Innovation Labs, Aleem Walji, in 2015 that observation and monitoring by the World Bank among 155 countries, half of the countries lacked recent poverty estimates. As per the IMF's General Data Dissemination System, two or more than two data points within a decade are required to give poverty estimates every 3 to 5 years. A study conducted by The World Bank in 2015 provide that out of 155 countries only 57 countries had less than two data points from 2002 to 2011, another 20 countries had two data points within one decade that are separated by more than five years, rendering the data which is inadequate for poverty estimates. It is impossible for the countries to design and implement appropriate policies due to lack of reliable poverty data.

Suggestions to Overcome Challenges :
The challenges discussed above can be overcome by developing an exclusive model for implementing, monitoring, measuring and reporting SDG related course of action. Though India has well established organizations such as the CSO to provide statistical data many times they are general and do not match specific requirements. Even in case of MDGs, India was not able to measure its achievement accurately because of lack of data. Therefore developing suitable indicators to assess the progress of SDGs and also simultaneously developing a system that can support this exercise by supplying the required data is of paramount importance.

A separate index for measuring the progress or achievement of SDGs can be developed by taking the Ibrahim Index of African Governance (IIAG) as a base.

1. Ibrahim Index of African Governance (IIAG)
The Ibrahim Index of African Governance (IIAG) measures the quality of governance in every African country on an annual basis. The IIAG was launched in 2007 and has evolved to be the most comprehensive assessment on African governance. As governance is not measurable directly, IIAG has developed the most suitable set of

proxy indicators for the purpose by making use of a variety of data sources and indicators. IIAG does not collect primary data, but rather collates data provided by respected external sources. The IIAG data set is updated every year when practical improvements are identified and the results are made available from 2000. Whenever new historical data are made available, or the structure of the IIAG is strengthened, the entire data set is updated back to 2000. The latest 2016 IIAG consists of 95 indicators from 34 data providers.

Techniques used in developing IIAG
Some of the techniques used in developing IIAG are worth noting and may be applied in the Indian context also.

- ***Clustered indicators***

Indicators measuring a specific governance concept are sometimes available from multiple sources. To improve the accuracy of the indicator measurement and avoid double counting, these measures are combined into a single clustered indicator, which is the average of its underlying sub-indicators.

- ***Handling missing data***

Most indicators included in the IIAG have missing data points over the time series. As this can have an effect on a country's aggregate scores, estimates are provided for missing data, following a statistical process called imputation. According to this process, if data is missing outside the time series, it is replaced by an existing data point. When data is missing inside the time series, these are replaced with numbers incrementally higher or lower than the neighbouring data points.

- ***Normalization***

Given that the data utilised in the construction of the IIAG come from 35 separate data providers that present their data on different scales, it is necessary to standardise all data. This is done through a statistical process called normalisation whereby raw data for each indicator are transformed by the min-max normalisation method. This process allows all scores to be published in common units and within the same bounds of 0-100, where 100 is always the best possible score.

- **Data aggregation**

The IIAG uses a transparent, simple and replicable method of data aggregation. A simple average is calculated using the structure of the Index to arrive at the Overall Governance scores.

All of the above four techniques are ideal and very much applicable for India. The Administrative system in India is highly bureaucratic with two Governments, one at the centre and the other at the state level. This has resulted in duplication of data. Even the available has gaps in it and suffers from errors of standardization. All this can be resolved by developing an Indian Index of Sustainable Development (IISD) by following the techniques discussed above. IISD can be developed for a period of 15 years from 2015-30. The data set can be updated every year according to recent developments and revised for all the 15 years by following the same pattern of Ibrahim index. This would ensure availability of the most recent data set.

2. Financing SDGs.

The challenge of financing SDGs can be resolved to some extent by strengthening the existing academic infrastructure in the nation. India is a regional hub for higher education and the home town of several renowned institutions such as IIT and IIM. These institutions have well developed infrastructure for research. These resources can be pooled and effectively utilised in designing, developing and measuring indicators meant for sustainable development.

In developing countries like India, there was some hesitation in reducing carbon emissions for two reasons, first their per capita emissions were lower, and second, it would mean compromising with the development of the nation. Therefore a *carbon trading system* was evolved among the countries of the world where firms were permitted to emit carbon within the prescribed limit and was assigned carbon credits for this purpose, if any firm wants to exceed the limit it can buy the unused credit from another firm. In this way the buying firm is penalized for exceeding its carbon quota and the selling firm is rewarded for reducing its emissions. Governments can consider the *idea of penalizing firms* with higher carbon footprints by making them finance the sustainable goal programmes in the developing and least developed countries.

3. The responsibility of implementing SDGs

With NITI Ayog expressing its doubt as to how far it would succeed in this laborious task it is high time the Indian Government decentralises this task and while doing so it must be borne in mind that SDGs aim at conserving and passing on the natural resources to the next generation. This cannot be done without involvement of the society. But a society so knowledgeable to use its natural resources in a perfectly ecologically sound manner is nearly impossibility. Changing social, political, cultural, technological and ecological conditions will exert new pressures on the natural resource base and the possibility of its misuse or overuse always remains. Therefore a political order in which decision making will be done by those who would suffer the consequences of those decisions would be ideal. A new system that would ensure participation from groups that are directly connected to the problem needs to be evolved.

Major Achievements

NITI Aayog, the Government of India's premier think tank, has been entrusted with the task of coordinating the SDGs. States have also been advised to undertake a similar mapping of their schemes, including centrally sponsored schemes.

In addition, the Ministry of Statistics and Programme Implementation (mospi) is engaged in the process of developing national indicators for the SDGs

Many of the Government's flagship programmes such as Swachh Bharat, Make in India, Skill India, and Digital India are at the core of the SDGs. State and local governments play a pivotal role in many of these programmes. State governments are paying keen attention to visioning, planning, budgeting, and developing implementation and monitoring systems for the sdgs.

NITI Aayog, the Government of India's premier think tank, has the twin mandate to oversee the adoption and monitoring of the sdgs in the country, and also promote competitive and cooperative federalism among States and uts

NITI Aayog, has been released SDG India index, with the task of coordinating the SDGs. The third edition of the SDG India Index was released by NITI Aayog in 2021. It has been developed in collaboration with the United Nations in India, tracks progress of all States and ut's on 115 indicators that are aligned to mospi's National Indicator Framework (NIF). Since it has been started in 2018, now in its third year, the index has become the primary tool for monitoring progress made by States and Union Territories towards achieving the sdgs and has simultaneously fostered competition among the States and Union Territories.

"From covering 13 Goals with 62 indicators in its first edition in 2018, the third edition covers 16 Goals on 115 quantitative indicators, with a qualitative assessment on Goal 17, thereby reflecting our continuous efforts towards refining this important tool," said Ms.Sanyukta Samaddar, Adviser (sdgs), NITI Aayog

Monitoring progress of localization: SDG India Index

First comprehensive measure of SDG performance and localisation with national and State/UT ranking

Goal-wise ranking of States/ UTs and overall ranking based on performance on all goals	Promotes competition among the States/ UTs in line with NITI Aayog's approach of competitive federalism	Enable States/ UTs to learn from peers
	Supports States/ UTs in identifying priority areas	Highlights gaps in statistical systems

Baseline report – 2018	V2.0 report – 2019-20	V3.0 report – 2020-21
13 goals	16 goals + qualitative analysis on goal 17	16 goals + qualitative analysis on Goal 17
39 targets	54 targets	70 targets
62 indicators	100 indicators	115 indicators
Goal-wise ranking on States/ UTs	Goal-wise ranking on States/ UTs + State/ UT profiles	Goal-wise ranking on States/ UTs + State/ UT profiles
Preceded National Indicator Framework (NIF)	Aligned with NIF; 68 indicators completely aligned, 20 refined, 12 new to cover goals 12, 13, and 14	Aligned with NIF; 76 indicators completely aligned, 31 refined, 8 in consultation with the line ministries

The SDG India Index computes goal-wise scores on the 16 SDGs for each State and Union Territory. Overall State and UT scores are generated from goal-wise scores to measure aggregate performance of the sub-national unit based on its performance across the 16 SDGs. These scores range between 0–100, and if a State/UT achieves a score of 100, it signifies it has achieved the 2030 targets. The higher the score of a State/UT, the greater the distance to target achieved.

States and Union Territories are classified as below based on their SDG India Index score:
- Aspirant: 0–49
- Performer: 50–64
- Front-Runner: 65–99
- Achiever: 100

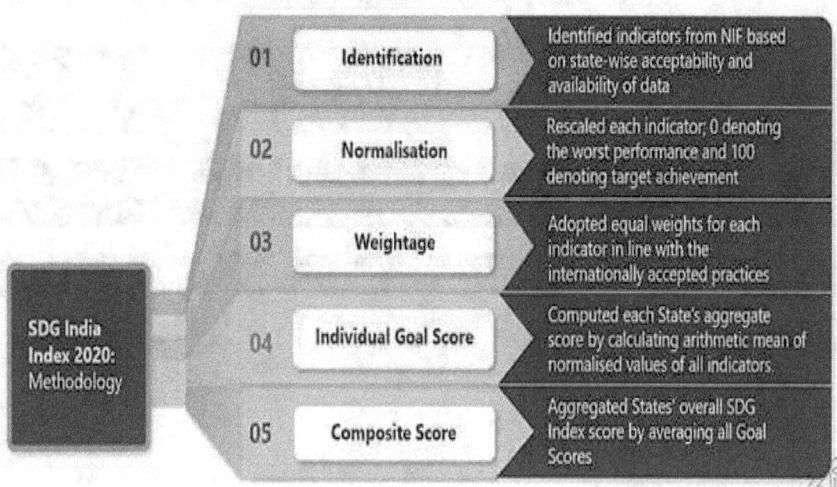

Overall Results and Findings

The country's overall SDG score improved by 6 points—from 60 in 2019 to 66 in 2020–21. This positive stride towards achieving the targets is largely driven by exemplary country-wide performance in Goal 6 (Clean Water and Sanitation) and Goal 7(Affordable and Clean Energy), where the composite Goal scores are 83 and 92, respectively.

Goal-wise India results, 2019–20 and 2020–21:

Greener Living

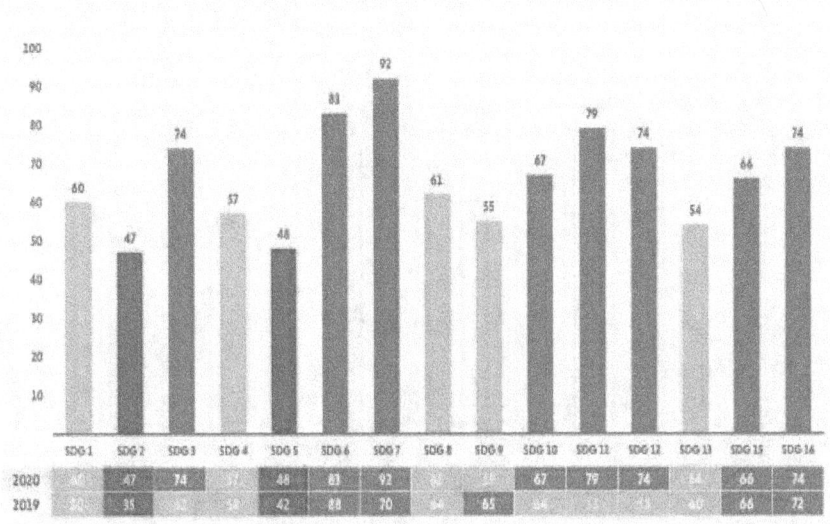

The top-five and bottom-five States in SDG India Index 2020–21:

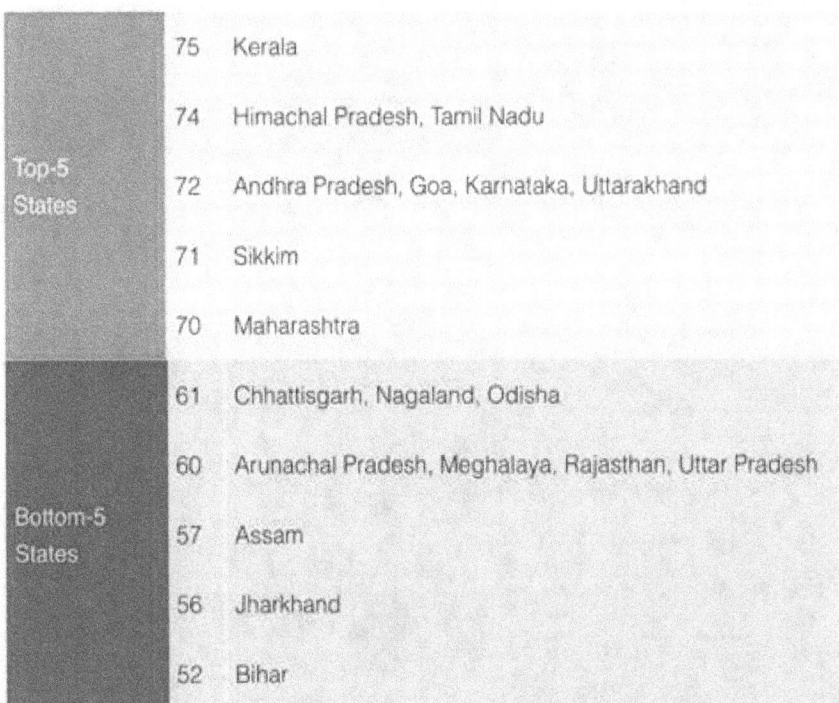

Greener Living

GOAL-WISE TOP STATES/UTs

Goal 1: No Poverty
Tamil Nadu, Delhi

Goal 2: Zero Hunger
Kerala, Chandigarh

Goal 3: Good Health and Well-being
Gujarat, Delhi

Goal 4: Quality Education
Kerala, Chandigarh

Goal 5: Gender Equality
Chhattisgarh, Andaman and Nicobar Islands

Goal 6: Clean Water and Sanitation
Goa, Lakshadweep

Goal 7: Affordable and Clean Energy
Andhra Pradesh, Goa, Haryana, Himachal Pradesh, Karnataka, Kerala, Maharashtra, Mizoram, Punjab, Rajasthan, Sikkim, Tamil Nadu, Telangana, Uttarakhand, Uttar Pradesh, Andaman and Nicobar Islands, Chandigarh, Delhi, Jammu and Kashmir, Ladakh

Goal 8: Decent Work and Economic Growth
Himachal Pradesh, Chandigarh

Goal 9: Industry, Innovation and Infrastructure
Gujarat, Delhi

Goal 10: Reduced Inequality
Meghalaya, Chandigarh

Goal 11: Sustainable Cities and Communities
Punjab, Chandigarh

Goal 12: Responsible Consumption and Production
Tripura, Jammu and Kashmir, Ladakh

Goal 13: Climate Action
Odisha, Andaman and Nicobar Islands

Goal 14: Life Below Water
Odisha

Goal 15: Life on Land
Arunachal Pradesh, Chandigarh

Goal 16: Peace, Justice and Strong Institutions
Uttarakhand, Puducherry

Mizoram, Haryana, and Uttarakhand are the top gainers in 2020–21 in terms of improvement in score from 2019, with an increase of 12, 10 and 8 points, respectively.

Top Fast-Moving States (Score-Wise):

State	2019-20 Score	2020-21 Score	Change in Score
Mizoram	56	68	12
Haryana	57	67	10
Uttarakhand	64	72	8

While in 2019, ten States/uts belonged to the category of Front-Runners (score in the range 65–99, including both) twelve more States/uts find themselves in this category in 2020–21. Uttarakhand, Gujarat, Maharashtra, Mizoram, Punjab, Haryana, Tripura, Delhi, Lakshadweep, Andaman and Nicobar Islands, Jammu and Kashmir and Ladakh graduated to the category of Front-Runners (scores between 65 and 99, including both).

	Aspirant (0-49)	Nil
OVERALL	Performer (50-64)	Manipur, Madhya Pradesh, West Bengal, Chhattisgarh, Nagaland, Odisha, Arunachal Pradesh, Meghalaya, Rajasthan, Uttar Pradesh, Assam, Jharkhand, Bihar
		Dadra and Nagar Haveli and Daman and Diu
	Front Runner (65-99)	Kerala, Himachal Pradesh, Tamil Nadu, Andhra Pradesh, Goa, Karnataka, Uttarakhand, Sikkim, Maharashtra, Gujarat, Telangana, Mizoram, Punjab, Haryana, Tripura
		Chandigarh, Delhi, Lakshadweep, Puducherry, Andaman and Nicobar Islands, Jammu and Kashmir, Ladakh
	Achiever (100)	Nil

Measures Taken by Indian Government for Implementing SDGs
1. Ratifying Paris Agreement
The 21st Conference of Parties (COP 21) under the **United Nations Framework Convention on Climate Change (UNFCCC)** successfully concluded in Paris after intense negotiations by the Parties followed by the adoption of the Paris Agreement on post-2020 actions on climate change. This universal agreement will

succeed the **Kyoto Protocol**. Unlike the Kyoto Protocol, it provides a framework for all countries to take action against climate change. Placing emphasis on concepts like climate justice and sustainable lifestyles, the Paris Agreement for the first time brings together all nations for a common cause under the UNFCCC. One of the main focuses of the agreement is *to hold the increase in the global average temperature to well below 2°C above pre- industrial level and on driving efforts to limit it even further to 1.5°.*

The Paris agreement requires each member country to prepare, communicate and maintain successive nationally determined contributions (NDCs) that it intends to achieve.

India's Nationally Determined Contribution (NDC) targets are to lower the emissions intensity of GDP by 33%–35% by 2030 below 2005 levels, to increase the share of non-fossil based power generation capacity to 40 % of installed electric power capacity by 2030, and to create an additional (cumulative) carbon sink of 2.5–3 billion tons of CO_2 equivalent through additional forest and tree cover by 2030

2. The Clean Development Mechanism projects in India

As on 4 January 2016, 1593 out of a total of 7685 projects registered by the **Clean Development Mechanism (**CDM) executive board are from India, which so far is *the second highest in the world with China* taking the lead with 3764 projects registered. Indian projects have been issued 191 million Certified Emission Reductions (CERs), 13.27% of the total number of CERs issued. These projects are in the sectors of energy efficiency, fuel switching, industrial processes, and municipal solid waste, renewable energy and forestry which spread across the country. About 90-95 per cent of the CDM projects are being developed by the private sector, facilitating investments of about R583, 751 core (US$ 87.77 billion) in the country, which is more than the total of multilateral grants available for climate change related activities.

3. State Action Plans on Climate Change:

The State Action Plans on Climate Change (SAPCC) aim to create institutional capacities and implement sectoral activities to address climate change. These plans are focused on adaptation with mitigation as co-benefit in sectors such as water, agriculture, tourism, forestry, transport, habitat and energy. So far, 28 states and 5 union territories (ut's) have submitted their SAPCC to the MOEF&CC. Out of these, the SAPCC of 32 states and ut's have been endorsed by the National Steering Committee on Climate Change (NSCCC) at the MOEF&CC.

3. Coal Cess and the National Clean Energy Fund

India is one of the few countries around the world to have a **carbon tax** in the form of a cess on coal. Not only has India imposed such a cess but it has also been progressively increasing it. The coal cess which was fixed at R50.00 per tonne of coal since 22 June 2010 and increased to R100.00 per tonne of coal in Budget 2014-15, was further doubled to R 200.00 per tonne in the 2015-16 Budget. Although, in July 2017, it was abolished with the introduction of GST and a new cess on coal production, at Rs. 400 per tone, called the **GST Compensation cess**, is being levied. **The National Clean Energy Fund (NCEF)** which is supported by the cess on coal was created for the purposes of financing and promoting clean energy initiatives, funding research in the area of clean energy and for any other related activities. Till date 56 projects have been recommended by the inter-ministerial group (IMG) with total viability gap funding (VGF) of R34,784.09 core spread over several years. For 2015-16, R4700 crore has been allocated in the Budget for NCEF projects. VGF is also being provided for Namami gange.

5. National Adaptation Fund for Climate Change

A National Adaptation Fund for Climate Change (NAFCC) has been established with a budget provision of I350 crore for the year 2015-2016 and 2016-2017. It is meant to assist in meeting the cost of national- and state-level adaptation measures in areas that are particularly vulnerable to the adverse effects of climate change. The overall aim of the fund is to support concrete adaptation activities that reduce the adverse effects of climate change facing communities, sectors and states but are not covered under the ongoing schemes of state and central governments. The adaptation projects contribute towards reducing the risk of vulnerability at community and sector level. Till date, the NSCCC has approved six detailed project reports (DPR), amounting to a total cost of I117.98

crore, submitted by Punjab, Odisha, Himachal Pradesh, Manipur, Tamil Nadu and Kerala.

6. Various measures announced in Budget 2022-23 on green energy

Sovereign Green Bonds : In 2022-23 budget it has been announced that the government will issue sovereign green bonds to mobilise funds to set up green infrastructure projects in the public sector and reduce carbon footprint. These funds will enable the government to achieve the 500 GW renewable energy target by 2030. This is just one of the many measures announced by the FM on green energy. FM also announced various measures to boost energy transition trough electric vehicles (EVs) and solar and green energy.

Battery Swapping Policy : For EV, the government has announced the launch of **a battery swapping policy**, which will create interoperability standards for batteries. The government will encourage the private sector to offer battery as a service by providing land resources.

Special Mobility Zones will be Developed for Electric Vehicles to promote clean technology and green mobility in public transport. Building laws and town planning will also be modernised for battery charging infrastructure. The budget will also promote energy saving and efficiency in large commercial buildings.

Additional duty of Rs. 2 per litre will being levied on unblended fuel from October 2022, which will encourage ethanol blending of fuel by oil marketing companies.

Aspirational Districts reach out : To improve citizens' quality of life in the country's most backwards districts Aspirational districts programme has been launched in 112 districts. 95% of these districts have made significant progress in key sectors such as health, nutrition, financial inclusion and basic infrastructure.

Conclusion

Sustainable Development is a historic opportunity for the world communities to deliver inclusive growth, eliminate poverty and reduce the risk of climate change by changing perspectives and approaches to economic development. For the sustainable development of India, it is necessary to achieve all the 17 SDGs. All the 17 SDGs are integrated and interconnected; action in one area will have at least some impact on others. Therefore, it is an enormous task to achieve all 17 SDGs up to 2030. Simultaneous achievement of these goals requires the effective involvement of every sector and each level of society. India has the second largest population in the world. For the achievement of SDGs, steps taken by India, matter a lot to the world. If India succeeds in attaining the SDGs it would mean a larger section of the world has achieved it. Therefore it is imperative for India to develop effective methods for implementing, monitoring and measuring the progress of SDGs. The major challenges for India seem to be the defining suitable indicators, data deprivation, financing SDGs, and to identify suitable method to measure the progress. To overcome these challenges an Indian Index for Sustainable Development (IISD) can be developed by taking the Ibrahim index as a base and It also requires major participation of public along with the Govt. in making efforts to achieve sustainable development.

References :
1. Prabhakar M. & David, Christopher; "Sustainable Development Goals (SDGs) - Challenges for India"; Vels University, Pallavaram, Chennai
2. Sharma , Suresh & Bothra, Manisha; "India and roadmap towards sustainable development goal 3: achievements and challenge";International journal of advanced research, oct. 2017
3. Prabhakar M; "Sustainable Development Goals (SDGs)- Challenges for India"Indian journal of public health Research and Development; Jan. 2018
4. https://www.iasexpress.net/sustainable-development-goals-sdgs-india/Sustainable Development Goals (SDGs) – India's Readiness & Challenges
5. https://www.niti.gov.in/verticals/sustainable-dev-goals
6. NITI Aayog Releases SDG India Index and Dashboard 2020–21

Assistant Professor (Economics)
Govt. College Bundi,
Rajasthan

20. Steam : Way forward the Future of Education

Mr. Neeraj Mohan Puri[1]
Dr. Rashmi Tyagi[2]

Abstract

This paper explores various dimensions of integrating arts with the STEM (Science, Technology, Mathematics and Engineering) curriculum at K12 school level. This paper highlights the purpose of inclusion of Arts in STEM. This includes various benefits of amalgamating Arts with STEM to accelerate the skills, competencies, promote creativity, innovation thereby by ensuring joyful learning experience for the learners giving them the ownership of learning. This paper presents few interdisciplinary projects combined with art which were held in Modern Sandeepni School to promote collaborative learning. The results of these pilot projects show positive correlation between the learning and performance of students with the inclusion of STEAM in school's core curriculum. Results of this study justify the fact that combining of various forms of art with science and technology at middle level and senior level has far reaching impact as compare to primary level, thereby making learning more enjoyable experience for the learners. This paper will be beneficial for extending further research and act as a corner stone for the school administrators, State and Centre to frame their policies on STEAM and design the curriculum.

Keywords : STEAM, Interdisciplinary, Best practices, K12 Schools, Projects.

Purpose of Study

The objective of this study is to explore the possibilities of integrating Arts with core curriculum through STEAM projects to develop 21st century skills and competencies among children. To discuss the best practices of STEAM being implemented in the schools. To identify the benefits of combining arts and STEAM for the young learners.

Methodology

The research methodology for this study involves reviewing the pre-existing scholarly articles, reports and government papers. Telephonic interviews of 15 PAN India Principals, 20 educators and 20 students who have implemented or participated in multidisciplinary art integrated projects in the STEAM disciplines were held.

1. Introduction

Future belongs to those who prepare for it today. Goals of education has been evolving continuously over centuries. New Education Policy of 21st century lays special emphasis on Sustainable Development Goal, with an eye to make Indian children Independent lifelong learners with lateral thinking having analytical skills. It is pertinent to note that each discipline of STEAM has its own implications and unique nature. Hence, its implementation at the school level needs impeccable planning.

1.1 STEM background

It was in late 90's, that National Science Foundation (NSF) coined an acronym "SMET," popularly known as "Science, Math, Engineering, and Technology." After the recommendation of certain officers the term SMET was reorganised as STEM. This is how this concept came into existence. With the passage of time need was felt to integrate Arts with STEM. Much of the latest literature advocates about synchronization of both the extreme disciplines together. This is not so because more students are entering the technology driven sectors but it is only through the arts that creative and innovative ideas can come on fore. Recent research studies propose that our prevalent educational system was prepared to meet the industrial needs of 20th century being designed like assembly lines, conformity and linearity. To prepare kids for the future we have to instill creativity, critical thinking, analytical skills, decision making and team players traits in them through core curriculum. Furthermore, the manpower engaged in the STEM disciplines admits that their arts experience plays vital role in personal and professional development.

Figure 1: *Image of STEAM*

1.2 Merger of Arts with STEM

Art is a diverse range of Human Activities to express our feelings, emotions, opinions and
ideas in visual, auditory, performing artifacts or written form. Broadly there are 3 forms of Art i.e Visual arts like painting, drawing; Performing arts like music, dance and literary arts like written text books etc.

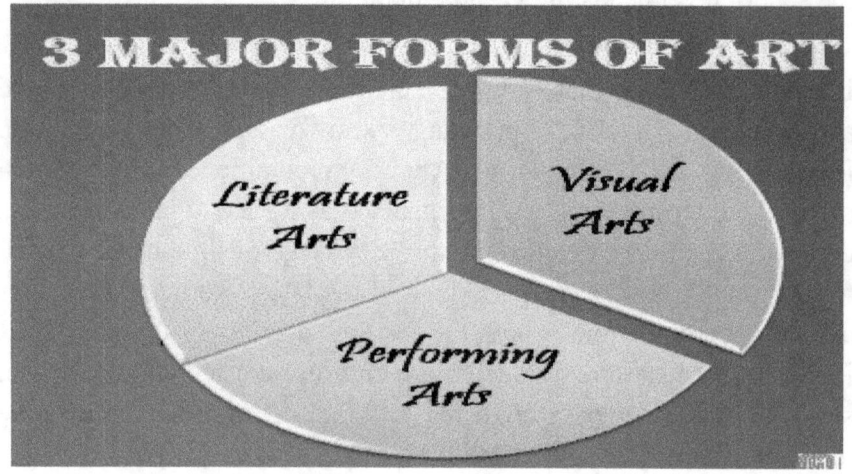

Figure 2: *Image of forms of Art*

The educationists who advocate to combine arts with STEM to make it STEAM propound that integration is indispensable not just to boost lateral thinking and innovation, but also it will help in the advancement of this discipline too. Indeed the connectivity between creativity and technology is on hike as most of the MNC's prefer human resources who have high end problem solving skills and have extraordinary designing competencies.

Procedure

During this unprecedented testing times Modern Sandeepni School, Punjab has introduced the multidisciplinary art integrated collaborative learning projects with peer review for the students of grade III to X. They have observed phenomenal results. Surprisingly, these projects were undertaken by students through virtual or online mode as students and instructors were not physically present in the campus. In order to ensure harmonious development of the children STEAM based cross-curriculum projects were assigned. In order to achieve the objective of outcome based learning, class was split in various teams. Each team comprised of boys and girls to avoid gender biasness. In addition, each team had students of every category like less advanced and more advanced this was to ensure the inclusion. When students of every background are included this allows children to respect the diversity. Later on, similar task with a deadline and clear instructions were allotted. Team members have to unanimously decide their team leader and team name. Task is equally distributed among all the members according to their skills and traits. Then learners work collectively and compile the project. Cross-discipline project covers every aspect of academics say social science, science, mathematics, languages with special emphasis on integrating any form of visual art like drawings or performing arts like dance, music etc. Finally, consolidated report is prepared with ICT tools and is submitted. Each team is assigned a mentor. Once the mentor receives the report they evaluate the project on pre-specified rubrics. The process does not end here. In next phase, the projects are interchanged and send for the peer review. In its last phase the result of the mentor and peer reviewer is averaged. This become the final score of a particular team.

In one of the art integrated cross curriculum project assigned to the team of grade vii students who were to work as a unit goes like this. The project is to make a design of the mask which is attractive, convenient to wear and fulfil the safety norms too. At the initial stage, they were to research about the fabric which is safe, comfortable to use, easily available and economical. Once decided, students have to brainstorm and draw various sketches or models which in itself involves art. Then they have to measure the dimensions of mask for various age groups. Later on they have to estimate the cost of manufacturing a single piece which involves various mathematical applications. Next stage they were to discover were the mask used by any civilization earlier, when and for what reasons? Moving on they were required to list down the merits and demerits of wearing mask. Team were to prepare a report of the whole process in English and their regional language. Finally, they were to compile the report using ICT tools and forward to the mentor. As an extended version scholars may be told to create a campaign to boost the use of the mask.

During this Pandemic period, Sandeepnites in school's ROBOTICS LAB designed and developed 2 models based on STEAM project namely (CARE- COVID ALERT RESPONSE ACTION and MUST-MULTI UTILITY SPECIAL TABLE). Both these models were based on programming, coding, robotics, aurdino, application of mathematics and science principles. These prototypes proved to be very effective and helpful for the CORONA Medicare warriors and general public. Children worked in a group and by heart quickly grasped various typical concepts which otherwise was difficult.

This highlights the fact that through a single project all round development of a child is possible. It started with research skills, moving on to art, mathematics, social science, science, languages. Learner is able to understand the concrete concepts through experiential learning which is outcome based developing numerous skills. This is perfect example of moving from abstract to concrete.

Observations

In an interview conducted for 15 Principals, 20 instructors and 20 students who had either conducted STEAM based projects or participated in it the results were impressive.

As per figure 3, 93% respondents strongly agreed that students' creativity should be a parameter to judge his academic excellence not he marks obtained through rote memorization.

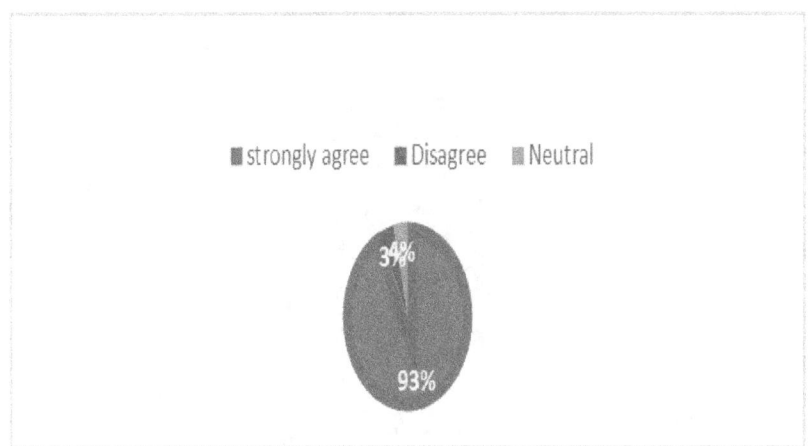

Figure 3: *Pie graph showing response of all the respondents*

As per figure 4, When this project was discussed with the teachers 17 out of 20 strongly agreed that this inquiry based learning will strengthen the understanding, knowledge of children as compare to traditional methods of teaching.

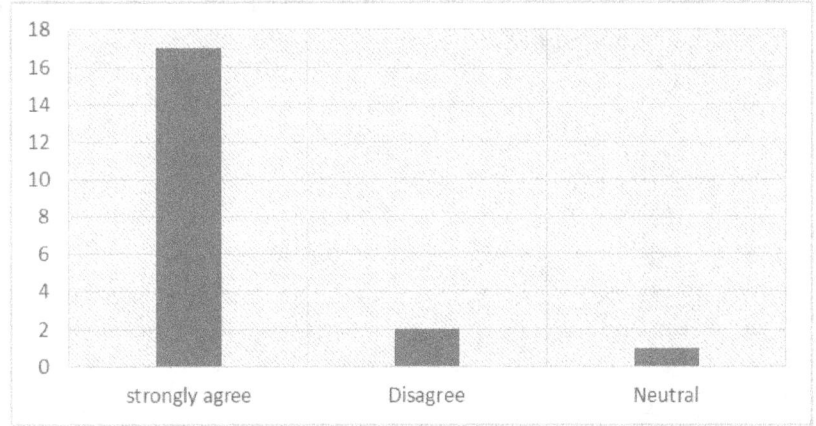

Figure 4: *Bar graph showing response of teachers*

Figure 5, result show that 90% teachers who were interviewed strongly agreed that children learn to share the resources, become team players, promotes brain storming and critically analyses the situation. This will enable schools to inculcate all the 21st century skills to make children employable.

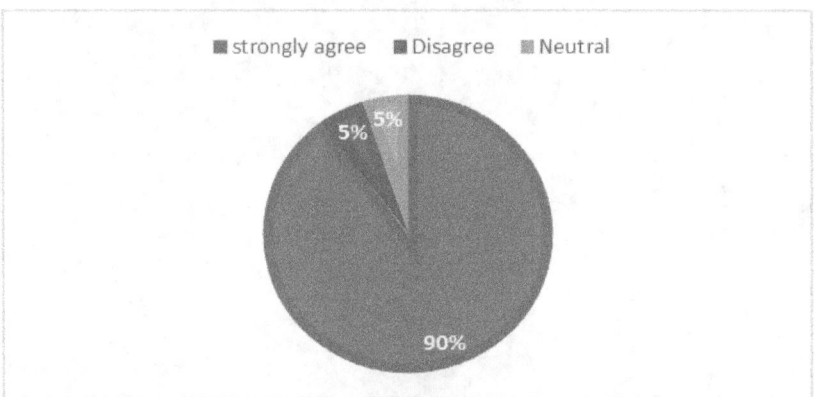

Figure 5: *Pie graph*

In figure 6, When 20 students were enquired, whether application of STEM and arts stimulate the creativity, innovation, imagination and scientific temperament of a pupil? 95% respondents strongly recommend the inclusion of STEAM in the core curriculum as it inspire students apply their classroom theory with real life problems. Learners admitted that Arts integrated STEAM projects arouse their curiosity, ignited them, sparked their creativity and above all generated their interest in studies.

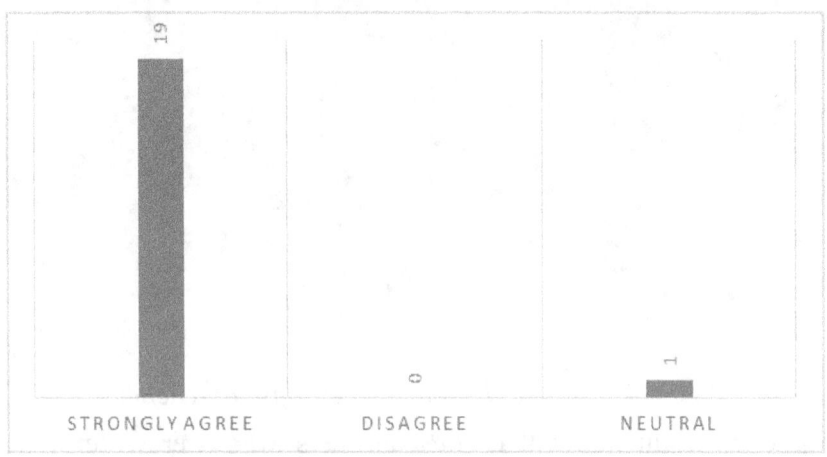

Figure 6: *Bar graph of students' reply*

Even a study of Missouri Public School in 2010 found that greater arts education led to fewer disciplinary infractions and higher attendance, graduation rates, and test scores.

Conclusion

Through this research paper, it is proven that combining arts and science will make children problem solvers, unique thinkers, researchers and all rounded personalities. Working in the arts help learners to grasp the concepts quickly, develop motor skills, language skills, social skills, decision-making, risk-taking and inventiveness. It increases the productivity of disengaged child. Teaching through the arts can present difficult concepts visually, making it easy to understand. This will not only improve their academic performance but also make education more knowledge oriented than marks oriented.

Further this approach of teaching learning acts as a social leveler providing an opportunity to less advanced children to perform at par with normal children. By introducing multi-disciplinary invention projects for the middle wing students we have obtained surprising results as all the learners demonstrated high level of creativity, engagement, self-discipline, joyful learning and also took sense of pride and self-esteem for their achievements in the STEM (*Science, Technology, Engineering, & Mathematics*) areas. Educators must be more creative with their instructional design and introduce different artistic concepts. In this approach of teaching there is transition from taking commands to making decisions, they take the onus of failure, learn to manage their defeat, accept the challenges, decode the problem statement.

In order to transform education system and to make art integration a reality nationwide efforts are desired. Educational institutes have to design the guidelines & to provide the necessary infrastructure to introduce this pedagogy, parents have to change their mindset and teachers need to undergo necessary trainings and stretch their imagination. Public awareness is very essential.

For self-sufficient (atamnirbhar), sashakat bharat we have to empower our children and prepare them for future jobs. Half the jobs that exist today, will perish by the time our students will enter the market space as a workforce. Future is about Big data, analytics, robotics, coding. Big question is, are we ready to take on the World's job market? Are our students' future ready? Are we skilling them for future?

To make this happen is not merely about curricular integration but more about changing the whole thought process. Finally, we are in a position to conclude that both these disciplines can co-exist to inspire and challenge the educators & learners. With the paradigm shift in the education there is no point to artificially keep both these streams apart, nor should they be aligned if not necessary. Even NEP 2020 says students are free to take any subjects of their choice by breaking the silos of streams. Resulting, the children to have stress free meaningful life thereby making this world a better place to live upon. This revolution can only happen if we work with a mission No Child Left Behind and a motto Every child Achieves.

References
Amir, N. (2021). Fostering Creativity and Joy of Learning Amongst Students in a Singapore Classroom Through Fun Design-and-Make STEM Projects. Academy of Singapore Teachers, Singapore. 51-53. DOI: 10.4018/978-1-7998-4658-1.ch003
Beal, S. (2013, July 11). *Turn STEM to STEAM: Why Science Needs the Arts.* http://www.huffingtonpost.com/stephen-beal/turn-stem-to-steam_b_3424356.html
Bidwell, A. (2014, Feb 5) *"Report: STEM job Market Much Larger Than Previously Thought."* US News & World Report, Feb 5, 2014: 31-32.
Neill, O.J., & Pollock, K. (2014, July 15). *"Education in the New Economy: STEM plus Arts."* St Louis Post-Dispatch, July 15, 2014: 15.
Sanders, M. (2009). "STEM, STEM Education, STEMmania." The Technology Teacher, 2009: 20-26.

[1]**Principal**
Modern Sandeepni School, Pathankot
neeraj.puri79@gmail.com
[2]**Director Academics**
Modern English School, Mumbai
tyagirashmi02@gmail

www.ingramcontent.com/pod-product-compliance
Lightning Source LLC
Chambersburg PA
CBHW050252010526
44107CB00003B/288